Ch. Basquaerie Bibelot,
owned by Mrs. Francis V. Crane

THE COMPLETE GREAT PYRENEES

The Board of Directors of
The Great Pyrenees Club of America
approves and endorses this book
and commends its authors
for a much-needed job well done

Champion Karolaska Glacier, 1967–1974, the top winning Great Pyrenees in America, with 10 Bests in Show, 111 Group placements, and two National Specialty wins. Owned by Edith K. Smith and handled by Robert Forsyth. — *Gilbert*

The Complete
GREAT PYRENEES

by Paul D. Strang
and James M. Giffin

FIRST EDITION
Second Printing – 1978

HOWELL BOOK HOUSE Inc.
230 Park Avenue
New York, N.Y. 10017

"To once own a Great Pyrenees is to want one always." — Mary W. Crane.

Library of Congress Catalog Card No. 76-51095
ISBN 0-87605-163-8

Printed in U.S.A.

With love to our wives
Edith Strang
and
Elizabeth Giffin

Ch. Azos Popette, and St. Girons Cupidon—on holiday in Connemara, Ireland.
— *Peter Gilbert*

Contents

Debra Ferguson with two future champions: Dastedke's Prima Donna, and Dastedke's Walloping Theodor.

Mrs. Francis V. Crane with eight of Basquaerie's outstanding brood bitches. From left to right: Ch. Rhune du Pic du Jer, Ch. Pastoure d'Arros, Ch. Bigorre du Pic du Jer, Ch. Gerita, Ch. Basquaerie Nana, Ch. Arizes de Soum, Ch. Munia du Pic du Jer, and lying in front, Ch. Koranne of Basquaerie, CD. One of the most important arrays of brood bitches ever assembled.

Foreword

Since the 1949 edition of my book, *The Great Pyrenees,* went out of print about ten years ago, there has been a real need and often expressed desire for a comprehensive volume to deal with the history, attributes and development of the breed. In this book, I feel that this need has been admirably met.

I am, therefore, proud and honored to be asked to write this dedicatory preface. It is my hope that the friends of the Great Pyrenees the world over will take pride in the accomplishment of its two authors, Paul D. Strang and Dr. James M. Giffin. From conception to successful conclusion, this book reflects their dedication to the breed, their experience, their outstanding qualifications for the assignment, their persistence and their great industry.

I hope this book will serve as well to inspire the newer generation to work for the perpetuation of the TRUE TYPE of Great Pyrenees. For without those beautiful, dark expressive eyes, that elegance of head and carriage, one just does not have a real Great Pyrenees.

So, long may the breed prosper and spread. And, so too, the joy of ownership, the devotion, companionship and intelligent protection to be offered by this, the world's most beautiful dog. For to once own a Great Pyrenees is to love and want one always.

MARY W. A. CRANE

Paul D. Strang.

James M. Giffin.

The Authors:

Paul D. Strang

Paul D. Strang's intimate association with the Great Pyrenees spans more than 50 years. As a student in Paris after World War I, Paul became enchanted with the breed's nobility and breath-taking beauty. He bought his first Great Pyrenees from a mountaineer. As his career as a linguist and correspondent led him to a life on the French Riviera, he found ample opportunity to add to his growing knowledge and expertise on weekend trips to various French kennels and breeding establishments.

In the 1930s Paul and Edith Strang returned to the United States and occupied the family residence at High Wyndham, in Bluemont, Virginia. Here they began to breed Great Pyrenees under the prefix CASTELLAN.

In 1972 Paul Strang and Mrs. Sonya Larsen joined forces to edit and publish a popular magazine, *The International Great Pyrenees Review,* widely read by members of the fancy in the United States and overseas.

Mr. Strang has been a member of The Great Pyrenees Club of America for over 40 years. He is the acknowledged English speaking authority on the origin and development of the breed in France, and has judged the breed both in the United States and abroad.

James M. Giffin, M.D.

Dr. James Giffin was born in New York City, lived in Connecticut, and was educated at Amherst College and Yale Medical School. Following his postgraduate training in Surgery at Barnes Hospital in St. Louis, Dr. Giffin entered the Armed Forces, serving as Chief of Surgery at the 45th Surgical Hospital in Vietnam.

He returned to Missouri in 1968 and founded his Great Pyrenees kennels in Springfield. Dr. and Mrs. Giffin became active in showing the breed and finished several champions. They have also campaigned a Best In Show winner.

Dr. Giffin serves on the Board of Directors of the Great Pyrenees Club of America. In 1975 he was elected to serve on the Committee to study the revision of the breed Standard, and was chosen as its Chairman. He is also a contributing Editor to the magazine, the *International Great Pyrenees Review.*

"As you look in those eyes, the immense moral
value of the breed pierces your soul."

Ch. Quibbletown Boleros Ravel
— *Shafer photo*

Introduction

IF WE WERE to name the best all-around dog for town or country, we would say, without hesitation, "The Great Pyrenees!" Possessing a breath-taking beauty, a wonderful disposition and a calm and stately bearing, no breed is more completely suited to fill the role of companion and guardian for the home.

And as a protector, no breed could be more sensible, wise or prudent. It has been said, truthfully, that his judgment of character can be relied upon absolutely. Tidy and fastidious by nature, he is easy to keep in condition and, despite his size, ideally suited to the life of a house pet.

Today the breed flourishes in his native France; and in the United States, Canada, Great Britain, Australia, New Zealand and South Africa—indeed from Europe to India and from the South Seas to the Arctic Circle. It would be difficult to find any place on the five continents where the Great Pyrenees is not known and loved.

For Mrs. Crane, who introduced the breed to America, the reason for the Pyrenees' spectacular and ever-increasing popularity is quite simple because, as she has often said, "This is the most beautiful breed in the world!"

For M. Senac-Lagrange, the French authority who once rescued the breed from the waters of oblivion, one of its principal attractions was to be found in the eyes. He wrote, "Only the true breed possesses this bewitching, almost indefinable expression in the eyes, both distant and caressing, contemplative and just a little sad. As you look in these eyes the immense moral value of the breed pierces your soul."

"The majesty of the Pyrenean is undeniable," wrote Dr. Will S. Monroe, the first president of the Great Pyrenees Club of America. "This is a dog of imposing size, regally clad in a mantle of ermine. He carries his head proudly. He stands fearlessly and when he moves, it is with power and authority."

Mme. Harper-Trois Fontaines, who introduced the breed to England, had this to say: "The Pyrenean Mountain Dog is a rugged individualist. He will take no pampering, other than his master's love."

And Marjorie Butcher, whose Cote de Neige Pyrenees played such a vital part in establishing the breed in the United States, often spoke of her joy at hearing his deep, sonorous bark: "That rumbling voice sounds like a lion's roar to the unwelcome stranger, but it turns to something more like a kitten's purr at his master's fireside."

"Rain, snow, ice and rough weather mean little to this breed," said the eminent French connoisseur, M. A. Cazaux-Moutou. "These dogs seem to prefer to sleep out in a gale in the coldest weather, rather than seek shelter under cover."

Thirty years ago, Mrs. Bruce Laymen of La Shan Kennels wrote, "No story of the Great Dog of the Mountains would be complete without a word about the puppyhood stage, for it is here that many of us make our first acquaintance with these dogs. As puppies, the Great Pyrenees are irresistible balls of white fluff, with small beady eyes that combine mischief with understanding, trust and adoration. They are lovable clowns and adorable in every way."

In the pages of this book we will attempt to give our readers an authentic and factual account of the Great Pyrenees—his history, traditions, and promise for the future. Perhaps you, the reader, are already a devoted fancier and need no further incentive to inspire your confidence and enthusiasm. In any case, we hope that in these pages you will glean something of the past and present glories of owning, or being owned by, one of these splendid creatures. And, in so doing, pass it along to the next generation.

THIS BOOK would not have been possible without the wonderful cooperation of many truly dedicated and unselfish Great Pyrenees fanciers who have contributed to these pages. We are especially indebted to Mrs. Francis V. Crane for her enthusiastic support. As the author of three editions of *The Great Pyrenees*, Mrs. Crane's unqualified permission to draw upon the contents of her life-long files made our task so much more pleasurable and rewarding. She is the author of two chapters.

Among those with whom we have conferred on the history of the modern Great Pyrenees in America, special recognition is due to the following: Mrs. Judith Bankus, Mrs. Bruce Hardy, Mrs. Waldemar Hauff, Mrs. Richard Kentopp, the Charles McConnells, Mrs. Melvin Rhoades, Mrs. C. Seaver Smith, Jr., Mrs. Ned Stuart, Mrs. Perry Valle and Mrs. Dorothy Wise.

In England, Mrs. Joyce Stannard, Mrs. C. R. Prince and Sqd. Ldr. Peter Gilbert (Retd.) have all made important contributions. Mrs. W. D. R. Calvert in Scotland, Mrs. Ranee Van Eck in Australia, Mrs. Lynlie Watson in New Zealand and Mrs. Denise Tudhope in South Africa have been of great assistance in gathering information and pictures about the breed in their respective countries. Mrs. Roy Addie has been particularly valuable in coordinating the chapter on the breed in Canada.

To Dr. Robert Brown, D.V.M., we are indebted for his chapter on Special Health Problems; to Whitney Coombs for researching the statistics on the production records of Great Pyrenees sires and dams at the American Kennel Club Library; to Roy Stehle for providing us with information on the Obedience Degree holders; and to Mrs. Frankie Glover for her suggestions on Grooming.

Mrs. Sonya Larsen has coordinated the gathering of overseas material and has made available to us pictures and information contained in her magazine, *The International Great Pyrenees Review.* Mrs. Bridget Olerenshaw, one of the top canine artists in Great Britain, drew the sketches for this book.

Mrs. Janet Thomas deserves special recognition for her long and devoted service in the preparation of this manuscript—our right hand gal!

To all of the above, and the many other friends who have contributed through correspondence, pedigrees and pictures, we wish to express our sincere thanks.

Finally, to Elsworth S. Howell, who gave us the opportunity to produce and publish a work on the Great Pyrenees, we are indeed grateful. We owe thanks to him, not only for the advice and encouragement he gave us during its inception and development, but also for the splendid job he has done in producing our book in its present form.

Paul D. Strang
James M. Giffin

Kimmie Kentopp with Tundra Gypsie of Karolaska.

17

In the Pyrenees—by Rosa Bonheur (1822-1899).

The Pyrenean Sheepdog, by Maude Earl, painted in 1901.
— *Courtesy, Mrs. C. Seaver Smith, Jr.*

18

The Shepherd Dog of the Pyrenees

by Ellen Murray

When day at last
Broke, and the grey fog lifted, there
I saw
On that ledge, against the dawning light,
My little one asleep, sitting so near
That edge that as I looked his red
barret
Fell from his nodding head down the
abyss.
And there, behind him, crouched Pierrot:
his teeth
His good, strong teeth, clenching the
jacket brown,
Holding the child in safety. With wild
bounds
Swift as the grey wolf's own I climbed
the steep,
And as I reached them Pierrot beat his
tail,
And looked at me so utterly distressed,
With eyes that said: "Forgive, I could
not speak."
But never loosed his hold till my dear
rogue
Was safe within my arms.

La Chasse Aux Loups, depicting two Great Pyrenees fighting a wolf. Painted by Jean Baptiste Oudry, the famous French animal painter, 1686–1775.

— *Courtesy, Mrs. Francis V. Crane.*

20

1

The Origin
of the Great Pyrenees

THE GREAT PYRENEES takes its name from the Pyrenees Mountain range between France and Spain. Here for centuries the dog served not only as the shepherd's chief ally in defending the flocks from wolves and bear, but also as a valued sentry for the chateaux of the area—ever vigilant to sound the alarm in case of enemy attack.

In his native France he is known as *Le Grand Chien de Montagne,* the Great Mountain Dog of the Pyrenees. To say he is great is to refer not only to his size, but also to distinguish him from the other shepherd's dog of the Pyrenees, *Le Petit Berger,* or the little shepherd, who drives and herds the sheep. As the Petit Berger is becoming known outside his native haunts it is well to keep the difference between the two breeds in mind.

Most pedigrees of Pyreneans with a mountain background show a confusing number of dogs called "Patou" and bitches called "Pastoure". These historic Gallo-Roman names, meaning the Shepherd and the Shepherdess, are part of the breed's ancestral heritage. To the mountain breeder they denote more fittingly than any other names the breed's unique supremacy for its age-old task. And so wherever Pyreneans are bred we find the names Patou and Pastoure often given in recognition of this link with the past.

In Great Britain and in other countries closely affiliated with the British Kennel Club such as Australia, New Zealand, and South Africa, our Pyrenean is called the *Pyrenean Mountain Dog.* The British standard for the breed is quite similar to our American standard, and neither differs, in essence, from the French standard. So whether we call it the Great Pyrenees, the Pyrenean Mountain Dog or the Patou we are talking about the same majestic, white-furred aristocrat. An aristocrat that at the end of the 19th century was thought to have passed from the scene—but in the 20th century has won the hearts of the canine world!

This increased popularity of the breed has sparked new interest and debate over its origins. Although his presence in the Pyrenees Mountains is documented as far back as Roman days, it is believed that his original home was elsewhere. Two theories have been developed. One is that the breed is a descendant of the Tibetan Mastiff. The other claims that his antecedents were the dogs of the ancient Sumerians.

The Tibetan Mastiff as Possible Ancestor

Robert Leighton in *The New Book of the Dog* (1911) points out that in spite of the fact that the Tibetan Mastiff is usually black, black-and-tan, or red, while our Pyrenean is mainly white, the two breeds do have much in common. He writes, "But for the difference in color, the Pyrenean bears considerable resemblance to the Mastiff of Tibet. Somewhat higher on the leg and perhaps less muscular, it has the same massive body, the same character and texture of coat, and the same form of head. The shape of the skull is precisely similar; so is the carriage of the ear, the set of the eye, and the form of the muzzle." And, he concludes, both are used for protecting rather than herding the sheep.

D. H. Mut and von Stephanitz, both German authorities, and M. B. Senac-Lagrange, the French Pyrenean master, all subscribe to the thesis that this Tibetan dog was the ancestor not only of the Pyrenean but also of the other large, mostly white, pastoral guard dogs of Europe and the Near East.

According to this theory, as the nomadic tribesmen of distant Asia migrated westward thousands of years ago, they were accompanied by their flocks and their dogs. The more intrepid pushed on to the Atlantic Coast and some must have settled in the Pyrenees. Others stopped along the way. And in each region where these tribes put down their roots, a new breed of flock-guarding mastiffs developed—all fathered by the original dog from Asia.

With the passing of the years, this legend of the assumed Tibetan origin of our Pyrenean and the other sheep-guarding breeds, came to be regarded as fact. A warning by von Stephanitz that the theory was based on assumptions and conjecture was nearly forgotten. But in some minds, nagging suspicions lingered. The question was, by what alchemy had the black dogs of Tibet been turned into the white shepherd dogs of Europe and the Near East?

One answer was given by C. Duconte and M. Sabouraud in *Les Chiens Pyreneens* (1970). These French authors maintain that environmental and climatic changes may well have brought about the color paling over the years, a trend which they believe is still in operation. For evidence, they point to engravings at the Chateau de Lourdes, made at the end of the last century, which show specimens having brown heads and areas of dark coloring on the body. The fact that our dogs have less coloring today is offered as proof of a gradual whitening of the breed.

But Columella, the Roman agricultural historian, in a work entitled *De Re Rustica* published in the second century A.D., tells us that, "Sheepherders in-

Pyrenean Mountain Dog, painted by Nina Scott Langley for *Hutchinson's Dog Encyclopedia.*

The Little Pyrenean Shepherds, co-worker of the Pyrenean Mountain Dogs. The big dogs were guardians of the flock, and the little dogs did the herding.

sist on white guard dogs for their flocks, for otherwise a dog could be struck during an attack through being mistaken for a wolf.'' So it appears that white sheep-guarding dogs have been known for nearly two thousand years! Any theory of gradual paling is put to doubt, to say the least.

The Ku Assa

Still another blow to the theory of the Tibetan Mastiff-origin of our breed is to be found in the recent emergence of a new contender for the honor. This is the Ku Assa, a pastoral guard dog of the ancient Sumerians. The Sumerian civilization began in the fertile Mesopotamian basin between the Tigris and Euphrates Rivers in Asia Minor.

"The Ku Assa Story,'' written by the Hungarian, Dr. S. Palfalvy, and translated by Dr. Edmond S. Bordeaux, appeared in the *Kuvasz Newsletter* in 1967. In 1974 Dr. Bordeaux published his book, *Messengers from Ancient Civilizations,* which gave further particulars. By deciphering cuneiform writing on clay tablets unearthed at Sumer in Southern Mesopotamia by British and French archeologists, Drs. Palfalvy and Bordeaux believe they have identified the Ku Assa as a pastoral guard dog employed by these agriculturists some thirty-five and forty centuries ago. And they maintain that the Ku Assa is the true ancestor of the European sheep-guarding mastiffs.

The Mesopotamian origin for this group is reinforced by the fact that today this region is the home of the Turkish Sheepdog, the Iranian Sheepdog and the South Russian Sheepdog.

Senac-Lagrange pointed out in his monograph on the Pyrenean in 1927 that the Turkish or Anatolian dog is astonishingly like the Great Pyrenees. It has, he says, the same powerful build and the same deep, but muted, voice. And it, too, was often equipped with an iron-spiked collar as protection against wolves.

But even more important, perhaps, is the claim by Palfalvy and Bordeaux that these ancient populations employed a small dog to herd the flocks. The big dog was the guardian and his little co-worker took care of the driving chores.

In Columella's time Asia Minor was part and parcel of the Roman Empire and his familiarity with the great white dogs becomes much more understandable if indeed their homeland was on his very doorstep rather than in far-off Tibet. Descendants of Columella's wolf-fighters are still found today in Italy, where they are known as the Maremma. With the Maremma is a little dog that does the herding, called the Bergamese Shepherd.

Robert Leighton, in the *New Book of the Dog,* pointed out that the Romans were advanced in their knowledge of the dog and its uses. So much so, that a classification was drawn up. Three main divisions were recognized: (1) *Canes villaica,* or watchdogs; (2) *Canes pastorales,* or sheepdogs; and (3) *Canes ve-*

24

Sir William Ingram's Tibetan Mastiff Bhotean, imported to England in 1906, as pictured by Robert Leighton in *The New Book of the Dog.*

Spiked iron collars worn by the European Mastiffs.

At right, worn by the Great Pyrenees, a broad iron collar with spikes an inch and a half long.

An articulated iron collar worn by the Anatolian Shepherd of Turkey.

natici, or hunting dogs. Of particular interest is Leighton's statement, "In their commerce with other countries the Romans acquired new breeds for particular purposes." British pugnaces, no doubt Mastiffs, were imported for the games at the Coliseum in Rome.

Another purpose for which the Romans needed exceptionally powerful and intelligent dogs was for use in the livestock provisioning camps which served as adjuncts to the numerous military posts set up throughout the far reaches of their Empire. And it is quite possible that, considering the evidence, the dogs from Asia Minor were selected.

Clockwise, round the countries of the Roman Empire, we find the following great white herd protectors: in Africa, the Atlas Mountain dog; in Spain, the Pyrenean Mastiff; in France, the Great Pyrenees; in Italy, the Maremma; in Germany, the old Pomeranian Sheepdog; in Hungary, the Kuvasz; in Czechoslovakia, the Chuvatch; in Poland, the Tatra Mountain Dog; in Turkey, the Anatolian Sheepdog—and there are still others in the Balkans and the Near East.

And in many of these countries we also find, in company with the big dog, a little, shaggy animated shepherd that leads and drives the sheep. Among them we can name the Pyrenean Shepherd in France; the Bergamese Shepherd in Italy; the Puli in Hungary; and the Valee or Nizinny Shepherd in Poland.

Does the presence of so many big white pastoral guard dogs and their little herding co-workers throughout so many of the areas of the Roman Empire really indicate a Roman connection? Or is it merely due to a strange coincidence? One thing is certain: whether his ancestors came from Tibet or Asia Minor, our Pyrenean Mountain Dog is definitely one of the oldest breeds in existence!

Development of the Breed

The Great Pyrenees has achieved his present status by two different stages. During the first, which lasted for many centuries, his working qualities were perfected by the mountain shepherds. The second stage is his recent emergence as a show dog.

Fanciers interested in our Pyrenean's show qualities tend to forget his past as a working dog. But we must recall the past to really understand the breed's essential character and special attributes.

Certainly the notion that mountain breeders in the old days were apt to breed anything to anything and hope for the best is in error. Actually, these peasant-shepherds usually imposed rigorous and severe standards of performance on their breeding stock. And only those dogs which met these stringent requirements were retained to produce the future generations.

As Columella pointed out nearly two thousand years ago, the first requirement was for a white dog that could easily be distinguished from wolves. Fur-

A Tatra Mountain Dog, photographed with Paul Strang in the
village of Zakopane in 1974.

A Czechoslovakian Chuvatch,
photographed by Mr. Strang in
1974. A breed favored by the
Russian army. And, judging by
the aplomb of this young man, a
breed that has the trust of its
owners.

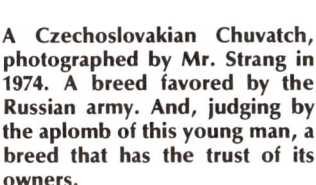

The historical Chateau de Foix — well guarded! — *Anthony Miles Ltd.*

thermore, the dog had to be big, strong, fearless and agile in order to cope with the enemy. Intelligence was required, not only to be able to act on its own initiative, but also to be able to understand and obey the shepherd's commands.

A rugged constitution and a weather-resistant coat were both essential—as the dog spent most of its life in the open. Excellent eyesight, an acute sense of hearing and a keen scenting ability were important. And a tremendous energy reserve was called for as the dogs had to stand duty around the clock—the hours of darkness being especially favored by the enemy predators.

J. Dhers, a breeder at the turn of the century who knew the dogs well, described the night scene in the following manner:

> As the evening shadows lengthen the sheep are assembled in the fold and the Patou, who may have drowsed a bit during the day, now becomes a protective demon. Head held high and tail wheeled over the back his keen nose bores into the darkness, first in one direction and then in another, as he circles the encampment. He listens intently for the slightest unwarranted rustling sound. At intervals he pauses to rest for a few moments and his deep bark sounds the signal that all is well.
>
> What controls his actions? Is it the shepherd's training or is it his atavistic hatred of the wolf and the bear? Does he know, or sense, that if either is allowed to approach, more sheep will be lost in a suicidal stampede than will ever be carried off by the attackers? In any case he will not sleep until, in the morning, the shepherd again takes charge of his flock.

We can be sure that such magnificent guard dogs were not produced by haphazard breeding, but rather through a centuries-old program of breeding only the best to the best. The shepherds have always prized their good dogs and parted with them only reluctantly.

The historian, M. Doublet, in a work devoted to the highwaymen and cattle rustlers that infested the Pyrenean region in the Middle Ages, tells of the great lords and landowners who frequently purchased the Pyrenean dogs for sentry duty in their castles. They were trained to hunt down brigands and thieves with the same eagerness with which they would attack a wolf or a bear. Thus the citadels of Lourdes, Foix and Carcasonne all had their troupes of Pyrenean dogs to protect the holdings.

And, according to legend, the troubadors—those lyric poets and minstrels who traveled from castle to castle throughout Provence—were often accompanied by the big white dogs. Perhaps this was for the strictly utilitarian purpose of affording them protection from the highwaymen, but it seems more likely that the artistic temperaments of the troubadors were drawn to the dogs because of their beauty of form and nobleness of character.

M. W. Byasson, an early judge of our breed, published a booklet at the turn of the century in which he tells how Patou's beauty ensnared another set of admirers—members of the French royalty:

> Mme. de Maintenon visited Barreges in 1675 accompanied by the young Dauphin, son of Louis XIV. In the countryside the boy made friends with a gorgeous male Patou about eight months old. The two became inseparable and eventually Patou and the Prince returned together to live at the Louvre.
>
> Two years later the Marquis de Louvois came to the Pyrenees and he, too, returned to Versailles with a magnificent male purchased at Betpouey. The dog became a great favorite at the court.
>
> From this time forward members of the nobility chose the Pyrenean above all other breeds.

After the French Revolution the Pyrenean retained his popularity and became, for the next century, one of the most sought after breeds on the large estates of France.

Turning briefly to the United States, we find that J. S. Skinner in *The Dog and the Sportsman* (1815) tells us that a Great Pyrenees was owned by a Mr. Beaudry of Delaware. The dog was pure white and stood 32 inches at the shoulder. Then in 1824 General Lafayette sent Skinner two other Pyreneans, being white with brown markings. Lafayette recommended them as being of inestimable value in all regions exposed to the depredations of wolves and sheep-killing dogs.

In the British Isles, Sir Walter Scott, in 1815, owned a cross-bred Pyrenean named Maida. His father was a Patou who had come to Scotland with soldiers returning from the Napoleonic Wars. His mother was a Scottish Deerhound of the famous Glengarry line. Robert Leighton's description of Maida is of considerable interest:

Neron, exhibited in the 1890s
by his owner, Mr. Remy of
Brussels, Belgium.

He was a magnificent animal, partaking of his Deerhound dam, but having height and power from his sire. The cross was of benefit to the breed, and from Maida came many of our best Deerhounds. Washington Irving described him as a giant in iron grey. But Landseer's portrait shows him to have been a white dog with a grey saddle mingled with black, extending into patches on the thighs.

Unfortunately, these early imports to America and Great Britain eventually disappeared without leaving a trace. Perhaps their size and strength were incorporated into other breeds, as happened in Scotland.

Two Pyreneans who came to Belgium in the late nineteenth century were destined to make a lasting contribution to our breed. A retired army officer by the name of M. L. Remy had visited the Pyrenees Mountains in the early 1890s. When he returned to Belgium, he brought with him two pure white pups named Neron and Diane. Diane was given to a Mme. Demaziere.

Organized dog shows, as opposed to informal expositions held in conjunction with country fairs, were just starting to get under way. Neron was entered in several European shows and his impact on the canine world was considerable. Dog fanciers fell in love with this "new" and magnificent breed.

Champion Alba, one of the
brood bitches at Zailea.

30

The dogs thus came to the attention of the distinguished canine authority, Count Henri de Bylandt, who was in the midst of writing a monumental encyclopedia on the races of dogs entitled, *Les Races de Chiens* (Brussels 1897). De Bylandt devoted several pages to the Pyreneans in his encyclopedia and included photographs of both Neron and Diane. He also drew up a standard for the breed, the first ever published, and included it in his text. All this publicity produced shock waves that reverberated throughout the canine world. Like lemmings heading out to sea, breeders from distant points headed for the Pyrenees to procure stock of these marvelous white-furred lords.

The effect of this sudden popularity was soon felt in the Pyrenees Mountains. In a few short years, most of the best breeding stock had been purchased by foreigners. This genetic drain placed the breed in perilous straits.

Reconstitution

In 1907, M. Th. Dretzen, accompanied by Count de Bylandt, went to the Pyrenees to study the breed on the spot. Once in the mountains they secured the help of M. W. Byasson. Among 350 specimens they examined, Dretzen reported that he found isolated in different parts of the mountains only six specimens who could be regarded as presenting the characteristics of the true race. In an effort to reconstitute the breed, Dretzen purchased these six dogs and moved them to his Zailea Kennels at Bois-Colombes, near Paris.

M. Dretzen's most famous dog was French Champion Porthos. In the words of Robert Leighton, "Porthos was exhibited throughout Europe, and it was perhaps with justification that last year this splendid specimen of his kind was introduced to the President of the Republic as 'the most beautiful dog in France,' for he was a truly magnificent animal."

The Dretzen-de Bylandt-Byasson party had focused attention on the need for some kind of community action on the part of the mountaineers to preserve the breed from further depletion. At that time there was no official standard for the breed in France. Although de Bylandt's standard was written in French, he was himself a Hollander. Mountaineers were disturbed by this "outside interference."

In defense of what they considered the breed's best interests, as well as their own, the mountaineers banded together in an effort to reconstitute the breed and produce an official standard of their own. But rivalries soon broke out and, as a result, different clubs were formed.

One group calling itself the Pastoure Club was formed in 1907 at Lourdes. Among the principals in this venture were Senac-Lagrange, Dr. Moulguet, J. Camjou and the President of the Club, Baron A. de la Chevreliere.

A second club, formed in the same year at Argeles, called itself the Argeles Club. This one included Byasson, Dretzen and de Bylandt.

Each group, by dint of further diligent searching, located about 50 or 60 dogs considered to be purebred. The Pastoure Club organized the first Pyrenean Specialty show. Fifty-five dogs were entered in competition for the various prizes. Both groups made serious efforts to control the breeding and sale of non-typical dogs to eager buyers. And both fought to maintain the size, dignity and vitality of the breed.

At this late date it is difficult to understand why the rivalries were so intense. Two different standards were drawn up, but neither differed very much from the other, and both only slightly from the first by de Bylandt. But this general division into two separate camps may have marked the beginning of the misconception that a different type of Great Pyrenees, derived from the so-called "mountain type," was developed for the show ring. In the Pyrenees, a good mountain dog has always been regarded as a good show dog—and vice versa.

Among the points of mutual agreement, those that have stood the test of time are: the use of the word "elegant" to distinguish the Pyrenees from the Saint Bernard and Leonberg; the addition of double dewclaws as a sign of racial purity; the addition of the color "gray" to the list of correct markings; and the statement that the tail is "carried over the back when the dog is going to attack."

Through the efforts of these two groups, the purity of the breed was restored and the Pyrenees appeared to be well on the way to future successes.

But World War I brought about an almost total collapse of the efforts of French breeders to revitalize the breed. Dretzen's Zailea Kennels at Bois-Colombes passed quietly from the scene. The two clubs ceased their activities and were virtually disbanded. Many of the dogs they had assembled were put down due to lack of food; the few that did survive were malnourished and often proved to be, at the end of hostilities, poor breeders.

After the War, registrations of Pyrenean Mountain Dogs in the *Livre Origines Francais*, the Stud Book of the Societe Centrale Canine in Paris, reflected the sad state of the breed. During ten years, only 20 Pyreneans were registered, all "without origins," i.e., of unknown ancestry and without pedigree.

An effort was made by a few mountaineers to restore size and substance by resorting to a cross with the Alpine Mastiff, but the results were disastrous. The specimens obtained totally lacked the majestic elegance so characteristic of the Pyrenean Mountain Dog. Heads were shorter and heavier; cheeks and stops too pronounced. Worse yet was the loss of the indefinable look which mountaineers called the "Pyrenean eye."

If it were not to be lost altogether, the cause of the Pyrenean Mountain Dog needed to be taken up seriously by a group of sincere fanciers. So it was at Lourdes, on the edge of the majestic region of Lebeda, cradle of the race, that a group of dedicated breeders met to consider the future of the breed. This was done, according to records of M. Senac-Lagrange, with very limited means and in the face of public indifference.

M. Dretzen's Pyrenean Dog, Champion Porthos, purchased in the Pyrenees about 1907. Named the most beautiful dog in France.

Gazost 1st. One of the dogs selected for the regeneration of the breed by the Argeles Club. Strong bone and arched toes. A typical mountain dog of the better type.

M. Bernard Senac-Lagrange at the judge's table, 1953.
— *Courtesy Mrs. C. R. Prince*

Toy de Soum. A beautiful bear-like head and superb Pyrenean expression — typical of his bloodline.

2

Development of the Breed in France

BERNARD SENAC-LAGRANGE, the man whose unflagging devotion to the cause gave us the Great Pyrenees as we know it today, was born in 1880 at Cauterets, in the High Pyrenees, and died in 1954 at Bastens-de-Bigorre, only a few miles away.

As a young man Bernard entered the diplomatic service, but cut short this successful career as he felt unsuited to its restricted life. Returning to his paternal family home, near his place of birth, he devoted the rest of his life to hunting, writing, and breeding dogs and horses. He was one of the best known all-around international judges, and officiated at field trials in both France and Europe.

His efforts on behalf of the reclamation of many breeds were crowned with success. He was named President of the Gers-Pyrenees Kennel Club, of the Blue Ticked Gascony Hound Club, of the French Pointer Club and the Club for Shepherd Breeds. He was Vice-President of the Central French Kennel Club (S.C.C.).

But for Pyrenean Mountain Dog fanciers, the years from 1920 to 1930 were the high point in his career. Under his leadership a new club was formed— *The Reunion des Amateurs de Chiens Pyreneans*, or Union of Pyrenean Dog Fanciers. This group, often referred to as the R.A.C.P., managed to combine in one club all the dissident factions which, in one way or another, were devoted to both the Mountain Patou and his little helper, the Petit Berger.

Aiding other breeders, particularly M. Cazaux-Moutou (de Soum) and Mme. Le Conte (de Langladure), he supervised their selection of breeding stock from the mountains and from the celebrated Betpouey Kennels of M. R. LaSalle, Lourdes, to aid in the establishment of France's foundation bloodlines.

As the work of reclamation continued, over a hundred fanciers joined Senac-Lagrange in his task. Named President of the Club, he immediately set about preparing an official standard for the Great Pyrenees. It was later published in the 1927 R.A.C.P. Yearbook. Here is the R.A.C.P. Standard:

The First Standard for the Great Pyrenees in France

GENERAL APPEARANCE: A dog of large size, imposing and strongly built, but not devoid of a certain elegance.

HEAD: Not too large in proportion to the size. The sides of the head fairly flat, the crown of the head oval and not very rounded with a scarcely marked central furrow, the line of the head sloping gradually to a broad muzzle of good length and slightly more pointed at its extremity. The upper lips falling but little, only just enough to cover the lower jaw: they are black or very strongly marked with black; palate black and the nose black. In a word the head of a brown bear, with ears falling down.

EYES: Rather small, intelligent and contemplative in expression, of an amber brown and placed a little obliquely in the head. The eyelids are close and bordered with black.

EARS: Placed at the height of the eye, rather small, triangular in form and rounded at their extremity, they fall flat against the head.

NECK: Strong, rather short with dewlaps but little developed.

SHOULDERS: Middling oblique, withers broad and muscular.

BODY: The chest not very low but broad and extending well to the rear. Sides slightly rounded. Back a good length, wide and straight. The croup slightly oblique with haunches fairly prominent. Flanks dropping but little.

MEMBERS: Front legs straight, strong, well-fringed. Fringes also on hind legs. The thighs are rounded but not low. The hocks are often too straight—they have double spurs on the hind legs and sometimes on the front.

FEET: Not long, compact with toes a little arched.

TAIL: Fairly long, thick and plumed. Carried low when in repose, just its extremity curled. When the dog is on the alert the tail is curled up above the back ("making the wheel," the mountaineers call it).

HAIR: Thick, flat, fairly long and supple, longer near the tail and around the neck where it can be slightly undulated (wavy). The hair of the quarters finer, more woolly and very thick.

COAT: White or white with spots; colour of a badger or pale yellow or wolf grey on the head, the ears and at the base of the tail. Spots like the badger are esteemed most. One or two spots on the body are not considered as faults.

SIZE: Females from 65 cms. to 72 cms. (25.59 to 28.34 inches). Males from 70 cms. to 80 cms. (27.55 to 31.49 inches).

WEIGHT: 45 to 55 kilos (99 to 121 lbs.).

FAULTS: Too heavy head, crown too much developed and front rounded; the stop of nose marked; bad dentition, unequal jaws; round eyes, too light or prominent; falling eyelids; light spots on nose and eyelids, insufficient pigmentation of mucous membranes; lips falling too low; long ears or with folds; tail not fully feathered or carried badly; short hair or curly; the hocks too straight (a common fault); other colours than those mentioned above denoting crossing; height and weight below minimum.

36

TO BE ELIMINATED: Absence of double spurs on hind legs.

SCALE OF POINTS:

Crown of head and muzzle (nose, lips, jaws)	15
Eyes	10
Ears	5
Neck, back rump	12
Shoulders, chest, sides	10
Legs and feet	10
Tail and carriage of tail	8
Coat, colour, pigmentation	15
General appearance (expression, height, movement)	15
	100

Commenting in *The Pyrenean Mountain Dog* (1927), Senac-Lagrange wrote:

The main preoccupation, then, of the members of the Reunion des Amateurs de Chiens Pyreneans was to prepare a standard which would put clearly in relief the points of the breed which could be endangered through the use of untypical specimens, or through any admixture of foreign blood.

Breeding which produces the correct head, the proper coat; the typical expression and gait earns 60 points out of a hundred. Anatomical perfection, however important, cannot rate higher than the points which are the main indication of the purity of the race.

As regards the general appearance we insist the dog, while strongly built, should nevertheless give a distinct impression of elegance.

The carriage of the tail is very characteristic. As soon as the well-bred dog, in good health, goes on the alert, the tail wheels over the back. In the patois of the region this is referred to as *arroundera.*

Let us mention, concerning the coat, two rather common mistakes. Certain persons believe the all-white coat to be the only orthodox one. Others regard the all-white dogs as degenerate and insist the *blaireau* dogs are the correct type. Both opinions are equally wrong.

There is nothing wrong with an all-white dog providing the nose, eyerims and mucous membranes are perfectly pigmented with black. As far as markings go, it is moreover certain that when they are present the dominant colour, the background, should be white. Most mountaineers prefer white dogs marked with badger on the head and perhaps a patch of the same colour at the base of the tail. In the dialect of Labeda this is *U Ca Pla P'Apat.* This means a well-marked dog.

Though dewclaws are perhaps of doubtful use, they have always, within living memory, been considered by mountain breeders as a sign of racial purity. Under these circumstances we must therefore insist that their absence must be considered a disqualification.

37

We will end these comments by adding that, at times, a Pyrenean dog adopts a gait like that described in literature on the horse and called not a "pace" but a "broken pace." In this gait the lateral bi-ped beat is in 4-time. As this gait may be observed in the little Pyrenean Shepherd Dog it must be considered as an adaptation to the mountain terrain.

As President of the French Club, Senac-Lagrange well knew that writing a description of a breed in dire straits was but the first step. Accordingly, he decided upon three further courses of action.

First, he persuaded other members of the Club to register their dogs with the S.C.C., and to breed only those specimens that met, in all respects, the requirements of the new standard.

Second, he drew up a list of judges he felt were competent to judge the breed. Uniform judging, he felt, would lead to uniform type. Furthermore, only six judges in all of France were considered to have the proper background to judge the breed with competence. Members of the Club were advised to take into account, in their breeding programs, only those dogs that won under these judges.

His third effort was directed at stopping the genetic drain through which, in the past, so many good dogs had been sold off to non-breeders and the public at large.

The importance of maintaining and controlling selected individuals for the future good of the breed was vividly pointed out in a newspaper article by Senac-Lagrange in 1929. He wrote, "Out of two hundred Pyreneans I have examined in the show ring since the end of the war, only about fifty could be taken into serious consideration." To have squandered this capital would certainly have further endangered the breed.

Great Pyrenees Type

Under the influence of Senac-Lagrange, a definite Pyrenean type was now emerging in the show rings and kennels of France and also in the mountains. It represented a significant advancement in the quality and consistency of the breed. Paul Strang wrote in the early thirties:

> Generally speaking, the show dogs are larger and more attractive than those found in the hands of the hard-working Pyrenean Mountain folk. Nevertheless, the latter do quite a business with tourists as these dogs never fail to command attention even though lacking some show points. On Fete days the peasants bring their best dogs to town to offer them for sale on the Esplanade or in the Grande Place. I remember seeing nine superior specimens thus offered one sunny morning in Bagneres de Bigorre. What with their glistening white coats contrasting so sharply with their black noses and dark eyes it was, to my mind, only natural that they should attract more attention than the official amusements.

With the publication of the French Standard in 1927, and its implementation by Senac-Lagrange and his associates, and the consequent emergence of Great Pyrenees type, the renaissance of the Great Pyrenees in France was well underway. At the same time, giant predators had been gradually disappearing from the Pyrenean Mountains and the dogs were no longer called upon to serve as they had in the past.

The Great Pyrenees, right arm of the lonely shepherd on the mountain steep, and chamberlain to the lords and ladies of the courts and chateaux of Medieval France, was now destined to become a show dog as well.

The Great Pyrenees Becomes a Show Dog

It was a bright morning in April. The year was 1933, and Pyrenean fanciers had turned out in force to witness the big event of the year—the judging at the prestigious Paris International. This year expectations ran high because the judge was the renowned Mme. Dretzen, who, with her husband, had founded the Zailea Kennels at Bois Colombes, over 30 years before.

The exceptional quality of the entries plus the acknowledged expertise of the judge served to heighten the suspense. As Madame Dretzen made her choices she, in turn, was being judged by the onlookers—not only the fanciers of the Paris region, but also the breeders from the High Pyrenees, men from Auch, Lourdes, Tarbes and Cauterets whose family ties with the breed went back through the centuries.

Perhaps the real importance of the event was not in the placings which were given that day, but in the fact here in one show ring were assembled all the famous bloodlines of the day. Bloodlines which history would later show were to be the power behind most of the later kennels of France, Belgium, England and America.

The males included Toy de Soum; the litter brothers Estat and Estagel d'Argeles; Athos de le Moriniere; Pastour d'Avron (of Careil bloodlines); Bastan de Soum; and Sancho de Langladure.

Among the females were to be found the litter sisters Luz and Monne de Langladure; "France" of du Givre breeding; Munia du Pic du Jer; Nive de Langladure; and the great Ariel de Soum.

Let us consider for a moment these great contenders and the kennels which produced them.

The stud dog, Toy de Soum, was well on his way to winning a French championship. He was out of Gazost de Betpouey, the most successful show winner of the previous decade. Gazost had won the Challenge Cup three times in five years, thus retiring the cup to his owner, M. Lasalle. The dam of Toy de Soum was Estom de Soum, who had won the Challenge Cup in 1926.

Merah de Langladure, owned by Mme. Le Conte. Merah was the dam of many splendid de Langladure offspring, including American Champion Mitsou de Langladure. Pictured in 1936.

Pastoure de Langladure. Foundation bitch at the kennels of Mme. Le Conte. Time: 1926.

Two young de Soum dogs.
— *Courtesy Mrs. C. R. Prince*

In the head and expression, Toy de Soum exemplified the perfection for which M. Cazaux-Moutou of Lourdes, in the Hautes Pyrenees, had long been noted. Toy was the sire of America's first champion and producer, Urdos de Soum, the founder of Basquaerie Kennels.

Always a close personal friend of M. Senac-Lagrange, M. Cazaux-Moutou had been in 1907 one of the founders of the Pastoure Club, and later when it collapsed, the R.A.C.P. He showed extensively all over France in the early years. He bred with extreme wisdom and care, and he registered all his stock with the S.C.C. in Paris. In the 1930s he was taken with ill health, but managed to keep some of his dogs intact through World War II. Thus the career of this distinguished gentleman spanned nearly a half century.

Mme. Le Conte, owner of French Ch. Ariel de Soum, was the proprietress of the ELEVAGE DE LANGLADURE. In 1933, this kennel was at its height, and almost no pedigree could be found in France that did not boast of de Langladure blood.

Ariel de Soum was of such a reputation that many described her as the best bitch France had ever bred. She was born in 1925 and won the Challenge Cup in 1929. She whelped her last litter at 11 years of age—still a grand old matron with everything visible that one could ask for in an outstanding Great Pyrenees bitch—type, expression, coat, soundness and character.

De Langladure dogs were of mountain origin, heavy in Betpouey, and closely allied to de Soum. The foundation stock had been carefully selected by M. Senac-Lagrange. In addition to Ariel de Soum it included Merah de Langladure, another top producer for the kennel.

Among the kennel's offspring, Yel de Langladure went to Holland where he was the foundation stud at Van Euskara. I'Nethou de Langladure was sent to England and became a major factor at de Fontenay. Champions Maya and J'Nive de Langladure played important roles at Cote de Neige and Basquaerie in America.

Shown that day at the Paris International was the beautiful brood matron, French Champion Monne de Langladure, owned by Mme. Carel of the DU VAL D'AURE Kennels. Monne was a bitch with an impressive pedigree: her dam was Ariel de Soum and her sire Toy de Soum.

A key mating between Monne de Langladure and Estat d'Argeles won fame for the Val D'Aure Kennels and made an important contribution to the bloodlines of France and America. This mating produced a remarkable litter of six puppies who were kept by the Carels and shown extensively throughout the continent where they won innumerable prizes. One male, Hermes, later became Champion of France.

Hermes was bred to his litter sister Halia—thus doubling up on the blood of d'Argeles and de Soum. This led to the birth of Ch. Ibos du Val d'Aure of Basquaerie, imported by Mrs. Crane in 1935 in advance of his grandfather

41

Estat d'Argeles. He was used extensively at stud in America, and thus left many progeny to carry on his bloodlines.

Perhaps the most famous Great Pyrenees to be shown that day—indeed one of the all-time great dogs—was the above mentioned Tri-International Champion Estat d'Argeles (Belgian, French, Luxembourg). With his litter brother Estagel d'Argeles, he was exhibited all over Europe in 1935 and 1936. Acclaimed the most perfect pair in France, Estat and Estagel were both stud factors of great force and value in their native land, and their voyage to America was also to prove of lasting value to the breed in this country.

They were owned by the American-born Countess de Bertier de Sauvigny, who divided her stay between her Paris residence and her French home in the historic Chateau de Morsang-sur-Orge near Chartres, where the dogs were often seen taking the country air in her gardens.

Mme. La Comtesse had made an extensive search throughout France in seeking her original breeding pair, and selected as foundation matron Estaube de Soum, a beautiful specimen whom she mated to the great show winner of 1929-1930, Rip de la Noe (M. Zivi), a true "dog of the mountains."

These two brothers were actually all that existed at the CHENIL D'AR-GELES. Madame La Comtesse had raised but one litter. Two sisters, equally fine, unfortunately went to homes as pets and never were bred.

The ELEVAGE DES LOUBONNIERES was another successful kennel of the day. It distinguished itself by combining de Langladure blood with a mountain outcross. Located at Grasse in the Alps Maritimes, it was owned by the two Crist sisters.

Mlles. Crist selected as their foundation matron l'Neige de Langladure who was among the last born to Ch. Ariel de Soum, then eleven years of age, and Ch. Estagel d'Argeles.

l'Neige was bred twice to an outcross male, a famous and successful stud, Fram de la Moriniere, of mountain ancestry. The first mating of these two dogs produced Krici des Loubonnieres. At one year of age, he won at the Paris Exposition and was crowned Champion of France. The second mating produced Lisey des Loubonnieres (of Basquaerie), who became an American champion and carried on her bloodlines in the States.

Des Loubonnieres exported dogs to the Chenil du Mont Picry, thus contributing to the establishment of this famous kennel in Belgium.

One of the Crist sisters was tragically killed in a freak accident after World War II when a war balloon alighted near her home. She was inspecting the balloon when someone lit a match and the balloon exploded.

Many of the French kennels of those early post-war years were kept by hotel and restaurant owners, butchers, and food concessionaires. Thus the dogs could be fed scraps from the tables, making it economically feasible to keep more than a handful. The CHENILE DE CAREIL was no exception. It was owned jointly by M. L. Janning and Mlle. Suzanne Luce.

The Famous Brothers. In the foreground Tri-International and American Champion Estat d'Argeles of Basquaerie, and in the background American Champion Estagel d'Argeles of Basquaerie.

Champion Mitsou de Langladure, a bitch of good type from one of France's best bloodlines, and an early Basquaerie import.

43

Originally the Manoir de Careil was located in Brittany and it was here that the foundation of the bloodline was laid. The brood bitch was Mirka de la Noe. She was mated to the stud dog Rip de la Noe, owned by M. Zivi; the mating produced the dog Patou—the first to bear the kennel affix.

While vacationing in Brittany in 1929, Mme. Harper Trois Fontaines had been drawn to The Manoir de Careil because of its famous cuisine. Here, for the first time, she saw the Great Pyrenees, and later wrote, "I fell in love with the noble creatures, who were as sweet as they were beautiful." She attempted to import a pair of pups but they both died in quarantine.

In 1933, M. Janning and Mlle. Luce moved their establishment to the Chateaux de Jacques-Coeur in Boisy. It was a typical and charming feudal castle, and after it was renovated it became a famous show place and one of the top flight inns of the day. During its career, it numbered among its guests both Madame Harper and Mr. and Mrs. Crane.

Mme. Harper returned to the Chenile de Careil in 1933 and persuaded M. Janning to part with Kop de Careil, whom he had intended to retain as a stud dog. In the background of Kop de Cariel was the blood of the mountains through his grandsire Rip de la Noe, who was also the sire of Estat and Estagel d'Argeles. Kop also combined, on his dam's side, Betpouey and de Soum. He became the foundation sire at de Fontenay.

It is interesting to note, therefore, that through the blood of de Soum and d'Argeles, admixed with the same mountain outcrosses, the basic bloodlines in England and America were nearly identical.

With the onset of World War II, M. Janning and Mlle. Luce dispersed their remaining stock and moved their hostelry to the French Riviera—thus writing a finis to one of the most colorful chapters in Great Pyrenees kennel history in France.

We turn now to another famous kennel of the day. Located a few miles outside the city of Lourdes, the dogs of DU PIC DU JER gazed across the beautiful Lac Lourdes to the distant snow-capped mountains bordering Spain. No more picturesque setting ever existed to found a kennel of Great Pyrenees. The proprietors were Mme. and M. Jos. Abadie-Toulet, who eked out a living tilling the soil and running a small refreshment concession for the summer tourists on the edge of the Lac. Litters were whelped in a barn, and the dogs were free to roam at will within the fenced boundaries of the yard, often going back into the mountainside with M. on his chores. Brood bitches were farmed out to the surrounding mountaineers. If a client wanted a good dog, M. Abadie-Toulet would mysteriously disappear into the mountains and return in a few days with a good specimen.

The foundation sire was Roland du Pic du Jer, a badger marked dog—sturdy, strong-boned and of mountain origin. The bitch was Fanchette. In all respects, du Pic du Jer was a typical mountain establishment.

Ch. Ibos du Val d'Aure of Basquaerie. A linebred grandson of Tri-International Champion Estat d'Argeles and a pillar of the breed in America.

Monne de Loubonnieres, a daughter of Ch. Krici de Loubonnieres, and considered one of the most beautiful bitches in France. Pictured here in 1939.

Ch. Aspe du Pic du Jer, one of the foundation bitches at Basquaerie, and the first bitch to win an American championship.

6481   Un éleveur de ch
       des Pyrénées et ses fav

M. Joseph Abadie-Toulet with two of his favorites at Du Pic du Jer.

One of M. Charles Fasquelle's du Givre dogs, pulling a cart.

The kennel prospered under the kindly supervision of the Toulets. By the late 1930s dogs had been exported to America, England, Belgium and Holland.

Bigorre, Rhune and Aspe du Pic du Jer were brought to Basquaerie, and Aspe distinguished herself by being the first female of the breed to win her American Championship. All left many descendants in the United States.

Baby du Pic du Jer became the foundation stud at De Mont Picry in Belgium, also winning a Tri-International Championship. Nethou du Pic du Jer was a popular stud and a champion in Holland.

Mme. Harper also bred heavily to the du Pic du Jer strain through the blood of her great stud, Labada du Mont Picry, son of Labeda du Pic du Jer. Thus the kennel had a far reaching effect on the early bloodlines of many lands.

M. Abadie-Toulet reported that during World War II he was able to keep his collection of dogs intact, although at great expense to himself, and privation of food on his part. After the death of M. Abadie, Madame was able to continue breeding for many years until, at the age of 87, in the year 1975, she too died and thus another great kennel passed into Pyrenean history.

At the CHENIL DE TRUCHARD, outside of the small village of Ussen-En-Forez, Loire, Mme. and M. Charet maintained a small collection of Pyrenees. The old dog of the kennel was Roland de Soum, a magnificent specimen and son of a fine sire, Tiarko, of mountain origins. The brood bitch was Pastoure de Bagneres. These two had produced a number of puppies, which were dispersed throughout France and the Continent. One of these was Arlette de Truchard of Basquaerie, who became an American champion and left many descendants to carry on her blood. The death of Roland and Pastoure in 1938 ended the breeding of Pyreneans at de Truchard.

The role played by M. Charles Fasquelle, founder of DU GIVRE, was a brief one; but of considerable importance. This gentleman led a somewhat double life. On the one hand he was an ardent devotee of the theaters, cafes and boulevards of "Gay Paree;" but he was also a serious and dedicated Pyrenees breeder.

Fasquelle had discovered the mountain dogs as a young man on vacation in the Pyrenees. He was especially impressed with the breed's size and strength and selected his breeding stock with these in mind. Many of his dogs were trained to pull wagons and sleds. Once, when taunted at a Paris dinner party for spending so much money on "good for nothing" dogs, he wagered his dogs could pull him from France to Spain. He won his bet by shipping dogs and a sled to the frontier and having his team pull him a hundred yards over the border.

The most renowned bitch of the Du Givre line was Blanchette who was imported by Mrs. Crane and became the dam of the first litter born in America.

Athos de la Moriniere, sire of Ch. H'Echez de Guerveur of Basquaerie. A combination of his bloodlines with those of du Givre gave rise to the de Guerveur strain of the Legers.

The Elevage de Guerveur. K'Eros de Guerveur, later to become an American champion, stands to the right of Mlle. Christine Leger. — *Courtesy, Mrs. Francis V. Crane*

48

Also present at the Paris show was the stud dog Athos de la Moriniere, whose qualities were brought to America through the de Guerveur-bred dogs, Ch. H'Echez de Guerveur of Basquaerie and Ch. K'Eros de Guerveur of Basquaerie. The ELEVAGE DE GUERVEUR was, in those days, run jointly by three sisters, the Mademoiselles Leger, one of whom, Christine, lived with her father in an apartment on the outskirts of Paris and attended to the sales and correspondence. The other two sisters resided at the kennel on the Belle-Isle-En-Mer, located off the coast of Brittany.

One of its principal values lay in its rather remote location which provided "cold" blood, not admixed with the strains of the late thirties. It therefore was considered a useful outcross for the de Soum and de Langladure strains.

Reports from de Guerveur in the late forties indicated that the kennel was still very much alive and going strong, sharing honors at the Paris shows with M. Delattre's Pontoise dogs. Today one still hears of dogs bearing the de Guerveur affix at shows in France. Therefore, this kennel ranks among the oldest in existence.

Perhaps every entry at the Paris International should have been a winner that day. But the dogs were not being judged by the historian. As Madame Dretzen stood back to consider her final choices, it was to be the great stud dog Toy de Soum, six years of age and in the magnificent bloom of his male maturity, who was to be given the honors. And as the winning bitch, Madame Dretzen chose the incomparable Ariel de Soum, then eight years old and every inch the Queen of France. Another Paris show had passed into history.

Thus the forces set in motion by B. Senac-Lagrange had unerringly brought together at Paris in 1933 a nucleus of bloodlines of such force and distinction that its influence on the breed in France would endure for years to come. With the founding of Basquaerie Kennels in the United States and de Fontenay in England, the type would blossom and propel the Pyrenean Mountain Dog around the world.

Mrs. Francis V. Crane marks her judge's catalogue at Morris and Essex, 1950. — *Evelyn Shafer*

Mrs. Crane with her first breeding pair, Champion Urdos de Soum and Blanchette du Givre, pictured in Needham, Massachusetts, in 1932.

50

3

Basquaerie Kennels— The Great Pyrenees Comes to America

by Mary W. A. Crane

As our chapter title implies, the story of the Basquaerie Kennels of Mr. and Mrs. Francis V. Crane is also the story of how the Great Pyrenees came to America. During its long and distinguished career, Basquaerie accounted for over 150 Great Pyrenees champions, a record which has yet to be broken. Mrs. Crane's contributions to the growth and betterment of the breed have been incalculable. We are particularly pleased to have this important story in her own words.

U NTIL THE FALL of 1930, my husband Francis and I were happily living in our home in Needham, Massachusetts with two imported English Cocker Spaniels—Desmond and Towser of Ware, and one Field Spaniel bitch—Dinah, for pets; little dreaming of enlarging our doggy family, founding a kennel, or introducing a breed to make history for the canine world.

But who, when they are dog lovers to begin with, can resist the charms of two ten-week-old Great Pyrenees puppies, all white and cuddly, seen for the first time, as were the brothers Bazen and Nethou de Soum, brought home from a summer spent in France by the Misses Hedge of Brookline, Massachusetts? The sisters had been visiting their aunt, Clara Perry, an American artist who lived part-time abroad, and who also happened to be a friend of our family. When Miss Perry next returned to France, it was with the instructions to buy a pair, suitable for breeding, to bring to the Cranes in the fall of 1931. And thus it was that Basquaerie was born!

An interesting side note, I think, was the fact that Miss Perry's interest in the breed stemmed from her enthusiasm for the "Seeing Eye" equivalent in France. Les Grands Chiens des Montagnes were in favor in France for this purpose, appreciated above all for their intelligence, keen eyesight and white color. The wetness of a long coat on stormy days did not seem to disturb the French people, as it has the Americans.

Thus arrived Urdos and Anie de Soum from the de Soum kennels of the eminent French breeder and judge, M. A. Cazaux-Moutou at Lourdes, Hautes Pyrenees. Improper and inadequate vaccination in France and ignorance on the part of the Cranes tragically cost the life of Anie from distemper the first winter, and the serious illness of Urdos who, fortunately, was saved. A second bitch, Blanchette du Givre, was brought over a year later, and thus the Great Pyrenees was launched in the United States of America.

As preparations to register the breed with the American Kennel Club were carried on, the breed name had to be condensed from the long official breed designation in France. Hence, "Great Pyrenees," derived from "The Great Dogs of the Pyrenees Mountains," was chosen.

Also, a kennel name had to be selected for registration. Proper names were out so, to try to give the feeling of the high Pyrenees, "aerie" (for high home of the eagle) was combined with "Basque" (for the dogs' homeland in France). The designation BASQUAERIE was registered with the American Kennel Club on April 17, 1933, thereby becoming the first Great Pyrenees kennels to be registered in the U.S.A.

Contacts having been made in France with various breeders through exchanges of correspondence, photographs, and personal contacts on the part of Miss Perry and myself, it was but a short time before other specimens were purchased and on their way to America. The next to come to Basquaerie were Patou (a real mountain dog) and Aspe du Pic de Jer, again from a peasant's farm, owned by Joseph Abadie-Toulet, up in the high mountains at Lac Lourdes. The third import was Mitsou de Langladure, from a well-known and long established breeding kennel owned by M. and Mme. Georges Le Conte, Chateau de Villechenay, located in the chateau country at Millancay in the Province of Indre. From here on, others followed in rapid succession, some from the mountains and some from kennels. Included among them were dogs of such notable contribution to the breed as Champions H'Echez de Guerveur, Pastoure du Pic du Jer, and Pastoure de Vieuzac.

From the start Basquaerie combined the strength and ruggedness of the true working type of peasant-owned and reared dog, and the more refined, polished and genteel type to be found in the French breeding kennels. This combination, I feel, gave a balanced refinement to Basquaerie's American-bred dogs that produced dogs of good temperament: strong in body, bone and conformation; correct in type and expression; elegant in stance and appearance.

This combination was the result of a fortunate set of circumstances, because the true peasant-bred dog lacks (and always has) a three-generation

Urdos de Soum, the first Great Pyrenees Champion in America, in 1934. His parentage: Toy de Soum — Lutour de Langladure. From a painting by Edwin R. Megargee.

Basquaerie Marsous, the first American-bred Great Pyrenees Champion. His parentage: Ch. Patou — Ch. Mitsou de Langladure. From a painting by Edwin R. Megargee.

TRI-INT. & AM. CH. ESTAT d'ARGELES of BASQUAERIE

Fr. Ch. Hermes du Val D'Aure

Ch. Ibos du Val D'Aure of Basquaerie

Ch. Basquaerie Ariel C.D.

Ch. Basquaerie Estagel

Ch. Basquaerie Beau Jacques

Ch. Sunset Knoll Basquaerie Beak

Ch. Basquaerie Corvina

Ch. Basquaerie Vicki Snow White

Ch. Basquaerie Gui de Noel

Ch. Basquaerie Bichon C.D.

Ch. Basquaerie Bibelot

Ch. Basquaerie Bijou

Ch. Basquaerie Bali

Ch. Balibasque Mister Big

Ch. Cote de Neige Symphony

Ch. Basquaerie Ballerina

Ch. Basquaerie Bali

Balibasque Beau of Karolaska C.D.

Ch. Karolaska Glacier

Ch. Basquaerie Boris

Ch. Cote de Neige Niverau

Ch. Quibbletown Mistigris

Ch. Quibbletown Gina

Ch. Quibbletown Ariette

Ch. Basquaerie Houx de Noel

Ch. Lawrence of Combermere

Ch. Loramo de La Colina

Ch. Lorvaso de La Colina

Ch. Quibbletown Good Time Charli

Ch. Quibbletown Jim Dandy

Ch. Balibasque Wooden Nickel

Quibbletown Bouncing Bett

Quibbletown April Sunshine

Ch. Quibbletown Impresario

Ch. Quibbletown Carlotta

Ch. Quibbletown Cavalier

Quibbletown Queen Bear

Ch. Karolaska Glacier

Ch. Quibbletown Impresario

Ch. Quibbletown Billy Wink

Ch. Chip 'N Tip Quibbletown Impy

Ch. Chip 'N Tip Sonny's Reflection

The descendants of Tri-Int. & Am. Ch. Estat d'Argeles of Basquaerie, showing the influence of this dog on contemporary bloodlines in America.

1
2
3
4
5
6
7
8
9
10
11

pedigree suitable or acceptable for official registration with both the French Kennel Club and the American Kennel Club. The peasant breeders, being far removed from the shows, and especially the Paris Show at which a win is required to attain a French title, were neither able to attend or sufficiently interested in showing to make the effort to meet the expense. At best, they kept very sketchy records of the ancestry of their dogs. Furthermore, they distrusted those in authority in the registering organizations in Paris. They could not, therefore, supply a buyer with a three-generation pedigree, nor did this disturb them at all.

Suffice it for them to know that their "Pastoure" was bred to M.'s "Patou" in the next valley or village. This simple exchange of breeding services between friends and neighbors accounts for the predominance in mountain pedigrees of Patous and Pastoures, followed by "de" (from), and then the proper name of the home territory of said animal.

At the beginning of the breed's introduction to the States, therefore, the American Kennel Club had to be liberal in lowering their standards to allow specimens to come into the country and to be shown and registered in spite of insufficient pedigrees. Otherwise, there would not have been enough breeding stock made available to assure strong and wise propagation of the breed.

Peasant-owned and reared dogs were selected for Basquaerie by M. Senac-Lagrange. He took charge of locating suitable specimens and getting them to the railroad station at Lourdes for shipment to America.

The following are important dates in the early history of the breed here:

1932: Urdos de Soum of Basquaerie carried the banner for the breed into the Miscellaneous Class at Boston's Eastern Dog Club Show on February 22.

1933: In February, the Great Pyrenees obtained official recognition as a purebred breed by the American Kennel Club. On April 4, the first separate classes for Great Pyrenees were offered at the Worcester show in Massachusetts. Records were made in quick succession. Urdos de Soum became the first Great Pyrenees to place in a Working Group (at the Ladies Dog Show on June 3). Two weeks later, the first litter of Pyrenees puppies, sired by Urdos, was born to Blanchette du Givre at Basquaerie Kennels.

1934: Urdos became the first American-crowned champion at the Eastern Dog Club Show in Boston. Champion Patou of Basquaerie won a Working Group — first Great Pyrenees to achieve this honor — at the Middlesex Kennel Club in Cambridge. On June 17, Aspe du Pic du Jer became the first Great Pyrenees bitch champion, winning her title at the Ladies Dog Club show in Dedham, Massachusetts. To round out this very active year, on December 2nd, The Great Pyrenees Club of America was formed.

1935: This year saw the championship of the first American-bred Great Pyrenees, Basquaerie Marsous, son of Champion Patou out of Mitsou de Langladure. Basquaerie Marie Blanque, a daughter of Urdos out of Pastoure du Pic du Jer, became the first Great Pyrenees to be registered and recognized in Canada.

Ch. Basquaerie Gui de Noel, a son of Ch. Ibos du Val d'Aure of Basquaerie, and a sire of nine champions. 1940.

Ch. Basquaerie Bichon CD, a son of Ch. Basquaerie Gui de Noel. He sired nine champions. 1943.

Ch. Basquaerie Bibelot, a son of Ch. Basquaerie Bichon CD. Note the outstanding type. Winner of 132 Bests of Breed. Bibelot sired six champions. 1948.

On September 10, the Great Pyrnees Club of America was voted a member club by the American Kennel Club. Mr. Crane became the delegate, a position which he held until 1948 when an illness forced his retirement.

In November, Great Pyrenees were shown at the Royal Winter Fair in Toronto, Canada, under National Kennel Club rules with separate classification for sexes. The breed was permanently launched in Canada.

During this year the breed was re-introduced to England by Madame Jeanne Harper Trois-Fontaines, who secured two males and one female from the Continent, and registered her de Fontenay Kennels with the British Kennel Club.

1936: The first American-bred Great Pyrenees arrived in England to begin its six-month quarantine. And at the Golden Gate Show in San Francisco, Belle of Basquaerie, daughter of Urdos and Blanchette, became the first registered Great Pyrenees to be shown in an AKC show on the Pacific Coast.

In the summer of this year Mr. and Mrs. Crane traveled to England and the Continent, visiting Mme. Harper and meeting her foundation stock, Nethou de Langladure, Kop de Cariel and Ianette de Boisy. They then went to Paris and, renting a car, drove into the Chateau and High Pyrenees Country, stopping to visit kennels and to seek out the breed in its home environment. Some of the movies taken on this trip have been reproduced for the Great Pyrenees Film Exchange and have been viewed by many in recent years.

This trip also brought to Basquaerie other imports including Maya de Langladure, Arizes and Azun de Soum, Arlette de Truchard, Khiva and Kaira du Val d'Aure, and some English Cocker Spaniels.

Over the next few years, I took further trips to the Continent: in 1937, France, Belgium and Holland; and in 1939, to Brussels to judge the Canine Exposition Internationale of The Societe Royale de Saint-Hubert. During this last visit I went to the kennels of Mme. Vandermousen in Frameries, which was near the Maginot Line. From Mme. Vandermousen I was able to purchase the bitch Koranne, a daughter of International Champion Baby du Pic du Jer. Koranne was destined to become one of Basquaerie's top brood matrons.

Mr. Crane joined me later in France and together we toured the French kennels, returning on the French liner Normandie. With us were six new additions to the kennel. Among these were Rhune du Pic du Jer and K'Eros de Guerveur of Basquaerie.

Perhaps no win did more to boost Great Pyrenees' popularity and prestige than that of Champion Ibos du Val d'Aure of Basquaerie. In June, 1939, Ibos won the Working Group at the North Westchester Kennel Club show which was held on the Sherman R. Hoyt estate at Katonah, New York. That this was the third largest show in America of the time added much glory; it was also the show considered that year as the Specialty Show of the Great Pyrenees Club of America.

57

Ch. K'Eros de Guerveur of Basquaerie, the first Great Pyrenees to win a Best In Show, on September 23, 1939, at the Eastern States Exposition. Owned by Mrs. Francis V. Crane. — *E. Morgan Savage*

Ch. Koranne of Basquaerie CD. The first Great Pyrenees Obedience title holder in America, in 1938. — *Percy Jones*

The following year, K'Eros de Guerver gained fame for the breed by being the first Great Pyrenees to win an all-breeds Best in Show, at Hartford, Connecticut, on April 20, 1940. Continuing along the road to fame came eight other champions: Basquaerie Gui de Noel, Basquaerie Beau Estagel, Basquaerie Bichon, C.D., Basquaerie Andre, La Shan Marc of Basquaerie, Basquaerie Bibelot, Sunset Knoll Basquaerie Beau, and Basquaerie Bali. All not only won Working Group firsts and consistently had other placements in the Group through their careers but most were also Best in Show winners.

While the Best of Breed winners were predominantly males, some of the great bitches over the years also deserve mention. The ones that especially come to mind are Champions Aspe du Pic du Jer, Mitsou de Langladure, Basquaerie Nana, Noella, Ballerina and Corvina; the latter two had the almost unheard-of distinction of defeating their male competitors at Club Specialty Shows!

One of the great bits of good fortune for Basquaerie and the breed in general was my meeting in Paris with Mme. la Contesse de Sauvigny, during which I was able to persuade her to part with her European Tri-International Champion Estat d'Argeles and his brother French Champion Estagel d'Argeles, and to send both to American in the fall of 1936. Estat had been proclaimed the most perfect and beautiful Great Pyrenees in all France in 1935. So, as the exemplification of correctness of head, expression and type, we commissioned Mons. Fath, a sculptor designated by the French Government as an official animal judge, to do a head study, and also a full length sculpture of him from life at his home chateau. One of the full length bronzes is in the library of the American Kennel Club in New York; the other at Basquaerie. The head study is known to all members of the Great Pyrenness Club of America as that on the club pin.

Mons. Fath also painted for us a full copy of the famous original by Oudrey, entitled "La Chasse Aux Loupes," depicting two Great Pyrenees fighting a wolf, which at that time hung over the grand staircase in the Chateau de Compiegne. This now hangs at the American Kennel Club also.

However, the greatest contribution, one that will be lasting, was the ability of the two famous brothers and their cousins from de Langladure to stamp their line with the correct Great Pyrenees' type and expression. This ability has come down directly through their descendants, all Basquaerie champions: Beau Estagel, Bichon C.D., Bibelot, Sunset Knoll Basquaerie Beau and Basquaerie Bali; then on to the Balibasque sires, among them Balibasque Beau of Karolaska C.D., El Amor Bruno Balibasque, and their offspring. These have been and are continuing to be the top producing lines for head and expression, without which, in my opinion, one just does not have a true and beautiful Great Pyrenees.

The only other strain that I have found consistently producing the same type is the inter-related de Soum, de Langladure and du Val d'Aure family. The progenitors of these are Champions Urdos de Soum, Azun de Soum, Ibos du

Val d'Aure, Gui de Noel and Basquaerie Boris. A mating of a son and daughter of Urdos de Soum was the foundation choice of Mrs. Butcher for her Cote de Neige Kennels.

Basquaerie pioneered in the field of Obedience training back in the early years of the movement in 1938. Champion Koranne of Basquaerie C.D. was the first obedience degree winner; Champion Basquaerie Amie, C.D., C.D.X., the first to gain the second degree in 1941. Spurred on by the interest in obedience training stimulated by the request for "War Dogs," classes were springing up all over the East, and by 1942 Basquaerie had five obedience title holders. They were: Champion Basquaerie Bichon C.D.; Basquaerie Kuri C.D.; Basquaerie Ariel C.D.; and the two females already mentioned. The services rendered by the "Dogs for Defense" are noted in Chapter 19.

Basquaerie's years of glory passed into history in the late 1950s. Never was there a sadder person than I when the realization came that the kennels must be drastically reduced and practically disbanded. This was due in part to Mr. Crane's health which necessitated a move to Florida for half of each year and the subsequent impossibility of finding suitable kennel management and supervision from such a distance.

However, in the dissolution of the large kennel family, representative breeding stock, male and female, of the famous and best producing lines went to Balibasque Kennels in Pennsylvania, and a few others to Soleil Kennels in Kansas. In both areas the lines carry on.

But Basquaerie has not and will not die as long as I live, for I have kept two brood matrons who carry on my favorite and best lines, as well as one youngster, Basquaerie Easter Bunny, daughter of my Champion Basquaerie Corla's Betsy II, who hopefully will make a name for herself in the show rings of the future. My fourth bitch is Champion Karolaska Babs of Basquaerie, daughter of Karolaska's famous foundation stud, Balibasque Beau of Karolaska, C.D. There just is NO FINIS to Basquaerie!

I am proud that through the years, Basquaerie has stood as a name of renown and honor wherever Great Pyrenees are spoken of, admired and loved. Dogs of our kennel prefix have gone, through the years, to foreign lands far and wide: England, Holland, Belgium, India, the Republic of South Africa, Brazil, Mexico and Canada.

We always attempted to do all in our power to establish and maintain the correct and true type of the Great Dogs of the Pyrenees Mountains. In the years before World War II, we bought up representatives of as many kennels and strains as possible, bringing them to Holliston, Massachusetts, in the hope of perpetuating the breed while the pressures of war threatened its very survival in its native land. We carried them safely over the war years, maintaining over one hundred individuals, breeding and showing whenever possible. We exhibited far and wide to acquaint the public with the breed's charm

60

and beauty. We stood ready to help new breeders with advice when asked, to assist breeding programs, and gave freely of our time to further the breed's proper promotion.

Basquaerie was the fountainhead from which all the early kennels sprang: Cote de Neige, Add-En-On, La Colina, La Shan, Robwood and Combermere.

Basquaerie is proud of the successes of the breed in America and believes that a bright future lies ahead IF breeders will put aside personal and petty jealousies and remain true to the authentic type, breeding for and rewarding in the show ring ONLY those dogs and bitches which carry the correct Pyrenean type and expression. Think of the head of a Polar Bear with the ears falling down; not a Brown Bear—for you want a substantial muzzle, not a short one. And refer to your club insignia for the correct head!

I want to take this opportunity right here and now to stress that it is NOT the nature of Great Pyrenees to be overly large, tall, or in any sense "immense." This choice of a translation word to describe the breed in the original standard was ill-chosen. The breed is a large breed, true, but neither excessively tall, slab-sided, short-muzzled, droopy-jowled, too narrow or too domed in the head, nor marked with a positive stop or a round-eye! They are of a large-medium size when compared with the few exceedingly tall and large breeds. So, please push far asunder any misconceptions you may now have concerning size. Let's not breed for ponies!

I bring this critique up because I have often been asked how the dogs of today compare in size with those early imports. My reply is that the average dog and bitch one sees are the same.

The initial interest in a tall Great Pyrenees came into vogue, I believe, with Champion K'Eros de Guerveur of Basquaerie, who did make a striking picture in the ring, and made himself famous by becoming the first to win Best in Show. But he was also a dog of correct Pyrenees type, not carrying the faults I mentioned above, and well deserving of his wins. However, size has become an obsession in the minds of some people ever since—but fortunately not in the minds of all! And not in the minds of those breeders whose interest centers on correctness of type and quality.

Unfortunately, all too many people are prone to speak out, giving their own ideas and appraisals to fit their own dogs. But how many who do this have really seen the dogs in their native land doing their natural chores? I say again, please don't pioneer for a new cause unless you are sure of your facts, from actual experience and not just hearsay.

Basquaerie has indeed had a long and colorful history, full of accomplishments, success and failures. We have had our share of happiness and sorrow, of good times and bad. But life, after all, means taking the bitter with the sweet. So we wish you all, newcomers to the breed and old alike, all successes in the years ahead. But PLEASE, one request—do not try to change the world's most beautiful and wonderful breed. The Great Pyrenees' delight and charm lie in its being what it is today. Keep it that way. And be proud of it!

Ch. Cote de Neige Echo, one of Marjorie Butcher's top winning bitches. Whelped in 1940.
— *Courtesy, Edith K. Smith*

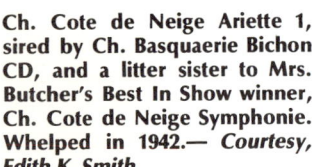

Ch. Cote de Neige Ariette 1, sired by Ch. Basquaerie Bichon CD, and a litter sister to Mrs. Butcher's Best In Show winner, Ch. Cote de Neige Symphonie. Whelped in 1942.— *Courtesy, Edith K. Smith*

Ch. Cote de Neige Ariel displays the perfection of type Mrs. Butcher sought in her bitches. Whelped 1942. — *Courtesy, Edith K. Smith*

4

Early American Bloodlines

THE BASQUAERIE IMPORTS of Mr. and Mrs. Crane provided a firm foundation upon which to build for the future. During the growing years, a number of well-known breeders and friends of the Great Pyrenees also made important contributions to the further development of the breed in America.

Cote de Neige

Among the early pioneering kennels, Mrs. Marjorie Butcher's Cote de Neige stands out as a dramatic example of just what can be accomplished by a truly gifted and dedicated breeder. During a rather brief period, little more than a decade, when Cote de Neige was at its height, no kennel produced more champions, or did more to establish correct type and soundness in its bloodlines.

Marjorie Butcher was born in Canada, educated in Switzerland, received training in the opera and sang for the Washington Opera Company. A great lover of dogs from early childhood, Mrs. Butcher moved to the Berkshires and, in Pittsfield, Massachusetts, acquired her foundation female. Ch. Basquaerie Fleurette promptly whelped a litter of puppies in a coat closet—much to the surprise of all concerned. It was obvious that she had indulged in a moonlight romance with her own brother! But Mrs. Butcher said, "We had a very nice litter from her. I could see no signs of nervousness, or what you might expect from inbreeding."

The following year Fleurette was bred to Ch. Patou of Basquaerie and produced two champions, Cote de Neige Patou and Joyeuse. The bloodlines of other imports were added, the most notable being Chs. Bazen de Soum and Maya de Langladure from France, and Ch. Zayda Van Euskara from Holland.

Bazen de Soum was the dog imported by the Misses Hedge in the fall of 1930. He later distinguished himself by doing sled work for the Grenville Mission in Newfoundland. And Ch. Zayda became the first Great Pyrenees to win a Canadian Championship.

The honor role of Cote de Neige champions, well over 30 in number, included many famous winners of the day: Cote de Neige Acteur, Ariel, Ariette, Berceuse, Echo, Guerrier, Nive, Nivereau, Pastourette, Symphonie, Zephire and others. Mrs. Butcher's musical interest explains the many musical names given her dogs; the floral names were the result of her great interest in song birds.

In 1944, Ch. Cote de Neige Echo became the first bitch to win the Will S. Monroe Memorial Trophy by going Best of Breed at the Great Pyrenees Club of America National Speciality. Two years later, Champions Cote de Neige Echo and her litter sister, Ariette, won the Best Brace at Westminister. The following year Ch. Cote de Neige Symphonie became the first American-bred Great Pyrenees to win an all breed Best in Show!

Mrs. C. Seaver Smith, a contemporary authority closely associated with Marjorie Butcher in the early fifties, recalls: "It would be difficult to find an American-bred Great Pyrenees today who does not have Cote de Neige in its background. La Shan, Esterhazy, Castellan, La Colina, Crete de Pins, Bon Chance, Robwood, Add-En-On, Be-La-Mar and Quibbletown all had, in their beginnings, at least some Cote de Neige stock.

"It would not be accurate to refer to Cote de Neige as a bloodline, as there was no true pattern of linebreeding or inbreeding. It cannot be denied, however, that through selective and perceptive breeding, Marjorie definitely established a Cote de Neige type, which we can still identify in the dogs of today. It is obvious in going over her records and photographs that the means to that end were the bitches of Cote de Neige. She seemed to have an unending supply of superb bitches and rarely was the kennel defeated in that sex."

In the forties Mrs. Butcher moved her dogs to New Canaan, Connecticut, where the kennel remained a small family-run operation with emphasis on quality. In the fifties she again moved to a new location, this time in Bedford Village. Since the new property was not well suited to a large breed, Mrs. Butcher turned to her other love, the Pembroke Welsh Corgi. In a short time time, Cote de Neige was to add to its fame through its top winning Corgis.

At the GPCA Fall Specialty Dinner in 1971, Mrs. Butcher revealed some of her guiding principles:

> "I'm a strong believer that the first litter you get from a bitch is going to be your best litter. I think if you're going to plan your first breeding, you should breed the very best you want to breed.
>
> "After my first litter which was inbred brother to sister, I've never bred that close again. I have bred father to daughter, but I'd rather skip a generation.
>
> "I believe that pigmentation problems are harder to correct than lack of bone. Again, I don't think a Pyrenees is a dog that should have clumsy, overly heavy bone. I think that it should be a moderately boned dog. It should be an agile moving dog with good, sturdy bone.
>
> "We often spayed our bitches after their first litter. They're much healthier if they're spayed. We were fortunate in being able to place our bitches in homes

Ch. Cote de Neige Starlight, a granddaughter of Ch. K'Eros de Guerveur of Basquaerie. She would be a top winning bitch in any era. Whelped 1945. — *Courtesy, Edith K. Smith.*

Frank Koller pictured with two of his Great Pyrenees. — *Courtesy, I.G.P.R.*

after breeding them. They didn't have to spend the rest of their lives in the kennels. There may be exceptions to this, but this was my policy.

"I think the coat of a Pyrenees should be really quite coarse hair lying absolutely flat. This coat sheds the dirt much better, and you can keep a dog with what I have called a 'correct' Pyrenees coat very clean with very little effort.

"I think that any little puppy that's brought into the world should have the opportunity to live. I do think that there are certain very serious faults that may warrant culling. But when you get a puppy which just hasn't quite made it, I think it's pretty sad if some good home somewhere can't be found. I think the puppy should be sold without papers along with a written agreement that it is never to be used for breeding. If you put a pet-quality puppy out and allow it to breed, then you will pull the breed quality down. A little puppy going without papers and with a signed agreement makes an awfully nice pet for someone who can't afford to pay the price for a show-quality dog."

Throughout her life Mrs. Butcher remained actively interested in the breed. Her devotion to the Great Pyrenees prompted her to serve on a Committee to study the Standard of 1971. Mrs. Butcher was recognized as one of the leading authorities on Great Pyrenees up to the time of her passing in 1973.

Castellan

The kennel prefix of the author, Paul Strang, came into being with the purchase of Ch. Cote de Neige Pataud from Mrs. Butcher.

While living in France in the 1930s, Mr. Strang owned a number of Great Pyrenees. These were selected from firsthand experience after visiting the shows, talking with the French breeders, and making several trips into the Pyrenees Mountains to study the dogs in their native environment.

Pataud came to Castellan Kennels in the spring of 1946 and before passing away some ten years later, this splendid dog sired innumerable litters that inherited, to a high degree, his beautiful head, keen intelligence and outgoing nature.

The goal of Castellan breeding, in the tradition of Pataud and his fine descendant, Castellan Coco, has always been to produce sound dogs of proper type and disposition, in the upper size range.

Add-En-On Kennels

The prefix of Dr. and Mrs. Carl Harris came into being in 1937 with the purchase of their foundation female, Basquaerie Hunnette, from Mrs. Crane.

Additional specimens were acquired from the Cranes and Marjorie Butcher. The first litter whelped in 1938, sired by Ch. Cote de Neige Zephire, was to establish the reputation of the kennel. Among seven puppies, six were champions by 18 months of age and one, Ch. Henry VIII, was a Group winner.

66

Ch. Lawrence of Combermere, the foundation stud at La Colina Kennels. A beautiful example of the breed. Owned by Dr. and Mrs. Fredrick Seward.

Ch. Lorvaso de la Colina set the type at Quibbletown. He sired 11 champions. Owned by Mr. and Mrs. C. Seaver Smith, Jr.

During the 12 years when Add-En-On was at its peak, the kennel played a major role in popularizing and promoting the breed, particularly on the East Coast, where modern pedigrees still show the Add-En-On influence. After the death of Dr. Harris in 1945, Mrs. Harris and her daughter converted their kennel into a boarding and training facility. Today they are the authors of the excellent *Add-En-On Kennels Course in Kennel Management*.

Bator de Esterhazy, Reg.

Born in Hungary, Frank Koller's kennel name celebrates the Esterhazy nobility of his native land. During a brief period in the late forties, this suffix was used by a Giant Schnauzer breeder and during this time Mr. Koller registered his dogs under the Zold Erdo prefix. Later, he reclaimed his rightful suffix and had it registered.

Frank Koller based his bloodlines on Basquaerie, La Colina and Cote de Neige. Ch. Vitz of Batour de Esterhazy and Nagy Feher of Batour de Esterhazy made an important contribution to the breed in this period. Chiogenes of Bighyo was the sire of Castellan Canichet.

Interbreeding between his foundation dogs, Frank Koller produced the sturdy, consistent Esterhazy bloodline that, with only occasional outcrosses, continues to this day.

Mr. Koller has been a consistent supporter of the Great Pyrenees for over 30 years. He became the Great Pyrenees Club of America's representative to the American Kennel Club in 1954 and held the position until he retired from the Club in 1966. He has watched the breed develop over the years, and he firmly believes that the present holds the reality of what in the past was only a wish. "Now is what we have always wanted and strived for. Now we have many Pyrenees, really good ones, and beautiful ones."

Mr. Koller continues to breed on a limited basis.

La Colina

Dr. and Mrs. Frederick Seward founded their La Colina Kennels at New Hampton, New York, in 1940. Ch. Lawrence of Combermere, purchased from Mr. and Mrs. George Lord's Combermere Island Kennels in Ontario, Canada, was the kennel's foundation stud dog. This was a truly beautiful dog, strong in de Soum and de Langladure bloodlines. Some fine bitches were purchased from Basquaerie and Cote de Neige.

The Sewards did not achieve instant success. Several of their younger stock were eventually shown to their championship, but on the whole Lawrence did not seem to be passing on his superlative qualities. Fanciers with less determination would have given up. Fortunately the Sewards persevered and for that we can be thankful. La Colina was, eventually, to go down in history as one of our breed's most oustanding bloodlines—and Lawrence as one of its great stud dogs.

Ch. La Shan Marc of Basquaerie, son of America's first Best In Show winner, Ch. K'Eros de Guerveur of Basquaerie. La Shan Marc was one of the breed's all-time top producers with 16 champion offspring. Owned by Homer H. Lee.

Ch. La Shan White Belle, also sired by Ch. K'Eros de Guerveur of Basquaerie, distinguished herself by becoming the first Great Pyrenees bitch to win the Working Group, at the Heart of America Kennel Club show, 1949. Owned by Mr. and Mrs. Eugene Noble, Aalii Kennels, Waterloo, Iowa.

Ch. Bazen — a son of Ch. Bazen de Soum. Bred by Marjorie Butcher and owned by Mr. and Mrs. Kenneth Evans of Val-Ken-Be Kennels, Portland, Oregon.

The "open sesame" to success came when daughters of Lawrence were bred to the outcross stud dog Ch. La Shan Marc of Basquaerie. Vano de la Colina and Ch. Vistoso de la Colina were produced in this manner. Ch. Lorvaso de la Colina, a grandson of Lawrence through his sire, was to pass his fine bloodlines on to Ch. Quibbletown Impresario.

As it turned out, Lawrence of Combermere became not only a pillar of the breed, but a testimonial to the fact that good breeders, such as Dr. and Mrs. Seward, with grit and perseverance, can turn adversity into success.

La Shan

The La Shan Kennels of Mr. and Mrs. Bruce Layman of Waynesboro, Pennsylvania, produced a number of show winners over a period of more than a decade. Their foundation bitch, Basquaerie Anamone, was purchased from Mrs. Crane in whelp by Ch. K'Eros de Guerveur in 1943. This breeding combined the French bloodlines of de Soum, de Truchard, and de Guerveur.

The mating gave birth to three champions: Ch. La Shan Marc of Basquaerie, Ch. La Shan White Belle, and Ch. La Shan K'Eros de Guerveur.

La Shan White Belle became the first Great Pyrenees bitch ever to win a Working Group, scoring at the Heart of America K.C. show in 1949. Only one other bitch in the breed has ever repeated this feat.

From their de Guerveur sire the La Shan dogs inherited great size and heavy bone and also the typical de Guerveur heads. To refine the heads in their line, the Laymans purchased the stud dog Ch. Combermere Capitan from the Lords in Canada. This dog was sired by Ch. Ibos du Val d'Aure, the result of a brother to sister mating by M. and Mme. Carel in France, made to capture the full effect of their parents, Ch. Estat d'Argeles and Fr. Ch. Monne de Langladure. Ch. Combermere Capitan thus brought the needed refinement to the La Shan bloodlines.

La Shan bloodlines were distributed from coast to coast: Ch. La Shan Damoiselle went to Mrs. Butcher; Ch. La Shan K'Eros de Guerveur to the Zimmermans in Minnesota; Int. Ch. La Shan Marc Aurelius to Mrs. Bethel Blendheim in Seattle, Washington; and Ch. La Shan White Belle to the Nobles in Iowa. Thus stock from La Shan, like that from La Colina, went to breeders throughout the country where they were to exert a powerful influence on behalf of the breed.

The Breed on the West Coast

To San Francisco must go the honor of hosting the first dog show in the United States at which Pyrenean Mountain Dogs were exhibited. This event occurred in 1915 at the great exposition celebrating the opening of the Panama Canal. According to a sharp-eyed newspaper man, there were also a number of other rare breeds on display including Basset Houds and the Russian Aft-sharkas. Of course, few if any of the breeds shown at this early gathering were pedigreed or registered wtih the American Kennel Club. However, it does point out the fact that San Francisco and California do have deep ties to dog shows in general, and to our breed in particular.

By the late 1940s, the breed on the West Coast was not only well under-way, but was actually represented by some of the finest specimens and blood-lines in America.

Contributing greatly to the size of the California dogs was the breeding done by Mavis Miller, of MILFRA GREAT PYRENEES, who imported the dog Ch. Zutano de la Colina from the Sewards in New York. Bitches at Milfra were obtained largely from two other distinguished West Coast kennels of that era, the VAL-KEN-BE Kennels of Mr. and Mrs. R. Kenneth Evans of Port-land, Oregon; and the BE-LA-MAR Kennels of Bethel Blendheim in Seattle, Washington. As noted earlier, the Blendheims' foundation stud was Ch. La Shan Marc Aurelius.

The Val-Ken-Be breeding program contained some of the finest bloodlines of its era. Their primary stud dog, Basquaerie Dijon, made a solid contribu-tion to West Coast Pyrenees.

The influence of his sire, Ch. La Shan Marc of Basquaerie, was even more considerable. This dog was sent to Homer Lee in northern California in 1950 by Mrs. Crane, with the hope that he would make a major contribution to Cal-ifornia breeding. This he did, siring 16 champions.

Among the pioneer efforts in southern California was Fran Bennet's PYR-HAVEN Kennels. Her first brood bitch, Ch. Princess Carla, embodied Bas-quaerie bloodlines. The first mating of Carla was to the famous stud dog, Ch. Basquaerie Monte Cristo, owned by the King-Smiths of Los Angeles. Three champions were produced from this mating in 1953. They included Prince Al-bert de Mont and Carlita de Mont, both of whom became key dogs in the Pyr-Haven bloodlines.

Ch. Basquaerie Monte Cristo was used at stud a number of times in both southern and northern California. In northern California, his influence is to be found primarily in the offspring of a litter whelped by Ch. Cordelia of Koch's Knoll, C.D. ("Trisky").

Trisky was bred by Mr. and Mrs. E. A. Koch and sold to the Melvin Rhodes (RHOPYR). She was bred twice. The first mating, to Monte Cristo, gave birth to three champions, one of whom was Ch. Montalvo of Rhopyr. In turn, Montalvo was the sire of the breed's top producer, Ch. Rogue La Rue, about whom more will be said later. Trisky's second mating was to Ch. Bas-quaerie Beau Mari. This breeding also led to champions who were to leave important descendants in California; namely Ch. Odin of Rhopyr and Ch. Euskaldun Rhopyr Gracieuse.

71

Another Pyrenees to top the list of California producers was Hendaye Euskalrho Laustan. He, too, sired 16 champions, and was the chief stud at HAI-LEE. His sire was Ch. Euskaldun Ramuntcho and his dam was Ch. Euskaldun Rhopyr Gracieuse.

Also contributing to the early bloodlines on the West Coast was the breeding of Ralph Ensign (RALFRANS). Champion Quibbletown Windsor was brought to California in 1956 by the Ensigns, where he sired Ch. Count Athos of Ralfrans. This dog, in turn, sired a great many leading California show winners. The Ensign's Jacquiline of Ralfrans was the dam of six champions, a number of them sired at the HAI-LEE Kennels of Mr. and Mrs. Merval Haile, by Hendaye Euskalro Lausten. The influence of these dogs continues to be felt on the West Coast.

The combination of the bloodlines of Basquaerie, La Shan and La Colina, that was to give the West Coast a well-deserved reputation for size, was further reinforced in 1962 by the arrival of the bitch Amelia de Fontenay. Amelia was the daughter of Irving de Pontoise de Fontenay, a French dog bred by M. Delattre of PONTOISE Kennels. Irving's sire was Ch. Drex de Pontoise, one of the truly large dogs of France.

In the late 1950s we find that three dogs of superior merit were taking the majority of the Bests of Breed at the leading California shows. Together, they embodied the best of the "old California bloodlines". They were: Ch. Odin of Rhopyr, owned by Mr. and Mrs. A. R. Hunter; Ch. Montalvo of Rhopyr, owned by Mr. and Mrs. Arthur Nevins; and Christine Palmer-Person's Ch. Euskaldun Ramuntcho, sired by Ch. Prince Albert de Mont out of Ch. Basquaerie Coquette II.

Ch. Euskaldun Ramuntcho's type was evaluated by Mrs. Crane in these words: "Never have I seen a lovelier or more typical Pyrenees head than Ramuntcho has. I would know just by looking at it that he had many crosses in his pedigree to the fine type of the famous old European Tri-International and American Champion Estad d'Argeles and his brother Estagel."

Speaking of the California dogs in general in another publication of the early sixties, Mrs. Crane wrote, "It is a real pleasure for me to write these few words about the status of Western-bred and owned Great Pyrenees, for I have, possibly unknown to any of their owners, sung their praises very loudly ever since my last visit to the Coast in 1959. At that time, I was fortunate to have shown under me a very imposing array of these dogs and I was particularly impressed with their size and well-proportioned appearance, their excellent type and their splendid coats."

Ch. Cordelia of Koch's Knoll, CD, a granddaughter of Ch. La Shan Marc of Basquaerie, sired by Milfra's El Gran Blanco Zutano. "Triksy" was the dam of six champions. Owned by Mr. and Mrs. Melvin Rhoades.
— *Courtesy, Dorothy Wise*

Ch. Montalvo of Rhopyr, the sire of the breed's Top Producer, Ch. Rogue La Rue. Owned by Mr. and Mrs. Arthur Nivens. — *Courtesy Dorothy Wise*

Ch. Euskaldun Rhopyr Gracieuse left important descendants in California. Owned by Mr. and Mrs. Douglas Miller. Pictured in 1960.
— *Courtesy Dorothy Wise*

73

The top winning Great Pyrenees in America. To the left, receiving Best of Breed, is Ch. Karolaska Glacier, owned by Edith K. Smith and handled by Bob Forsyth; to the right, receiving Best Opposite Sex, is Ch. Karolaska Polar Bonnie Bear, owned and handled by Carol Kentopp, at the GPC National Specialty in '72. The judge is Mrs. Maynard Drury. Both Pyrenees were bred at Karolaska Kennels. — *Gilbert*

Five French bitches at the Elevage de Comte de Foix, M. and Mme. Giralt, in 1975.

5

The Great Pyrenees Standards

The Official American Kennel Club Standard of the Great Pyrenees

(Approved February 13, 1935)

General Appearance:

A dog of immense size, great majesty, keen intelligence, and kindly expression; of unsurpassed beauty and a certain elegance, all white or principally white with markings of badger, gray or varying shades of tan. In the rolling, ambling gait it shows unmistakably the purpose for which it has been bred, the strenuous work of guarding the flocks in all kinds of weather on the steep mountain slopes of the Pyrenees. Hence soundness is of the greatest importance and absolutely necessary for the proper fulfillment of his centuries' old task.

Size:

The average height at the shoulder is 27 inches to 32 inches for dogs, and 25 inches to 29 inches for bitches. The average length from shoulder blades to root of tail should be the same as the height in any given specimen. The average girth is 36 inches to 42 inches for dogs, and 32 inches to 36 inches for bitches. The weight for dogs runs 100 to 125 pounds, and 90 to 115 pounds for bitches. A dog heavily boned; with close cupped feet; double dewclaws behind and single dewclaws in front.

75

Head:

Large and wedge-shaped, measuring ten inches to eleven inches from dome to point of nose, with rounding crown, furrow only slightly developed and with no apparent stop. **Cheeks:** Flat. **Ears:** V-shaped, but rounded at the tips, of medium size, set parallel with the eyes, carried low and close to the head except when raised at attention. **Eyes:** Of medium size set slightly obliquely, dark rich brown in color with close eyelids, well pigmented. **Lips:** Close-fitting, edged in black. **Dewlaps:** Developed but little. The head is in brief that of a brown bear, but with the ears falling down.

Neck:

Short, stout and strongly muscular.

Body:

Well-placed shoulders set obliquely, close to the body. **Back and Loin:** Well coupled, straight and broad. **Haunches:** Fairly prominent. **Rump:** Slightly sloping. **Ribs:** Flat-sided. **Chest:** Deep. **Tail:** Of sufficient length to hang below the hocks, well plumed, carried low in repose, and curled high over the back, "making the wheel" when alert.

Coat:

Created to withstand severe weather, with heavy fine white undercoat and long flat thick outercoat of coarser hair, straight or slightly undulating.

Qualities:

In addition to his original age-old position in the scheme of pastoral life as protector of the shepherd and his flock, the Great Pyrenees has been used for centuries as a guard and watchdog on the large estates of his native France, and for this he has proven ideal. He is as serious in play as he is in work, adapting and molding himself to the moods, desires and even the very life of his human companions, through fair weather and foul, through leisure hours and hours fraught with danger, responsibility and extreme exertion; he is the exemplification of gentleness and docility with those he knows, of faithfulness and devotion for his master even to the point of self-sacrifice; and of courage in the protection of the flock placed in his care and of the ones he loves.

76

SCALE OF POINTS:

(a) Head, 25 points comprised as follows:

Shape of skull 5

Ears 5

Eyes 5

Muzzle 5

Teeth 5

(b) General Conformation, 25 points comprised as follows:

Neck 5

Chest 5

Back 5

Loins 5

Feet 5

(c) Coat: 10 points.

(d) Size and Soundness: 25 points.

(e) Expression and General Appearance: 15 points.

TOTAL number of points, 100.

Some Observations on the
Revision of the AKC Standard

With the introduction of the breed to the United States in 1933, a standard was required to register the dogs with the American Kennel Club. As a temporary measure so that the breed could be recognized and shown, Mr. and Mrs. Crane persuaded their artist friend living in Paris, Miss Clara Perry, to consult with M. Senac-Lagrange and obtain an English translation of the French Standard. The essential points were discussed, and after making minor changes Senac-Lagrange gave his approval to its final form. It was adopted by the AKC, but remained in force for only two years, after which it was replaced by our present Standard.

The current American Kennel Club standard will be found to be, in the main, an extension of the French view. But there are certain important differences.

The Standard contains none of the breed faults listed in the French version. The inclusion of at least some of these would have been of considerable aid to American judges and breeders, unfamiliar with the finer points of the Pyrenees dog.

Next we come to the AKC Standard's description of the dog's gait: "In the rolling ambling gait it shows unmistakably the purpose for which it was bred . . ." A further explanation of this passage appears in order because to many these words have implied that pacing is a common breed characteristic.

We must recall that the French version did not give a gait description. So when one was required for the AKC Standard, an attempt was made to locate an appropriate source. This led inevitably to M. Senac-Lagrange, who had firmly maintained in his notes that *at times* the Pyrenean Dog adopts a gait like that described in the literature on horses (Senac was an authority on this subject also). This he described as a "broken pace", in which the lateral bi-ped beat is in 4-time, and not 2. He was quick to point out that the same applied to the Petit Berger, a breed also given to long hours of work on the mountainside. It would seem that what Senac was describing was not the pace, with its exaggerated side-to-side rolling body motion, but a modification of it more akin to the single foot. This is undeniably a resting gait which conserves energy and momentum and can be maintained effortlessly for long periods. It must be added that Senac-Lagrange did not condone pacing in the show ring. And when a gait description did eventually appear in the French Standard, as we shall see shortly, it did not include a roll, an amble or a shuffle.

The classical working gait of the Great Pyrenees will be taken up in a later chapter.

Next, two changes were made in the dog's size and balance. The first was the lowering of the minimum height for both sexes by ½ inch. The second was the specification that the shoulder height must equal body length (from withers to root of tail), thus giving a compact and well-balanced silhouette.

One significant omission is found in the head section, in which our present Standard does not specify the structure or length of the muzzle. As the French state, it should be strong, of good length, slightly pointed towards the nostrils and with a *black* nose. A person reading our current standard would be perfectly free to breed a Pyrenees with a short, square muzzle (without pigment)—yet this would be completely uncomplimentary to the breed type. The Standard also does not mention that a correct Pyrenean bite is one in which the incisors meet in either a scissors or an even manner.

With these thoughts in mind, in 1938 the Great Pyrenees Club of America published a *Concise Guidebook on the Breed* which was distributed to members and judges. The Guidebook contained a list of Proposed Changes to the Standard as well as a list of *Peculiarities Characteristic of the Breed* which aided considerably in the matter of interpreting the Standard. Unfortunately, the Guidebook went out of circulation years ago. An in-depth look at the Standard will be taken up later in this book.

Current Standard in France:
(R.A.C.P. 1970)

General Appearance: That of a dog of large size, imposing and strongly built, but not devoid of a certain elegance.
Faults: A general appearance of heaviness, without distinction, or indicating a resemblance to the Saint Bernard, Newfoundland or Leonberg. Sluggish, over-weight dogs, or those having a dangerous look.

Size: Males: 70 to 80 cms. (27.55 to 31.49 inches). Females: 65 to 72 cms. (25.59 to 28.34 inches). A tolerance of 2 cms. above these sizes is admissible for subjects of flawless type.

Head: Not too heavy in comparison to the size. The sides of the head are fairly flat; the skull is slightly rounded; the peak of the occipital bone, being visible, gives the posterior portion of the skull an ogival, vaulted form.
The breadth of the skull at its widest part is about equal to its length. There is a gentle slope to the broad muzzle which is of good length, slightly pointed at its extremity. The lips hang but little, just enough to cover the lower jaw; they are black or very strongly marked with black, as is the roof of the mouth. The nose is entirely black. The head is that of a brown bear with the ears pressed down.
Faults: Head too heavy; over-enlarged skull; fore-skull protuberant; a heavy or marked stop; insufficient pigment of the mucous membranes; lips sagging too much; a square head.
Disqualification: A nose other than completely black.

Teeth: A full set of healthy, white teeth is required. The incisors meet like the blades of a scissors, the uppers just overlapping the lowers without losing contact. An even bite is acceptable.
Disqualification: An undershot or overshot bite.

Eyes: The rather small eyes, of intelligent and contemplative expression, are amber brown in color. They are surrounded by tight lids, bordered in black, and placed slightly obliquely. The look is gentle and dreamy.
Faults: Round eyes, too light and prominent (staring); drooping eyelids; an evil or haggard expression; insufficient pigment around the eyes.
Disqualification: Missing pigment on the eyelids.

Ears: Placed at the height of the eyes; fairly small, triangular in form and rounded at the tips; they fall flat against the head; carried a little higher when the dog is on the watch.
Faults: Long ears, poorly formed, folded, placed too high (above eye level).

Neck Strong, fairly short, with the dewlap little developed.
Faults: Too slender and weak, too long, too much dewlap.

Shoulders: Medium oblique. Withers broad and well muscled.

79

Body: The chest does not come down too far but is broad and of good length. The ribs are slightly rounded. the back is of good length, broad and straight. The rump is slightly oblique with the haunches fairly prominent. The flanks drop but little.
Faults: Sway or roached back.

Legs: The forelegs are straight, strong and well fringed. Fringes on the hind quarters are longer and thicker. The thighs are rounded but not low. The hocks are strong, clean and sharp, of medium bent. The back legs carry well formed double dewclaws.
Faults: Straight hocks. Poor front alignment; toeing in or out.
Disqualification: Absent dewclaws; single dewclaw or poorly developed dewclaw.

Feet: Not long, compact, with slightly arched toes.
Faults: Feet too long.

Tail: Fairly long, well-plumed; carried low when not at attention, preferably with just the extremity curled; raised over the back (making the wheel according to the Mountaineers) when the dog is on the watch.
Faults: A tail too bushy or badly carried; a tail too short or too long, without plumage; not making the wheel in action.

Coat: Rather thick, flat; fairly long and supple, longer on the tail and about the neck where it is sometimes slightly waved. The hair of the pants is finer and more woolly and very thick.
Faults: A short or curly coat. Lack of undercoat.

Color: White or white with spots of gray or badger color (*blaireau*), pale yellow or wolf-gray on the head, the ears and the base of the tail. The markings of the badger are esteemed the most. A few spots on the body are permitted.
Faults: Other colors than those indicated above, which denote cross-breeding.
Disqualifications: Black markings reaching to the root of the hair.

Gait: In spite of his size, the Pyrenean moves easily, without plodding or heaviness, but on the contrary with elegance; due to his angulation he moves without tiring.
Disqualifications for Males: Monorchid and cryptorchid dogs, that is to say, those having only one testicle or none at all.

SCALE OF POINTS:

Skull and muzzle (nose, lips, jaws) 15
Eyes 10
Ears 5
Neck, back, loin, rump 12
Shoulders, chest, sides, flanks 10
Legs and feet 10
Tail and carriage of tail 8
Coat, color, pigmentation 15
General appearance (expression, size, gait) 15
                                                                  100

Some Observations on the
Revision of the French Standard

This standard, compiled by M. Duconte and M. Delattre, is basically an attempt to update the Senac-Lagrange standard of 1927. *(See Chapter 2.)* Two new sections have been added: one on dentition and correct bite; the other on gait. A few notes have been added to the Head section. Despite the changes, it is quite apparent that every effort has been made to safeguard the *true* French type. In the words of M. Duconte:

> "The type, which is the result of head, coat, markings, pigmentation, expression and gait will earn 60 points out of 100. These are the principal indications of purity, and they should never be sacrificed to the anatomical points, no matter how important the latter may be. Regarding the general aspect of the Pyrenean Mountain Dog, we insist that it lack that overall heavy appearance which is common to most big dogs, such as the Saint Bernard. This is why he is qualified in the standard as being a dog with a certain elegance."

Great importance is given to the tail carriage which is regarded by the French connoisseur as a positive sign of good breeding. As soon as the dog goes on the watch, he must lift his tail quite frankly and curl it over his back in such a way that the crook at the very end reaches the back at the level of the loins. This is the *arroundera* or "making the wheel" as the mountaineers say.

The French also insist that the top of the ears be level with the eyes and lie flat against the head to give the skull its distinctive contour.

Great emphasis continues to be placed on strong pigmentation, which in France must also cover the roof of the mouth.

A scissors bite, in which the upper and lower incisors are touching, is preferred. An even bite is admissible.

There has been no loss of regard for the Pyrenean eye, which must be gentle and dreamy (the far away look).

Regarding the gait, the remarks of M. Mansencal will suffice:

> "It is while the dog is trotting that one can best judge good gait and bearing, the "arroundera', and the elegance and pride of the Pyrenean Mountain Dog. Besides the build of the Mountain Dog, which should be established by working upwards, how can a plethoric dog, which often has short legs and loose skin, be elegant?
>
> "In order to have an idea of this natural elegance and pride, one needs to have seen a Mountain Dog, head held high, tail arched, trotting the Lord knows where across the grass of a Pyrenean meadow far from all human habitation."

The British Standard

The first standard for the breed in Great Britain was approved by the British Kennel Club in 1936. It remained identical to the American standard until 1955 when a policy decision by the Kennel Club (England) called for the removal of the table of points from all standards having them.

In the late sixties, British fanciers became aware that without a points designation, or a list of well-considered faults, judges were finding it difficult to decide on the relative merits of the various dogs they saw in the show ring. Under the able direction of Sqn. Ldr. Peter Gilbert (R.A.F. Retd.), who served as Secretary of the Standard Working Party and later became the Chairman of the Pyrenean Mountain Dog Club, a new standard was formulated and approved by the Kennel Club in 1972. Several important and necessary clarifications were made. A number of faults are now included, being graded in accordance with their severity. Here is the current standard for the breed in Great Britain:

Current Standard for the Pyrenean Mountain Dog
in Great Britain

Characteristics: The Pyrenean is a natural guard dog and was originally employed as a protector of the shepherd and of his flocks.

General Appearance: The Pyrenean should possess great size, substance and power, giving an impression of an immensely strong yet well-balanced dog. These qualities should be accompanied by a certain elegance resulting from a combination of the attractive coat, the correct head and a general air of quiet confidence. It is of the utmost importance that nervousness or unprovoked aggression should be heavily penalized.

Head and Skull: It is very important that the head should give an impression of strength with no sign of coarseness; it should not be too heavy in proportion to the size of the dog. The top of the skull, as viewed from front and side, should show a definite curve so as to give a somewhat domed effect and the breadth of the skull at its widest point should be about equal to the length from occiput to stop. The sides of the head should be nearly flat and of a good depth. There should be no obvious stop and only a slight furrow so that the skull and muzzle are joined by a gentle slope. The muzzle should be strong, of medium length and with a slight taper near its tip. The nose should be absolutely black. When viewed from above, the head should have the general form of a blunt "V" well filled in below the eyes.

Eyes: The eyes should be almond-shaped and of a dark amber-brown color. The close-fitting eyelids should be set somewhat obliquely and should be bordered with black. Drooping lower eyelids should be penalized. The expression should be intelligent and contemplative.

82

Bergerie Knur, Supreme Best In Show, Crufts, 1970.
— *Courtesy Mrs. C. R. Prince*

A classical example of the "arroundera", in which the wheeling tail touches the loin on either side of the back, seen in this lovely South African Pyrenees, Ch. Pendragon Pretty Please, owned by Mr. Jon Matthews of Capetown. — *Adshade S. Africa*

83

Ears: The ears should be fairly small and triangular with rounded tips, the root of the ear being on a level with the eyes. Normally the ears lie flat against the head, but may be slightly raised when the dog is alert.

Mouth: There should be a complete set of healthy even teeth, the incisors meeting in either a scissor or a pincer bite. The two central lower incisors may be set a little deeper than the others but this should not be rgarded as a serious fault.

The lips should be close fitting, the upper ones extending downwards just sufficiently to cover the lower. They should be black or heavily marked with black in common with the roof of the mouth.

Neck: The neck should be fairly short, thick and muscular. Some dewlap is permitted.

Forequarters: The shoulders should be powerful and lie close to the body. There should be medium angulation between the shoulder blade and the upper arm. The forelegs should be straight, heavily boned and well muscled. The elbows should not be too close to the chest nor should they stand off too far from it, so that a good width of stance and a free striding movement are obtained. Pasterns should show flexibility, but no weakness.

Body: The chest should be broad and of sufficient depth to reach just below the elbows. The sides should be slightly rounded and the rib cage should extend well to the rear.

The back should be of a good length, broad, muscular, straight and level. Dogs usually have a more pronounced waist than bitches, giving a greater curve to the lower body line.

Hindquarters: The loins should be broad and muscular with fairly prominent haunches, the rump should be slightly sloping and the tail should be set on so that the topline curves smoothly into it. Male animals should have two apparently normal testicles fully descended into the scrotum.

The thighs should have great strength and be heavily muscled, tapering gradually down to strong hocks. The stifle and hock joints should both have medium angulation as seen from the side.

The hind legs should each carry strongly-made double dewclaws and lack of this identifying characteristic is a very serious fault.

The hind feet may turn out slightly, but the legs themselves when viewed from behind should be straight. Pronounced cow-hocks should be heavily penalized.

Feet: The feet should be short and compact, the toes being slightly arched and equipped with strong nails.

Gait: It is very important that the gait should be unhurried, and one should gain the impression of a large dog propelled by powerful hindquarters moving steadily and smoothly well within its capacity, yet able to produce bursts of speed. At slow speeds the Pyrenean tends to pace.

Tail: The tail should be thick at the root and should taper gradually towards the tip, which, for preference, should have a slight curl. It should be of sufficient length to reach below the hocks and the thick coating of fairly long hair should form an attrac-

84

tive plume. In repose, the tail should be carried low with the tip turned slightly to one side, but as the dog becomes interested the tail rises and when he is fully alert it should be curled high above the back in a circle.

Coat: The undercoat should be profuse and composed of very fine hairs whilst the longer outercoat should be of coarser texture, thick and straight or slightly wavy but never curly or fuzzy. The coat should be longer around the neck and shoulders, where it forms a mane, and towards the tail. The forelegs should be fringed. The hair on the rear of the thighs should be long, very dense and more woolly in texture, giving a "pantaloon" effect. Bitches tend to be smoother-coated than dogs and usually have a less developed mane.

Color: (a) Mainly white with patches of badger, wolf-grey or pale yellow, and (b) White; (a) and (b) are of equal merit and judges should show no preference for either. Areas of black hair, where the black goes right down to the roots, are a serious fault.

The colored markings can be on the head, the ears and at the base of the tail, but a few patches on the body are permitted.

The nose and eyerims should be black. The presence of liver pigmentation or pink is a serious fault.

Weight and Size: The shoulder height of a bitch should be at least 26 in. (66 cm) and of a dog 28 in. (71 cm). Most specimens will exceed these heights by several inches and great size should be regarded as absolutely essential, provided that correct type and character are retained. The weight of a bitch should be at least 90 lb. (40 kg) and of a dog 110 lb. (50 kg). (These weights apply only to specimens of minumum height and taller ones should weigh considerably more.) Weight should always be in proportion to height, giving a powerful dog of great strength. Excess weight due to fat should be penalized.

A family group living on a sheep ranch in Virginia. — *Linda Walraven*

6

Character of the Great Pyrenees

"I SAW my first 'animated snowdrift' some ten years ago" wrote Mr. Strang in 1935, "stretched in front of a busy Paris cafe, taking up considerably more than his share of the sidewalk. He struck me then as the most beautiful dog I had ever seen and a more intimate association with the Great Pyrenees since has convinced me that his character is on a par with his looks."

The Pyrenean character, to which Mr. Strang refers, has been clearly set forth in the breed Standard. Let us consider these two passages:

First, *A dog of immense size, great majesty, keen intelligence and kindly expression . . .;*

And second, *In addition to his age-old position in the scheme of pastoral life as protector of the shepherd and his flock, the Great Pyrenees has been used for centuries as a guard and watchdog on the large estates of his native France, and for this he has proven ideal. He is as serious in play as he is in work, adapting and molding himself to the moods, desires and even the very life of his human companions, through fair weather and foul, through leisure hours and hours fraught with danger, responsibility and extreme exertion; he is the exemplification of gentleness and docility with those he knows, of faithfulness and devotion for his master even to the point of self-sacrifice; and of courage in the protection of the flock placed in his care and the ones he loves.*

Maxwell Riddle, the respected American judge and author, in his book *The New Complete Shetland Sheepdog* wrote the following on Sheltie character. It applies for all breeds:

Is a dog loyal who follows the children to school? Is it one which shadows its master? Will it attack the charging bull which threatens its owner? If the owner engages in a fight with another, will the dog attack the owner's opponent? Will the loyal dog rush into the street and drag a child out of the path of a car?

87

Dogs do these things. But they rarely have the chance to prove themselves. The dog which shadows its master may do so out of innate fear of being alone; rather than out of loyalty. Similarly, the dog which barks when strangers approach may be doing so out of fear, and may feel no sense of loyalty.

Similarly, it is the rare dog in any breed which does not show affection for its master and family. This is a quality of being a dog. So, as in the case of loyalty, this tells us nothing about the breed's character.

So, in attempting to describe the qualities that set the Great Pyrenees apart from other breeds, we must take into account three special qualities which are either stated or implied by the breed description. They are:

* He is a working dog bred for a specific purpose.
* He is a natural guardian. This aptitude has been refined through genetic selection.
* His keen intelligence is reflected in his innate ability to discriminate between friend and enemy—in a word, dependability.

While no one can deny that the Pyrenean's benevolent expression and a certain bear-like lovability are part of his charm, to the peasant and shepherd who developed the breed as we know it today, a working dog needed something more than charm. Let us consider the historical background of our present day Pyrenees. What are the attributes of character we expect to find in today's dog? This account, written by Robert Leighton in *The New Book of the Dog* (1911) will serve as an example:

> In the beginning of the summer the Pyrenean shepherds moved their flocks from the lowland pastures to the mountains, where they remained for a period of four to five months, often at an altitude of five thousand feet above the sea level. The dogs accompanied them, and in a country infested with bears and wolves there could be no better or more faithful and courageous guardians. Gifted with an exceedingly keen sense of hearing and an excellent nose, the Pyrenean Dog was accustomed to mount sentry at night over the sleeping flocks; and if a marauding Bruin should approach, or a stealthy pack of wolves draw nigh, he knew it from afar, and was ever alert to warn his master, or himself hasten to the attack, and the wolf or bear who should face him would have to deal with an exceedingly formidable foe, whose quickness of decision and adroitness in combat might be compared with the trained skill of the fighting dog of the arena.
>
> So trusting was this canine guardian of the fold, that the shepherd could with confidence leave him at intervals of two or three days at a time, knowing that during his absence the dog would tend the sheep unaided, never deserting his post of duty.

For yet another description of Pyrenean character, we turn to the description given by the Argeles-Gazost Standard of 1907:

> Possessing a courage against all odds, combined with immense strength and the power of his jaws, nothing stops him or makes him retreat. At night he continues to bark to show he is on guard. He does not sleep for a moment. He in-

spects the surrounding neighborhood without wandering too far, unless he finds the trail of a dangerous animal, and only returns when he knows the danger to the flock is over. The true Pyrenean never sleeps at night, but rests and sleeps during the day in case his vigilance fails (during the night). He distinguishes himself from other large breeds by his devotion to everything he is expected to guard, principally children.

To quote M. J. Dhers, a French connoisseur of the late twenties and thirties, "The characteristics of this true type are their utter fearlessness, a total lack of nervousness, and an apparent desire to mind their own business and have strangers do likewise."

From these accounts it is not hard to picture the character of the dog. First, he put duty above all else. He worked in extremes of weather, in gales of rain or snow—often alone. Isolated on the mountain slopes with just his sheep to protect, he was expected to show reserve towards strangers. Under the right circumstances, he must be suspicious, even hostile. A stranger could be a thief. And a shepherd would never consider leaving his flock, if he were not sure it was well protected by his Pyrenean guards.

In turn, each dog would need to recognize its master and his helpers and submit to their orders.

A Pyrenean would have to act with boldness and determination when the wind brought the scent of an enemy. A shy or nervous animal would lack the self-confidence to react appropriately to a plausible threat. An overly dependent dog who shadowed his master could never be relied upon to take over in the absence of his owner. The shepherds expected these things from their dogs, and bred them for it.

A dog that attacked or bit without provocation would have been a menace to everyone including the villagers. Lady Morris once remarked after a visit to the mountains, "I never met a mean dog," and certainly a shy or untrustworthy Pyrenees would not have been tolerated in the restricted economy of the herdsmen.

So we find that a Pyrenees of correct character is steadfast, responsive and self-sufficient. He has inherited, to an uncanny degree, an understanding of man's ways. Lithe and quick of action, he is capable of enduring hardship, exposure, and any degree of activity. He is undisputably one of the most intelligent dogs in the world and certainly one of the most picturesque and beautiful. He exemplifies, as no other breed can, the attributes one looks for in a devoted companion and worker.

More than just a guardian of the flock, the Great Pyrenees is a superb watchdog. From the chronicles of the early life and adventures of the Pyrenees dogs on the royal estates of France, three, narrated by M. Duconte, a French authority and breed historian, show how the Pyrenean performed this time-honored service. The first is the story of the Chateau de Foix:

This castle was built on steep rock, difficult of access. Its prison cells and secret dungeons were continuously occupied by brigands and highwaymen who tried to hold up and rob travelers passing through this area to Spain. Thieves also attacked mountain flocks which were insufficiently guarded. So many were these brigands that there was scarcely room for them in the prison nor sufficient men to guard them. So a certain number of Pyrenean Mountain Dogs were brought in, their keen sense of smell and nocturnal vigilance making them proof against any surprise. The Pyrenean shepherds had, in fact, for a long time beforehand, trained their dogs to chase thieves as well as wild animals. And so Foix acquired its guard of Pyrenean dogs; and from then on it was well guarded.

The second account is based on a document in the National Library of France, telling that in 1407 the Chateau de Lourdes had both a square and a round tower, both of which were surrounded by a high wall. Between the wall and the towers was an open passage, round which Pyrenean dogs patrolled on watch to give the alarm:

> The dogs seemed endowed with intelligence enough to recognize suspicious behavior of criminals and yet never to attack any honest man. These qualities were particularly precious at a time when a cowl literally made the friar. But there was one occasion when it didn't work as planned! One of the officers of the castle, wishing to put the guard dogs to test, disguised himself in the garb of a wandering friar and then made his nightly rounds. He was set upon by the angry dogs in the twinkling of an eye, and was in grave danger when luckily the clever beasts recognized him and so he was spared.

Still another ancient document, found in the archives at Fuxeennes, relates that in 1391, following a treaty of succession to Gaston Phoebus, Comte de Foix, King Charles VI decided to go and pay a visit to his cousin who was waiting for him in his castle at Mazeres:

> Before getting to Mazeres the King rode through a region stocked with huge white cattle wearing silver bells about their necks. Knights disguised as shepherds were running in all directions trying to get the herd out of the way. Enormous mountain dogs with thick long coats were engaged in helping them. Suddenly a bull charged the King! One of the shepherds attempted to catch it by the horns and pull it to the ground, whilst the dogs, hanging onto its ears, dragged it back to the herd and so saved the King!

Thus we can vouch that our Pyrenean has always been considered an ideal watchdog, even from the earliest times. Only a person who knows dogs very well would dare to advance upon a Great Pyrenees on guard. The sound of a warning growl, not to mention the explosive bark which follows, would cause any trespasser to keep a respectful distance.

A Pyrenees is adept at cannily blocking the approach of a suspicious intruder. His bushy mane rises in anger and he merely raises his lips to expose a fang. He is skillful at cornering and holding until help arrives. His keen intel-

An antique steel engraving showing a Pyrenees. Done expressly for Godey's Lady's Book by F. Humphreys, in 1851.
— Courtesy, June Palmer

Mrs. A. Croxton Smith, wife of the Chairman of the British Kennel Club, with Pandora, about 1912. — Courtesy Mrs. C. R. Prince

John Foyster Grantham in his robes as "gentleman commoner" at Oxford, with his Pyrenean companion.
— Courtesy Joan Gross

91

A hard-working Pyr in the traces, but a lazy wagon master.

Going for a walk is Matt Burke, of Cleveland Heights, Ohio.

ligence and powers of discrimination allow him to distinguish the suspicious intruder from the friend who belongs.

A charming account of Pyrenean character is found in *The Power of the Dog* (Maude Earl), a piece written by A. Croxton-Smith as a tribute to his beloved Pandora:

As the heavy train steamed into Willesden, sounds of barking directed me to the compartment in which the pup was traveling. When the hamper was opened the most delightful little Teddy Bear imaginable bounded out and proceeded to introduce herself. A mass of white fluffy down, with here and there a splash of lemon, eloquent dark eyes, and plump as the proverbial partridge. That was Pandora as we first knew her. Time only served to strengthen and crystallize the early impressions. With manners as charming and irreproachable as her looks, before many days had passed she had won all hearts, becoming an important member of the household. That wise head of hers held brains which led her instinctively to adapt herself to her surroundings, and fall in with the habits and wishes of the human gods who formed her little world. Visitors, though tolerated as necessary evils, were regarded with signal disapproval, heavy bark and bared teeth warning that no evil intent must be harbored towards the inmates of the home.

As Pandora grew older the downy coat was shed, profuse long hair taking its place in gradual transition, and she became more and more intelligent, until we agreed that we had never, among our host of canine friends, met one so sensible. None, too, could be more expressive. When on mischief bent she displayed it with a roguishness of demeanor that earned absolution for the misdeed almost before it was perpetrated.

Greatly did she delight in a game of "catch as catch can" on the lawn with the children. Entering into the spirit of fun she would romp around in endless gyrations, bushy tail extended to the full a few inches from hands ready to grasp, but she could calculate to a fraction, twisting and dodging with the art of a football player, until pity impelled her to pretend she could go on no longer.

One could fill a book relating Pandora's escapades, but further recital might weary. Let mention of her adventure with the garden hose suffice as an example of the rest. The curious serpentine length stretching out on the lawn interested her vastly, and when she heard the sizzling noise made by the air escaping from the nozzle as the water came on, down went her nose to investigate. A sudden jet full in the face caused a precipitate retreat, and now as the hose appears there is much commotion at a diplomatic distance.

Certainly no other breed is more ideally suited for the role of child's companion and protector than is the Great Pyrenees. Perhaps in the joy and carefree abandon of a child, a Pyrenees sees a kindred spirit. In the company of children he seems sublimely happy whether enjoying a romp, a tussle, a game of tag, pulling some kind of conveyance or merely doing nothing but listening to their chatter. Ever conscious of his own strength, he seems more gentle than the smallest lap dog, yet, should danger appear in the form of a molesting stranger, thief or trespasser, his deep warning bark is usually enough to handle the situation. If not, his size, strength and fury most certainly will.

When a Pyrenees wants attention he has a way of slapping you with his paw. He always sleeps with his back against a door which opens inward, so as not to be taken by surprise; a fact which caused the shepherds to refer to their Patous as "mat dogs."

The breed gets along well with other dogs and household pets. A Pyrenees would much prefer to ignore the harassment of a smaller dog and will usually fight only as a last resort. However, two mature Pyrenees of the same sex often do not get along well together as housepets. This is particularly true of males.

When a Pyrenees turns his attention to the affairs of his family, his powers of deduction are uncanny. Let something out of the ordinary happen, such as packing a suitcase, and a Pyr becomes all eyes and ears. An alert family will go to almost any length to conceal their plans from their household Pyr—but he always finds them out! Even the accidental jingle of a choke collar brings any Pyrenees, napping in a remote corner, straight to the door, insisting upon a walk. A Pyrenees reads your dress and mannerisms as you read the evening paper—and for much the same reason: to find out what's going to happen next. The difference is, the Pyrenees is usually right, and you aren't.

There is no doubt that the Great Pyrenees is a highly intelligent animal. He always knows what's expected of him and his ability to understand the subtle nuances of his master's voice and expression are second to none. Add to this a desire to do everything required to win his handler's praise, and you have a dog who is easy to train for obedience work.

To train a Pyrenees, one should approach the task in a leisurely fashion and keep the exercises, at first, reasonably brief and varied. As with any intelligent species, perfunctory and repetitious exercises are apt to bore.

A part of the breed's innate intelligence is an almost uncanny prescience, an ability to know or sense danger well in advance, and to take action to safeguard, as illustrated in this anecdote: One evening in the late 1930's Mrs. Carl Harris, of Add-En-On Kennels, was traveling with her husband and their dogs in Mississippi when they decided to stop for the night, by the side of the road, to camp. She then set out to take her favorite dog, Henry VIII, for his nightly walk, and had gone only a short distance when suddenly Henry sat back and refused to go any further—indicating his desire that they return at once to the camper. Mrs. Harris became quite exasperated and tried to coax him to continue, but the wise dog steadfastly refused and they eventually returned to the trailer. The following morning Henry again went for a walk with his mistress and in due course they returned to the same spot as the night before. There, before the pair, was an abandoned cistern! Had Henry not sensed the danger the night before, the two would have continued on (according to Mrs. Harris) and plunged to their deaths.

Kimberly Mardi Gras and friend. Owned by Brenda Judson, Carabrae Kennels, England.

Happy Days, with Champion Ariel Charm's Cor.

Cavalier Malachi makes himself protector of his youthful charges.
— Breck Smith

Perhaps the character of the breed is best exemplified by the intelligent and kindly expression to be found in the eye of the well-bred dog. A look which has been classified as far-away, contemplative, perhaps a little melancholy, yet possessing, too, a serenity acquired through association with the high, wind-swept, mountain slopes and distant vistas that make up the magnificent grandeur of the Pyrenees Mountains.

The vocabulary of the Great Pyrenees is a subject which has interested fanciers for many years. With a little experience one can learn not only which dog is barking, but can tell, within limits, just what he is talking about. The joyous bark of greeting is different from the short, excited yapping of the same dog chasing a rabbit. The plaintive whine of an uneasy dog in trouble is quite different from the wheedling whine of a dog overjoyed by attention.

The range of different barks is certainly extensive. The dog is hungry or has overturned his water bucket and is thirsty. Another animal is running loose; there is a snake in his pen; he smells fire; he has caught his feet in the fence; he is answering the call of another dog in the distance on a moonlit night; each emotion is qualified by a particular bark. And besides barking, whining and howling, our dogs growl; there are different growls for different occasions. Greeting, with suspicion, another dog; protective growling in defense of his property, master, food pan or bone; the low grumbling, deep-in-the-throat growl when angered and about to attack.

But of all the different vocalizations of which our dogs are capable there is one that stands out above all others. This is the voice of authority that, in the night, calmed restless sheep in the fold, assured the shepherd of the area's security and told potential trouble-makers that the camp was well-guarded.

Writers, from the earliest days of our breed's history have spoken, in passing, of this distinctive Pyrenean bark. This remote ancestral trait is certainly a vital characteristic of our breed.

Calm, low-registered, powerful but muted, this is the voice of the Great Pyrenees at his age-old post, telling us—all is well.

APPEARANCE. Immense size; majestic, elegant; keenly intelligent; kindly; sound; heavily-boned

EARS V-shaped; tips rounded; medium size; set parallel with eyes; carried low, close to head

NECK strongly muscular; short; stout

BACK and Loins: Well-coupled; straight; broad

RUMP sloping slightly. Haunches fairly prominent

TAIL well-plumed; carried low in repose; hangs below hocks; curled high over back ("making wheel") when alert

GAIT rolling; ambling. Legs strong; large-boned; sound

COAT: Heavy, fine, white undercoat; long, flat, thick, coarse outer-coat—hair straight or slightly undulating

COLORS: All white; principally white with badger, varying tan-shades or gray markings

HEAD large, wedge-shaped; resembling brown bear with ears hanging; measuring 10"-11" from dome to point of nose; rounding crown; no apparent stop. Cheeks flat

EYES medium size; set slightly obliquely; dark, rich brown; close eyelids, well pigmented

LIPS close-fitting; edged with black

DEWLAPS developed but little

SHOULDERS set obliquely; close to body; well placed

CHEST deep

DEWCLAWS double behind, single in front

FEET close-cupped

RIBS flat-sided

SIZE huge; Height, males, 27"-32"; females, 25" to 29". Average length from shoulder blades to tail root the same as height. Girth, males, 36"-42"; females, 32"-36". Weight, males, 100-125 lbs ; females, 90-115 lbs

98

7

An In-Depth Look
at the Standard

NO PYRENEES has yet been bred who can fulfill all the ideals of our breed standard. No dog is perfect. Yet some are better in type than others. In the Standard, we find both an incentive to correct breeding and a measure by which success in the show ring can be acknowledged.

The character of the Great Pyrenees has been discussed in the preceding chapter. As a trusted guardian and a worker of single-minded purpose, no other breed is his rival. However, this discussion will not deal primarily with the character of the dog, except that where character is a quality of the part we are discussing, it is reason enough to insist upon the perfection of that part.

General Appearance and Size

The Great Pyrenees, like other breeds, has its own unique composition. The Standard describes our breed as a dog of immense size, great majesty, unsurpassed beauty and a certain elegance. We should note that this is all part of the dog's immediate appeal and, indeed, it is inseparable from his composition. Good composition adds not only to the esthetic appeal of the dog, but also allows the dog to carry on with his appointed tasks under circumstances in which the poorly constructed one falters or breaks down. Hence, as the Standard says: *"soundness is of the greatest importance and absolutely necessary for the proper fulfillment of his centuries' old task."*

A Great Pyrenees of proper proportions will tell us at a glance that he can pull a cart, climb a mountain, pack a load or attack a predator—all with equal ease and determination. His conformation must be judged by the principle that he is, above all, a powerful and well-coordinated working dog.

The Standard gives the shoulder height of males at 27 to 32 inches, and females at 25 to 29 inches. We would suppose that in any breed such as ours in which the height of the specimen is not defined within a narrow range, a

A well balanced dog with a level back.— *Peter Bickle*

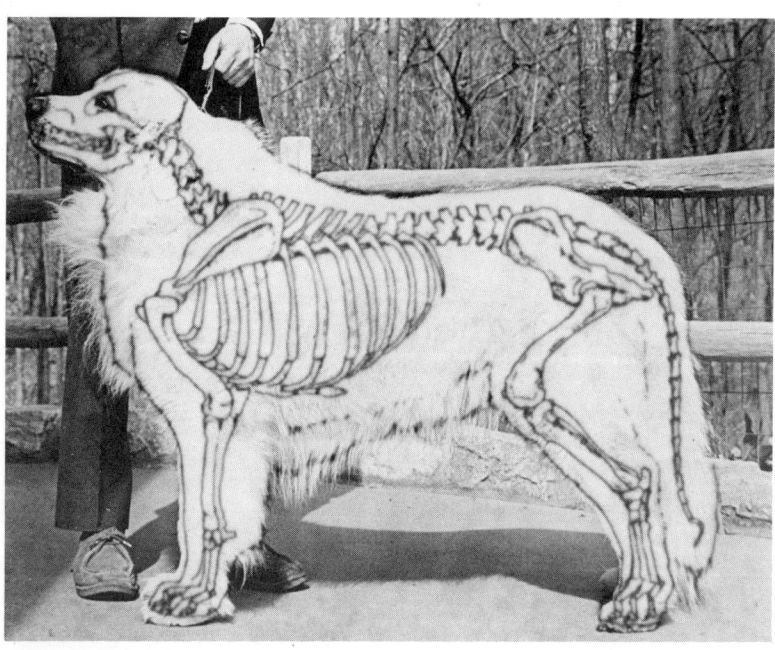

A photograph of a living Great Pyrenees showing the angulation and skeletal structure of a correct specimen. — *J. Clawson*

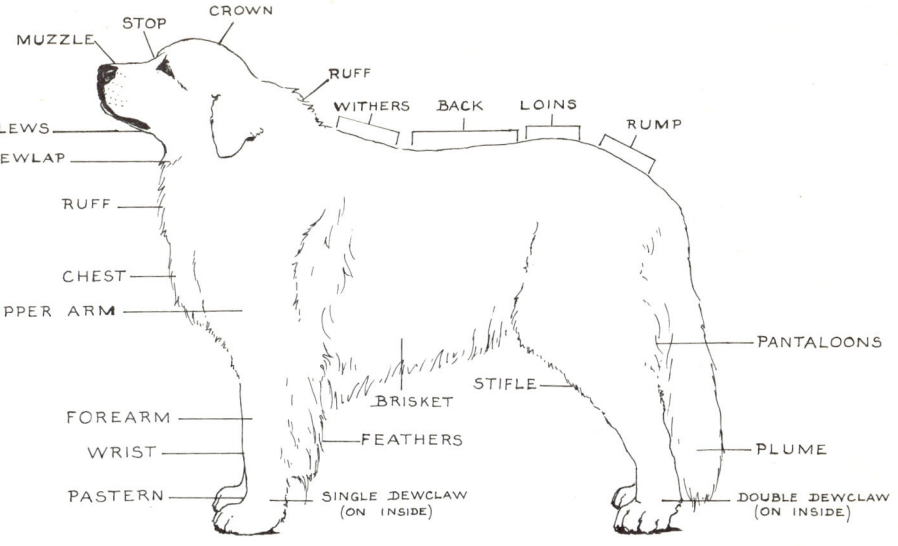

MUZZLE STOP CROWN

RUFF
WITHERS BACK LOINS
RUMP

LEWS
DEWLAP

RUFF

CHEST

UPPER ARM

PANTALOONS

BRISKET STIFLE

FOREARM

FEATHERS

WRIST

PLUME

PASTERN

SINGLE DEWCLAW
(ON INSIDE)

DOUBLE DEWCLAW
(ON INSIDE)

Topographical Anatomy. — *Bridget Olerenshaw*

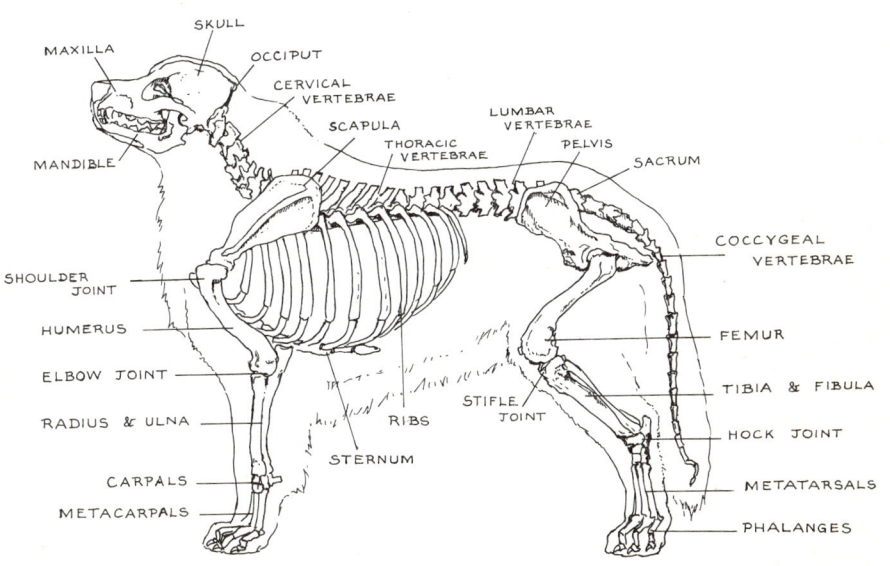

SKULL

MAXILLA OCCIPUT

CERVICAL
VERTEBRAE

SCAPULA

THORACIC
VERTEBRAE

LUMBAR
VERTEBRAE

PELVIS

SACRUM

MANDIBLE

COCCYGEAL
VERTEBRAE

SHOULDER
JOINT

HUMERUS

FEMUR

ELBOW JOINT

TIBIA & FIBULA

STIFLE
JOINT

RADIUS & ULNA

RIBS

HOCK JOINT

CARPALS

STERNUM

METATARSALS

METACARPALS

PHALANGES

Skeletal Anatomy. — *Bridget Olerenshaw*

101

strong current of opinion will exist within the fancy as to what constitutes the ideal height. At least this has always been the case in our breed, not only in today's fancy, but in bygone years. A glance at the old breed descriptions will show that height ranges among the older Standards have not always been in agreement.

Whatever height the dog attains, it can only be part of the complex of qualities which confer to the Great Pyrenees his imposing appearance. A tall, rangy dog who lacks substance and coat will not appear immense. We would need to consider not only the dog's height, but his correct weight, muscular development, angulation, girth of bone, his balance and coat—for all of these are part of the dog's grandeur, charm, appeal in the show ring, and success in the field.

The Standard gives a maximum weight for bitches (115 pounds) and for dogs (125 pounds), but specimens of both sexes will sometimes weigh more. Weight is difficult to gauge because a heavy boned, muscular Pyrenees will weigh far more than a light boned fat one. Each dog has its own ideal weight, which must be taken into account when determining its overall balance.

The Standard describes the Pyrenees as heavily boned. The purpose of bone is to provide strength and support for the attachment of muscle and tendon. In general, we would expect that as bone girth increases, muscle mass does likewise. Extra bone without the muscle to move it makes for a clumsy animal. A Pyrenees can have too much bone, just as he can have too little.

The properly balanced Pyrenees, the Standard tells us, is one in which the average length from the shoulder blade to the root of the tail is the same as the height in any given specimen. From this we can infer that in silhouette the dog will present a compact, symmetrical outline. The back and loin are well coupled, straight and broad. The ideal topline is straight and level.

In skeletal structure, a slight dip near the junction of the thoracic and lumbar vertebrae is necessary to provide flexibility to the vertebral column. If the back is broad and well-muscled, as it should be, this dip will not be noticeable. There is a slight tuck-up which is more pronounced in males.

The neck is strongly muscled, being of sufficient length to carry the head proudly. There is little dewlap.

Bitches are more refined in every way than dogs.

Head and Expression

The pride and elegance of the Pyrenean Mountain Dog is to be found in the perfection of his head, expression, carriage and bearing.

The head attains its look of perfection by the way in which its parts are joined by smooth curves rather than abrupt angles. A good Pyrenean head will never appear coarse. Nor will it appear massive. It should always be in good proportion to the size of the individual dog. The crown is only slightly rounded when viewed from the front. From the side, the skull and muzzle are joined by a gentle slope. The occipital bone at the back of the skull forms a charac-

THE BROWN BEAR HEAD—Note the characteristic length and shape of the muzzle. — *Bob Weir Studio*

THE PYRENEES HEAD—That of a brown bear, but with the ears falling down. A substantial muzzle of good length, tapering slightly towards the black nostrils. Notice the similarity in skull shape between these two species. There is no apparent stop.
—*J. Clawson*

teristic protuberance for the attachment of powerful neck muscles. The skull should not, therefore, fall away abruptly at the back.

At the crown, the skull is about as wide as it is long. In keeping with a wedge-shaped head, the muzzle should be broader at its root and then taper slightly towards the black nostrils. The muzzle should be of good length. We should guard against a muzzle which is too short relative to the overall length of the head. This is why the Standard qualifies the head as, "In brief, that of a brown bear, but with the ears falling down."

Eyes are almond-shaped, medium sized and dark brown in color. The lids should be tight, black, and slightly oblique. The eyes are "smiling" and the expression more engaging, if the slant is directed slightly upwards. The look, which is both kindly and intelligent, is highlighted by a fine line formed by the meeting of the hair on the upper and lower face which extends backwards from the corner of the eye towards the ear.

Ears are V-shaped, rounded at the tips, medium in size and carried low and close to the head. The placement of the ears, set on at the level of the eyes, is most important. They should also be placed towards the rear of the skull, where they are more easily carried low and close to the head, often half hidden in the neck ruff. Ears set too high, or too far forward, detract from the dog's characteristic expression.

As carriage of the ears is most important, the term "raised at attention" may prove misleading. It is merely a comparative term as ears so placed can never be raised to a great height in the sense of a terrier's ears. But Pyrenean ears do come forward and up, giving a different expression when the dog is "on the watch." Very subtle changes in the position of the ears can tell us volumes about the dog's mood. A Pyrenees should not have to raise his ears frankly in the show ring to show that he is attentive.

Lips must be tight and close-fitting, the uppers dropping just enough to cover the lowers. Loose lower lips which sag away from the teeth allow for an unsightly drool of saliva.

Teeth are strong and regular, the canines being especially well developed. The incisors touch in either a scissors or even bite. Malocclusion of any type is a serious problem.

Pigmentation in a white-coated breed such as the Pyrenees is of great importance. Black is to be found on the lids, eye-rims, lips, and nose. The eye should be a dark rich brown.

Pigment should be even and, where required, symmetrical. Snow-nose is sometimes excused by exhibitors because it is said to be a temporary condition; but, from a genetic point of view, we would all do well to continue to regard this as a sign of pigment breakdown.

Forequarters

The Standard asks for *"well placed shoulders set obliquely, close to the body."* If we refer to the anatomical picture we can see how the shoulder

A lovely head and expression—Champion Basquaerie Nuvalari, bred by Mr. and Mrs. Bruce Hardy.

A fine shot of a good Pyrenean head in profile, showing crown and muzzle in two parallel planes. — *Peter Bickle*

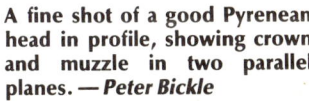

Insufficient length of skull, plus the bulging eye and pronounced stop, makes this an incorrect head.

A slightly rounded crown as seen from the front, that would be acceptable to most breeders. Notice the position of the ears—set at a level with the eyes and carried low and close to the head. — *Peter Bickle*

High-set ears give the crown a flat look. These ears are also folded, standing out from the side of the head.

The round eye with the loose eyelid shows nothing of the desired "slightly oriental" look. A third membrane is visible.
— *Peter Bickle*

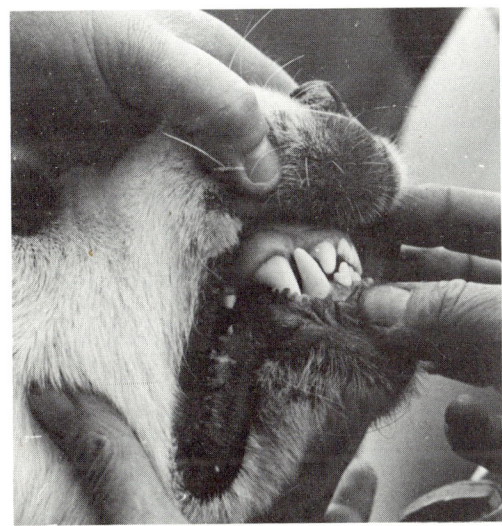

A good mouth with strong teeth, meeting in a scissors bite.
— *Peter Bickle*

The loose, drooling mouth that makes wearing a raincoat necessary if you want to ride in the car with your dog. — *Peter Bickle*

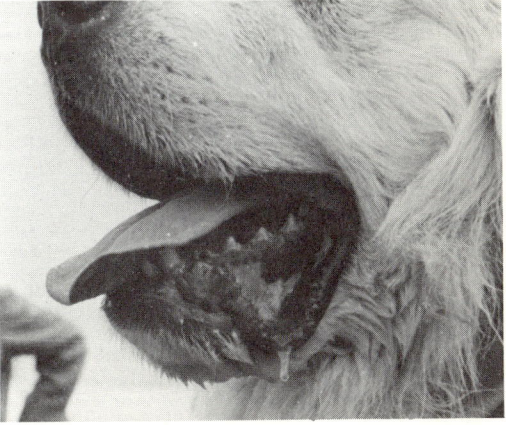

blade is set (at about 45 degrees) and how the upper arms meet the shoulder blade (at about 90 degrees). In adhering to the concept of the well-angulated front assembly, we are reminded that in bounding down a slope the entire weight of a dog is borne by the forequarters. A sound front assembly becomes a "must" in a breed specifically designed for this sort of strenuous activity.

An essential feature of the well-constructed front is a strong pastern with enough bend, or slope, to take the weight off the column of bones at the moment of impact, thereby transmitting the shock via tendons and ligaments (which yield and absorb) rather than via cartilage and bone (which don't). For mechanical reasons, the extremely steep or straight pastern may cause knuckling over at the wrist joint. On the other hand, a weak pastern slopes too much, thereby stretching the ligaments and breaking down the foot.

Chest

The chest is described as deep. The proper depth of chest is determined by the brisket in relation to the elbow, which the brisket must reach or come slightly below. The Standard asks for flat-sided ribs, which means that the ribs are flat in their midsection, although well-sprung from the spinal column. Characteristically, the rib cage extends well to the rear.

The width of the chest is seen from the front. A correct width is one in which the column of support beginning at the shoulder joints and falling vertically to the foot pads places all the bones and joints in a straight line. The front legs are parallel. A chest which is too wide or too narrow for the particular individual throws the elbows "in" or "out" of alignment with the joints above and below. The effect is easily apparent when the dog is gaited towards the observer.

Feet

The close-cupped feet of our dogs should be well arched and thickly padded to provide good leverage and freedom from injury. A working Pyrenees with a long, thinly padded or splayed foot, is "off on the wrong foot" as far as his structure is concerned.

As double dewclaws on the hind feet are a breed "must," it stands to reason that they should be of some use and not merely decorative appendages. They ought to be sufficiently strong and placed rather close to the foot so that they can be an asset in climbing and braking. Loosely attached or floppy dewclaws tend to be set higher on the foot and are often associated with the very long harefoot instead of the compact catfoot.

A foot structure, peculiar to the Great Pyrenees, is to be found in the inherent tendency for the back feet to "toe-out" slightly in action. It appears to have been a useful mechanical adaptation to hard work up and down steep mountain slopes, providing traction and balance. Only the toes should turn out. The legs themselves when viewed from behind should be straight. Cowhocks are a common fault but should not be confused with this slight toeing-out which is a breed characteristic.

Good front alignment with proper width of chest for the individual shown.

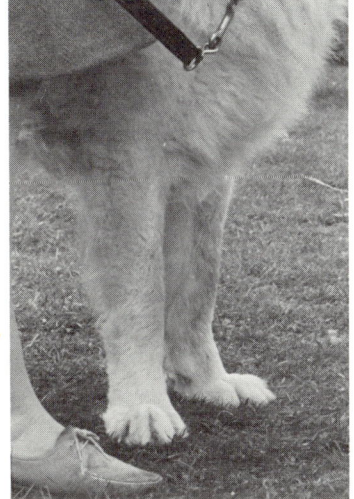

Flat feet with splayed toes and an east-west front. The chest is too narrow for the individual dog.
— *Peter Bickle*

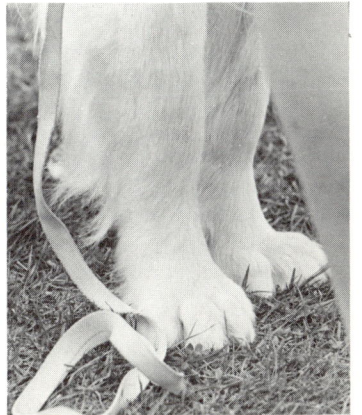

Strong pasterns—sloping slightly. Close-cupped feet. — *Peter Bickle*

Broken-down pasterns. Mechanically un-sound movement. — *Peter Bickle*

This cow-hocked rear makes proper drive difficult.—*I.G.P.R.*

A sound rear assembly showing legs straight and parallel.

Too straight in the stifle—a common fault. Fails to provide drive, reach, spring, absorption of impact. Makes for a stilted, restricted gait and side-stumbling.

The Hindquarters

As the majority of the dog's weight is carried on his forequarters, the purpose of the hindquarters is to provide stability and a strong drive. For this, a sound rear is an absolute necessity. The cornerstone in the rear assembly is the pelvis which is described as slightly sloping. It should slant at about 30 degrees. In addition, it should be broad and thickly invested with muscle as this stabilizes the rear end and provides for sound hip joints.

The thighs should be heavily muscled, "rounded but not low" as the French say, and should taper to strong substantial hocks. The stifle should slope at about 45 degrees. The tibia and fibula should set at about 90 degrees to the femur. The reader is again referred to the anatomical photograph.

The hock joint is the dog's true heel. Between it and the toes, we find the long metatarsal bones. We may conveniently refer to this entire assembly as the rear pastern. The rear pasterns are parallel and nearly perpendicular to the ground when the dog stands naturally.

Tail

The tail is fairly thick at the root and should be of sufficient length to reach to the level of the hocks or slightly below. It is well feathered, the hair being somewhat longer near the tip where it serves to form an attractive plume. A characteristic kink at the end of the tail ("shepherd's crook") has always been a much sought after attribute by the French. It is not required by our Standard. However, it is a most becoming feature. By turning the tip of the tail to one side, it displays the plume.

When a Pyrenees is gaited, his tail either flows out behind him or is curled over the back quite frankly, "making the wheel." A wheel is usually an indication that the dog is aroused. At the same time, when moving from place to place at a steady gait, the tail is often carried in the lower position. Most Pyrenees' fanciers agree that in the show ring it is appropriate for the dog to carry his tail in either manner.

Coat

For the coat to be functional and attractive, both the undercoat and the outercoat should be well exhibited. The underpart is heavy and fine, more woolly along the sides and back of the thighs. The outercoat, which is supple and weather resistant, is especially long on the tail (the plume), and back of the thighs (the pantaloons), the back of the front legs (the feathers) and over the rump.

A ruff of longer hair about the neck and shoulders, more pronounced in males, is highly characteristic and gives foundation to the expression so often heard, "Oh, he looks just like a lion about the head." It contributes greatly to the beauty of the dog and gives added protection in battle to an otherwise vulnerable point.

The coat is either straight or slightly wavy—but never curly or fuzzy. It should lie flat. The combination of a dense coarser top coat and a heavy fine underpart, as described by the Standard, carries a natural lustre and is easier to keep groomed than an overly long or silky-textured coat which mats and tangles.

Color and Markings

The Standard describes the Pyrenees' coat as either *"all-white, or principally white with markings of badger, gray, or varying shades of tan."* The color "badger" is generally accepted to be a grizzled-gray with an admixture of yellow.

Common usage has given us the term "blaireau" to describe any dog which carries one, or a combination of more than one, of the above markings. *Equal value should be given to the blaireau and all-white dog in the show ring, as both are equally correct.*

Markings are characteristically found on the head, the ears, and at the base of the tail. A few body spots are sometimes present. The undercoat may be white or shaded. Markings on the head and ears are usually even and symmetrical.

When we consider the merit of a dog with profuse markings, we must remember that the Standard gives the specific guidelines that the dog must appear principally white. Correct markings serve to enhance the beauty and expression of the specimen. Profuse markings, which give the impression that the dog is an off-color, must be regarded as less desirable.

Gait

In his carriage and bearing, the Pyrenees attains a look of elegance. In his gait we should expect to see both the pride and majesty of a Pyrenean Mountain Dog at his age-old duties of patrolling and defending the flock; as the Standard says: *"showing unmistakably the purpose for which he was bred."*

In a restricted show ring having a large entry, space must be made to exhibit the attributes of the dogs as they are gaited individually. Pyrenean movement is both efficient, ground-covering and tireless. The Pyrenees does not move ponderously; nor does he pace in the show ring. The stride should never appear awkward, stilted or restricted.

Because of his angulation, the Pyrenees moves smoothly and steadily, showing a well-balanced reach both fore and aft, with legs tending towards the center line as speed increases. The rear feet, carrying dewclaws, will never move so close as to interfere. Movement is rhythmic and free-flowing, without a sloppy side-to-side roll of the body.

In summary, the Great Pyrenees should give the impression of a dog of great size, substance and power; propelled by strongly driving hindquarters; moving well within his capabilities.

Correct movement, smooth and efficient, showing a good balanced reach both fore and aft.
—*J. Clawson*

Diagonal pairs of legs moving in unison, propelled by strong hindquarters.
—*J. Clawson*

Mrs. C. Seaver Smith with her first puppy, Ch. Cote de Neige Guerrier.

Three early Quibbletown Champions benched at Westminister. Pictured left to right are Hermia, Parfait and Mistigris. Champion Quibbletown Mistigris went Best of Breed at this show in '54, '56 and '57. Owned by Mr. and Mrs. C. Seaver Smith, Jr. — *Stephanie Rancou*

8

The Modern
Great Pyrenees
in America

WITH THE DISAPPEARANCE of Cote de Neige, La Colina and some of the other early kennels from the show scene in the late forties, the banner of the breed in America passed into the hands of a new generation.

Foremost among the current show and breeding kennels in America is QUIBBLETOWN, owned by Mrs. and Mrs. C. Seaver Smith, Jr. of Taunton, Massachusetts.

This kennel came to the forefront in the very early 1950s. During the next 25 years Quibbletown bloodlines have continued to maintain a place of national prominence in the show rings from coast to coast. Quibbletown is now second only to Basquaerie in the number of champions produced and, like Basquaerie, Quibbletown is the foundation upon which a good number of United States kennels have based their breeding programs. To date, over 100 homebred champions have been produced at Quibbletown.

Edith Smith acquired her first Great Pyrenees over 30 years ago while still an undergraduate at Radcliffe. Cote de Neige Guerrier was a familiar figure on the college campus and at the Fogg Museum at Harvard. As an art major, Mrs. Smith spent many hours at the museum. Her Great Pyrenees shared her dormitory room.

Two years later, when Mrs. Smith married, she and her husband decided to show Guerrier and he became their first champion. Between 1951 and 1955, the Smiths began their kennel by acquiring all the best stock owned by Marjorie Butcher.

''The kennel got its name,'' Mrs. Smith tells us, ''while we were living at New Market, New Jersey. There was a marker in the town which explained that, in colonial days, it had been called 'Quibbletown,' since the farmers would bring their produce to the square and then quibble over the prices.''

Two of the early stand-out bitches at Quibbletown were Ch. Cote de Neige Actrice and her daughter, Ch. Cote de Neige Ariette II. They were direct descendants of Ch. Cote de Neige Ariette I, a litter sister to America's first home bred Best In Show winner, Ch. Cote de Neige Symphonie. Mrs. Smith recalls: "Our early breeding efforts were plagued with problems which don't exist today. Vaccines were less than reliable, and more than one promising puppy was lost to disease. In 1951 hepatitis struck many American kennels, and Quibbletown came close to being wiped out. Those dogs who survived had hard-pad and lived thereafter with damaged feet. The battle against parasites was difficult and discouraging, without the aid of today's more sophisticated drugs. We relied heavily on 'Early Bird Puppy Wormer.' While sulfa drugs were available, as well as the early antibiotics, their side effects were damaging in many cases. When we watch our veterinarians in surgery today, with complex anesthesia procedures and total life support systems available, we remember the days when few veterinarians owned an X-ray machine and surgery meant an ether cone."

Quibbletown dogs made an immediate impact on the show scene. In the fifties and early sixties Ch. Quibbletown Easter Token, and Ch. Quibbletown Bon Chance campaigned by the Linewebers, swept the National Specialties with seven combined wins. Ch. Quibbletown Mistigris, one of the early distinguished winners, achieved 105 Bests of Breed and 37 Group placements.

One of the most successful Quibbletown show winners of this period, and a dog whose production was to be of great significance to the breed in the years to follow, was Ch. Quibbletown Impresario. Impy holds the record at Quibbletown with 18 champion offspring, many of whom have been outstanding winners and producers in their own right.

While Impy was making his mark in the East, Ch. Quibbletown Chanson de Geste was being campaigned in the Midwest and became the first Quibbletown Best In Show winner for his owner, Mrs. Hubert Everist, in Iowa.

After Impy was retired, Ch. Quibbletown Jim Dandy began his career by winning a National Specialty from the classes at 15 months of age. Mrs. Smith said, "This beloved dog was our friend, companion, house dog and resident character of 12 years and is still sorely missed by his family." Dandy left a legacy of ten Quibbletown champions.

Ch. Quibbletown Billy Wink was a multiple Group winner and placer who was campaigned in the middle 1960s. After his tragic death at the age of six, the Quibbletown banner was carried by Ch. Quibbletown Falstaff, owned by Francis Glover.

One of the great bitches at Quibbletown was Ch. Quibbletown Dutchess, BOS winner at the National Specialty in 1961. Two of her offspring, Ch. Quibbletown Beaucoup II and Ch. Quibbletown Chanson de Geste, each won the Working Group before they were two years old. Mention must also be made of Ch. Quibbletown Carlotta who whelped nine champions. Several famous winners and producers out of the Impresario–Carlotta breeding made a

116

Ch. Quibbletown Carlotta is shown winning under judge Wm. L. Kendrick on way to a Group placement at Camden County Kennel Club show, 1964, just three weeks before she whelped. The breed's Top Producing Dam with nine champions to her credit. Owned by Mr. and Mrs. C. Seaver Smith, Jr. —*Shafer*

Champion Quibbletown Jim Dandy at 12 years, pictured at Laneway Farm with his owners, Mr. and Mrs. Smith in 1974.

117

profound impression on the modern Great Pyrenees in America and Canada. These will be discussed later. Carlotta currently heads the list as the breed's Top Producing Dam.

Another Quibbletown bitch who deserves special recognition is Quibbletown Queeka Bear, owned by the Kentopps of Anchorage. Queeka was the dam of two Best In Show winners in the 1970s as well as a Group-winning bitch.

In 1971, for the second time in the history of Quibbletown, the Smiths campaigned a dog who did not bear their kennel prefix: Ch. Karolaska Glacier. The first dog so campaigned was Ch. Lorvoso de la Colina. Glacier came to live with the Smiths in 1971. He shattered all marks with an awesome 10 Bests In Show, 56 Working Group Firsts, 61 Group placements, two National Specialties and two Regional Specialties, to become the top winner of all time! Mrs. Smith wrote, "The record could not have been made without the dedication and devotion of Frankie Glover and Ed Cloud and the ring presence and showmanship of Glacier and Bob Forsyth. This team traveled approximately 65,000 miles in three years in all kinds of weather to achieve this record." Glacier's phenomenal career was tragically terminated at its height by his untimely death from bone cancer.

Quibbletown's record at National Specialties from 1953–1973 began with Ch. Quibbletown Easter Token (3), and continued with Ch. Quibbletown Small Fry (2), Ch. Quibbletown Meringue (1), Ch. Quibbletown Bon Chance (4), Ch. Quibbletown Beau Olard (1), Ch. Quibbletown Jim Dandy (2), Ch. Quibbletown Falstaff (2), and Ch. Karolaska Glacier (2) for a total of 17 Nationals in 20 years.

Mrs. Smith states:

> "Quibbletown is a true bloodline, not merely a kennel prefix. Because we stood almost alone in the early years here in the East, we developed and maintained perhaps a larger colony than we would have liked. We determined to be totally self-sufficient, to linebreed—with extensive culling—in an effort to produce litters even in size, type and soundness. Via our Cote de Neige stock we had the type we wanted, since those early dogs were almost all close to the lovely Estat d'Argeles of Basquaerie.
>
> "In the late 1950s we added our one outcross dog, Ch. Lorvoso de la Colina, who corrected any deficiency we felt we might lack in soundness. Laurie finished his championship in 1958, at the age of nine years, and also won the Working Group. This dog produced hindquarters, balance and good feet with remarkable consistency. Once Laurie had been incorporated into our breeding program, we felt we were on the right track. Laurie was the sire of 11 Quibbletown champions, including Impresario.
>
> "Our hope has always been that, within our linebred colony, we can afford the luxury of purely visual breeding, and that any dog and bitch may be mated without danger of a genetic disaster. Though we do not offer stud service, we have always welcomed Quibbletown-bred bitches who are brought back to be bred and thus continue a linebreeding pattern.

118

Ch. Quibbletown Mistigris went Best of Breed 105 times in the early 1950s and won 37 rosettes for Group placements. Pictured here winning the Group at the Chester Valley Kennel Club Show in 1956. Owned and handled by C. Seaver Smith, Jr. — *Brown*

Ch. Quibbletown Billy Wink was a Group and Specialty winner in the late '60s. Owned by Mr. and Mrs. Smith. — *Roberts*

119

An array of Soleil and Skeel champions pictured at the Spokane Kennel Club Show, 1969. *Left to right:* Ch. Skeel's Bonnie, handled by Carrie Stuart Wells; Ch. Soleil Serein Ami, owned and handled by Jack Magoffin; Ch. Soleil Ami Sustenter, owned and handled by Evelyn Stuart; Ch. Woodruff of Skeel, owned and handled by Mrs. Edward Daniel; Auld Reekie's Sheila of Skeel, owned and handled by Mrs. A. D. Rennaker. — *L. Roberts*

Ch. Soleil Serein Ami is shown proudly winning the Working Group under judge Maxwell Riddle at the Mid-Del Tinker Kennel Club show on October 4, 1970. Owned and handled by Jack Magoffin. — *Petrulis*

"We are pleased that our stock has been wholly or in part the foundation of many of today's most respected kennel names: In the fifties, BEAU KAY Kennels in Oklahoma (Cote de Neige Sunburst, Ch. Cote de Neige Berceuse, Quibbletown Chloe of Beau Kay); TIP 'N CHIP (Ch. Tip 'N Chip's Quibbletown Impy, Ch. Quibbletown Chanson de Geste); BON CHANCE (Ch. Quibbletown Bon Chance, Ch. Quibbletown Simba); CAVALIER (Ch. Quibbletown Cavalier, Ch. Quibbletown M'Appari); LIMBERLOST (Ch. Quibbletown Valkyrie, Ch. Quibbletown Applejack); BARQUEILL (Ch. Quibbletown Terrible Tyrant, Ch. Quibbletown Patrician, Ch. Quibbletown Falstaff); KAROLASKA (Quibbletown Queeka Bear, Ch. Quibbletown Sock It to Em); ELYSEE (Ch. Quibbletown Oliver Twist); MARANTHA (Ch. Quibbletown Glacier Mist); HANDWERK (Ch. Quibbletown Neige Deese, Quibbletown de Blitzard). All go back, at least in part, to Quibbletown. Via their efforts the line has spread and blended into the breeding of others, and has contributed to the type and soundness we have tried so hard to preserve."

While Quibbletown was getting underway on the East Coast in the fifties, a second kennel, 1800 miles to the west, began a modest breeding program which was to grow in prominence over the next twenty years, culminating in a major contribution to the show scene in the early seventies.

This was SOLEIL, owned by Mr. and Mrs. Jack Magoffin of Sterling, Kansas. Jack and Dorothy became actively interested in breeding and showing in the late forties. Their first Pyrenees, Sunshine O'Combermere, left a permanent legacy in her name—"Soleil," the French equivalent for "Sunshine"— which became the kennel prefix.

The next Pyrenees to arrive at Soleil was Ch. Basquaerie Marechal, purchased from Mrs. Crane after he finished at the National Specialty in 1947 under judge Mme. Harper Trois Fontaines. The vibrations of Marechal were felt in the Midwest in the late forties, where he was campaigned successfully to a number of Working Group placements.

Next came Lady Jeanne, Sunshine's puppy who finished in 1949, and Basquaerie Jacquiline, daughter of the multiple Best in Show-winning Ch. Basquaerie Beau Estagel, who was writing the record book in the East.

In the late fifties, the Magoffins began to campaign their dogs in the manner which won fame and admiration for the breed in the plains states. Jack and Dorothy drove hundreds of miles each weekend, usually with four dogs in their station wagon, often to find little if any competition at the shows. A display of Soleil Great Pyrenees at a benched show in the Midwest, where the breed was virtually unknown to visitors, was always an impressive sight.

Ch. Pondtail Raphael of Basquaerie and Ch. Pondtail Tattoo of Basquaerie joined the family in 1958. Raphael was a son of Eng. Ch. Bedat de Monda. Tattoo was his grandson. Raphael sired Ch. Soleil Baron out of Ch. Soleil Coquette. Tattoo sired Ch. Soleil Rayon. Thus the Magoffins blended the English bloodlines of Bedat de Monda and Pondtail into the Soleil strain.

Ch. Soleil Baron was greatly admired in the Midwest show rings and achieved multiple Working Group placements. In 1965, he was named the breed's first Top Producing Sire.

Ch. Cobberidge Adam, a top producer with 14 champion offspring. Co-owned by Mrs. Joann Teems and Mrs. Betty A. Wade and Dr. Betty Hohmann. — *Dai*

The acquisition in the sixties of Ch. Rogue La Rue, bred by Mr. and Mrs. Floyd Bolden of southern California, was to be a major factor at Soleil. In Rogue's background were to be found some of the best of the early Basquaerie bloodlines in California.

Ch. Rogue La Rue is the Top Producing Sire in the breed. His first offspring began to finish in 1965. By 1975 he had produced 27 champion offspring. Among his most famous sons and daughters are Ch. Soleil Serein Amni, Ch. Soleil Rouelle, Ch. Soleil Mon Dieu, Ch. Soleil Ami Sustenter, Ch. Soleil Winni Too of Skeel and Ch. Skeel's Bonni.

Ch. Soleil Serein Ami opened doors for the breed in the Midwest. He was the Top Winner in 1967 and the lifetime holder of 29 Group placements.

The most widely known of the Rogue sons is Ch. Soleil Pierre de Blu Crest. Bred by Jack and Dorothy Magoffin, Pierre was acquired by Vic and Sue Capone of POCO PYRS Kennels. Under the able campaigning of owner Vic Capone, Pierre brought new attention and excitement to the breed in the early seventies. On November 14, 1970, Pierre broke the more than five years' hiatus during which a Great Pyrenees had not won a Best In Show, achieving this singular honor under judge Fairfield Pope Day at the Sussex Hills Kennel Club Show. Pierre followed with four more Best In Shows, a total of 87 Group wins or placements, three National Specialty wins, a Regional Specialty win, and innumerable Bests of Breed. One of Pierre's most poignant wins was at the 1974 National Specialty at Rock Creek in Maryland under English judge Mrs. Joan Passini-Birkett. At ten years of age, Pierre came out of retirement to win first the Veteran's Class and then the Breed. His record as a sire, at Poco Pyrs, includes 13 champion offspring. During his amazing career, Pierre was indeed a true Pyrenean pathfinder, paving the way for contemporary Pyrenees in the Working Group and Best In Show circles.

Additional Soleil champions to distinguish themselves in the Working Group are: Ch. Basquaerie's Clown by Golly, Ch. Soleil Rayon, Ch. Soleil King's Image, Ch. Soleil Gai Lance and Ch. Cobberidge Adam.

Soleil stock has been dispersed widely and has founded, at least in part, a number of fine contemporary kennels, including SKEEL in Idaho, MARWELL in Alaska, COBBERIDGE in Wisconsin, BASQUAY and CHANTILLI in Utah, SNOWMASS in California, and VENTISQUERO in British Columbia.

In the words of Dorothy Magoffin, "The tall fragrant cedars that are on the north side of Soleil have become the final resting place for those wonderful, affectionate friends who, like troopers, went many miles with us. In 31 years the names are many and I wouldn't say that one was greater than another, for each had the qualities that set them apart, to us and to the breed."

The Great Pyrenees fancy sustained a major loss with the passing of this great and generous lady on May 17, 1974. The Soleil line continues in a reduced capacity under the direction of her husband.

Ch. Tip 'N Chip Sonny's Image, pictured winning the Breed at the Wheaton Kennel Club Show under the late judge Earle Adair. A ranking producer with 16 champion offspring. Owned and handled by Mrs. Judith G. Bankus. — *Booth*

The TIP 'N CHIP Kennel of Mrs. Roy Peavey and her daughter, Mrs. Judy Bankus, has earned a reputation for producing and showing a distinguished line of Great Pyrenees winners. This kennel came into being in 1948 with the acquisition of its foundation bitch, Basquaerie Dawn, bred by Mrs. Crane. Two more females who were to play an important role in the Tip 'N Chip bloodlines were Basquaerie New Dawn and Soleil Ting Tang Paddy Wack.

In the late 1950s the kennel came to the attention of the fancy with the breeding of Ting Tang Paddy Wack to Ch. Soleil Rayon. A trio of top winning Pyrenees was produced: Ch. Tip 'N Chip's Gentle Ami, Ch. Tip 'N Chip's Massif Mont-Blanc and Ch. Tip 'N Chip's Mountvalea. The first and third were shown as a brace; a fourth pup from this mating won both his championship and a CD degree.

The next important influence on the kennel strain came in 1963 when a litter out of Gentle Ami was sired by the well-known Ch. Basquaerie Bali. This produced four champions, including Ch. Tip 'N Chip's Luchon, a Best of Breed winner at the National Specialty under Mrs. Crane in 1967.

In 1966 Ch. Tip 'N Chip's Mountvalea was bred to the Best In Show winner Ch. Quibbletown Chanson de Geste. This mating gave birth to another newcomer, Ch. Tip 'N Chip's Mount-Chanson ("Sonny"). The kennel then added a Quibbletown female, Ch. Tip 'N Chip's Quibbletown Impy ("QT"), a product of the well-known Impresario-to-Carlotta breeding of Mrs. C. Seaver Smith. This, then, was the basic material which gave rise to the contemporary Tip 'N Chip winners and producers.

Mrs. Bankus writes, "Sonny (Mount-Chanson) left a definite impression on the breed in his short life. He died at 20 months of age after siring only three litters. Among these, one truly outstanding litter whelped by 'QT' was born on March 18, 1968. Sonny was a Top Producing Sire in 1969, with a total of eight champions, two of whom were Group winners."

The Sonny-QT litter mentioned above included six puppies who were raised by a foster mother, a Collie, because of milk toxicity. They were: Ch. Tip 'N Chip Sonny's Reflection; Ch. Tip 'N Chip Sonny's Image; Ch. Tip 'N Chip Sonamara Chanson; Ch. Tip 'N Chip Sonny's Pride and Joy; Ch. Tip 'N Chip Sonny's Angelique; and Tip 'N Chip Sonny's Impression CD.

Champion Tip 'N Chip's Quibbletown Impy, the dam of this litter, was also BOS at the 1967 National Specialty and Top Producing Dam in 1969. To her credit is one other champion: Tip 'N Chip Sonny's Ques-Tor, a multiple Group winner.

The reputation of the kennel was now given further stimulus by the show success of Ch. Tip 'N Chip Sonny's Reflection who completed his championship from the puppy class and went on to win a Group fourth. He then won the Midwest Specialties back-to-back in 1970 and '71. His show career encompassed 112 Bests of Breed, 6 Group Firsts and 35 Group placements. His career as a producer began in 1970. In 1973 he was declared the year's Top Producing Sire. Among other accomplishments, he sired the Top Winner in

At right is Ch. Tip 'N Chip's Mont-Chanson, owned by Mrs. R. E. Peavey and Mrs. Judith G. Bankus. The first in a line of "Sonnys". At left are Ch. Tip'N Chip's Gentile Anie, Ch. Tip'N Chip's Massif Mont-Blanc and Ch. Tip 'N Chip's Mountvalea, at one year of age, all also owned by Mrs. Peavey and Mrs. Bankus.

Ch. Tip 'N Chip Sonny's Reflection won 112 Bests of Breed, 38 Group placements, and six Group Firsts. Owned by Judith G. Bankus and Mrs. R. E. Peavey.
— *Booth*

Ch. Tip 'N Chip Sonny's Sundance Kid, the year's Top Producer in 1975 with seven champion offspring. Pictured winning Best of Breed at the first Colorado Specialty, 1976, under judge Paul D. Strang. Owned by Judith G. Bankus and Louise Quinn. — *Booth*

Ch. Trottenfox I'm a Tuff Tip 'N Chip is pictured winning the Puppy Class at the Great Pyrenees Club of California Specialty, April 25, 1976, under English judge Peter Gilbert. Two weeks later, "Tuffy" made history by becoming the first Great Pyrenees to win a Working Group First from the Puppy Class, at the Oshkosh Kennel Club Show under judge Thomas Gately. Owned by Mrs. Judith G. Bankus and Miss Nan Hall Hamilton (pictured above). — *Schley*

Ch. Tip 'N Chip Sonny's L'Air, going Best Opposite Sex at the Midwest Specialty, in 1976. The judge is Mrs. Brenda Judson, of England. Owned and handled by Jean Groves. — *Booth*

Ch. Tip 'N Chip Sonny's Quaes-Tor winning a Group Second under judge Mrs. Peter Guntermann at the Columbus Kennel Club show, May 1975. Owned and handled by Mrs. Stuart Blandford. — *Twomey*

1975, Ch. Pyrstrom's Ringmaster. His total production, at the time of this writing, is 13 champions.

Three Sonny's Reflection daughters have won at the Specialties. They are: Ch. Starlaxy Ursa Minor (WB National '73); Ch Tip 'N Chip Sonny's L'Air (BOS Midwest '76) and Trottenfox Little Bit 'O Sonny (BOS Colorado '76).

Ch. Tip 'N Chip's Sonny's Image is another producer who deserves special recognition. He is also out of the Sonny-QT breeding. He has sired 16 champions, which ranks him as the third Top Producer in the breed. Three of Image's daughters have won at the Specialties. A son, Ch. Tip 'N Chip Tam Tam's Diamond, is a multiple Group placer. A full sister of Image, Ch. Tip 'N Chip Sonny's Angelique, won BOS at the Midwest Specialty in 1971.

Continuing in the tradition of his sire, Sonny's Reflection, is Ch. Tip 'N Chip Sonny's Sundance Kid. He was BW at the National Specialty in 1973 and BOB at the Colorado Specialty in 1976 under judge Paul Strang. In 1975 he was the year's Top Producing Sire with seven champions. Five of these were out of Ch. Tip 'N Chip's Roxanne. Together these two produced another National Specialty winner, Ch. Tip 'N Chip's Sonny Side Up.

Mention, too, must be made of the production record of Ch. Tip 'N Chip's Roxanne. Her offspring now total eight champions with two more expected to finish soon.

Tip 'N Chip Kennels has owned or produced 55 champions. Another 26 have been bred by Tip 'N Chip sires. Four dogs are Specialty winners; ten are Group placers; six are Group winners; and one has gone on to a Best In Show.

Tip 'N Chip bloodlines have played a major part in the development of several other kennel programs.

Mrs. Louise Quinn and Mrs. Bankus co-own Ch. Tip 'N Chip Sonny's Sundance Kid and Ch. Tip 'N Chip's Roxanne. Seven Pyrenees' champions in Mrs. Quinn's kennels have borne the Tip 'N Chip prefix.

Miss Nan Hall Hamilton of TROTTENFOX co-owns with Mrs. Bankus a Sonny's Reflection son out of Ch. Soleil Merrie Coquette. This is Ch. Pyrstrom's Ringmaster, the Top Winning Great Pyrenees in 1975 and leading the field in 1976. He recently joined the Pyrenees honor roll by winning a Best In Show. His record to date includes 13 Group Firsts and 48 Group placements. These two also co-own the promising young dog, I'm a Tuff Tip 'N Chip, sired by Ch. Pyrstrom's Ringrouser out of Tip 'N Chip's Chevaux Chalet. Tuffy became a new star in the kennel's line of Group winners by winning (for the first time in the history of the breed) a Working group from the puppy class.

Mr. and Mrs. Waldemar Hauff of BASQUALERO Kennels in Colorado purchased their first Tip 'N Chip dog from the kennels in 1972. They currently own four Tip 'N Chip champions including Ch. Tip 'N Chip Dandy Lion who has placed several times in the Groups. They are also the owners of Ch. Tip 'N Chip Sonny Side Up. This young Group winning dog made history in 1976 by going BOB at consecutive Specialties: The first Independent National Spe-

128

cialty judged by Mrs. Crane; and the following day the California Specialty under judge Peter Gilbert of England. He finished his championship in Canada on July 4, 1976, by winning a Best In Show at the Lions Gate Kennel Club Show, in British Columbia, under judge Gerhardt Plaga.

Mr. and Mrs. Stuart Blandford are the owners of PEERAGE Kennels in Georgia. The Blandfords co-own and handle two top winning Great Pyrenees: Ch. Tip 'N Chip Tam Tam's Diamond and Ch. Tip 'N Chip Sonny's Ques-Tor. "Quint's" record from 1975 through the first half of 1976 is eight Group placements and two Group Firsts. Six Blandford champions have pioneered the breed in the Southeast.

Tip 'N Chip has provided foundation stock for other kennels as well, including STARLAXY, WOLFSONG, EDGINBAR and WILDWOOD.

Mrs. Bankus says, "Our family is continuing into its third generation with Pyrenees. My two daughters, Marcy and Laurie, have started to take an active interest in grooming and showing. Laurie won first place in Junior Handling with Tuffy—whom she trained herself."

Thus it would appear that Tip 'N Chip is in safe hands for at least another generation of Bankus offspring.

The story of the BALIBASQUE Kennels of Mr. and Mrs. Bruce Hardy began with the acquisition of Ch. Dji Dji Bator de Esterhazy in 1960. During the next few years, during which time the health of Mr. Crane made it desirable for the Cranes to move to a warmer climate, Carolyn and Bruce Hardy gradually acquired several of Mrs. Crane's finest dogs.

The first of these was a female, Ch. Basquaerie Clown's Folly, who arrived in 1961. Shortly thereafter came Ch. Basquaerie Bali—the dog who gave his name to the Balibasque prefix. They were followed in order by Ch. The Willows Dutchess; Ch. Basquaerie Tyna; Ch. Basquaerie Jolly Clown; Ch. Basquaerie Vicki's Snow White; Basquaerie Winter's Fog; and Basquaerie Laika. All of these were of Mrs. Crane's breeding except the first.

When Mrs. Crane sent Ch. Basquaerie Bali to Carolyn Hardy he had already acquired his reputation as a winner and a Working Group placer. When his pedigree arrived, it was seen to carry in the hand of Mrs. Crane the following words: "This is the very finest of Basquaerie pedigrees—containing all our most famous names and bloodlines." Bali lived up to his reputation. He was the sire of ten champions. His influence, in succeeding generations, was to have a far-reaching effect.

A mating between Bali and Clown's Folly led to the acquisition by Mrs. Passini-Birkett of the American import Ch. Basquaerie Nuvalari of Pondtail. Nuvalari added much to the breeding picture in England. Among other accomplishments, he was the grandsire of England's Supreme Champion Bergerie Knur.

Bali was next bred to Mrs. Ruth Eveland's foundation female, Ch. Blancura of Bator Esterhazy. This mating provided a useful outcross to the Bas-

Ch. Tip 'N Chip Dandy Lion, owned by Mr. and Mrs. Waldemar Hauff.

Balibasque Beau of Karolaska CD—Sire of two Best in Show Great Pyrenees and a Group Winning bitch. Bred by Mr. and Mrs. Bruce Hardy and owned by Karolaska Kennels.

Ch. Basquaerie Vicki's Snow White, Winners Bitch at the National Specialty in 1970, pictured with her owner, Mrs. Bruce Hardy. — *Evelyn Shafer*

130

quaerie line in the strain of Frank Koller's Esterhazy. The result was to be Ch. Balibasque Mister Big.

Another strain which proved to be important in the bloodlines at Balibasque began with the acquisition of Basquaerie Jolly Clown in 1962. He, too, provided a blending of Basquaerie and Esterhazy, his sire being Ch. Basquaerie's Clown By Golly and his dam, Ch. Zold Erdo Posey of Basquaerie.

The story of Jolly Clown is an interesting one. He was originally sold to Sargent Shriver by Mrs. Crane. When Mr. Shriver was named to head the Peace Corps by President Kennedy in 1962, the Shrivers were obliged to move to Washington where they took up residence in an old mansion complete with hand-made tapestries, needlepoint and antique furnishings. To complicate matters, Jolly enjoyed making informal visits to a nearby Veterans Hospital across a busy thoroughfare. This proved to be a rather difficult setting in which to keep a Pyrenees. So when Mr. Shriver contacted Mrs. Crane to find a new home for Jolly, she referred him to Mrs. Hardy.

Another Balibasque dog with a singular career was Ch. Basquaerie Vicki's Snow White. Vicki went to Florida with the Cranes. However, as the hazards of heartworm were not well known in the early sixties, Vicki became a victim. Back to Boston she came with a clump of worms obstructing the flow of blood through her heart. She entered the Massachusetts General as a patient and underwent surgery to remove the mass. Mrs. Crane was warned, "Another bout of heartworm will do her in!" So no more Florida for her. Mrs. Hardy took her and showed her to her championship. But the highlight of Vicki's career came a few years later, and it was to provide her mistress with one of the greatest thrills of her lifetime. The gal who had survived an open-heart operation was named Winners Bitch at the Great Pyrenees Club of America National Specialty in 1969.

Breeding at Balisbasque has always centered principally on the bloodlines of Basquaerie. Mrs. Hardy writes:

> There is one important physical characteristic of the Great Pyrenees that so impressed us that we decided to concentrate our efforts to retain it true to the Standard. That's the physical appearance of the head. The Pyr head is likened to that of the brown bear but with the ears falling down. The pigmentation must be excellent. In our opinion, this is what identifies the Great Pyrenees and keeps him from being just another big, long-haired dog. Bali had one of the most beautiful heads we have ever seen. He always seemed to hand the same excellent type down to his offspring. And to Ch. Jolly Clown goes credit for producing puppies with beautiful black pigmentation. To start with such excellent stock was sheer luck, but it has taken planning to continue these qualities.

> The first son of Bali handled to his championship by us was Ch. Balibasque Mister Big. It was a tragedy that this dog's life was cut short by a rapidly growing bone sarcoma, but he passed the fine qualities of Bali through to his sons, Ch. Balibasque Wooden Nickel ("Nicky") and Balibasque Beau of Karolaska CD ("Chief"), both out of Ch. Basquaerie Vicki's Snow White.

In turn, Nicky produced some fine offspring including Ch. Balibasque Roland; and Ch. El Amor Bruno of Balibasque owned by Carol and Rick Kentopp.

But possibly the best known grandson of Bali is Balibasque Beau of Karolaska CD who has sired five champions, three of whom were top winners: Glacier, Nero and Bonni Bear.

The key to the success of the KAROLASKA Kennels of Mr. and Mrs. Richard Kentopp is to be found in the fortuitous blending of the bloodlines of Quibbletown and Balibasque. While luck may have played a part at the beginning, only a perceptive application of good breeding practices can account for the consistent winning of this kennel during the past decade.

Rick and Carol Kentopp came to Alaska in 1967 to homestead a wild tract on the side of a mountain overlooking the harbor at Anchorage. With them came their foundation pair from North Carolina, Balibasque Beau of Karolaska CD and Quibbletown Queeka Bear. During the first winter, while the Kentopps lived in a rough cabin, the dogs were required to haul tanks of propane gas up the mountainside. The original homesite has been replaced by a modern home and up-to-date kennels. But the dogs are still expected to pull their share of the load when the need arises.

The first Karolaska litter was born the following summer. The first puppy born was to become a champion and a Best In Show winner. This was Ch. Karolaska Polar Nero, currently owned by Dr. and Mrs. James Giffin. The next litter, a repeat breeding, gave birth to Ch. Karolaska Glacier, the Top Winning Great Pyrenees in the breed in America. A sister of these two, Ch. Karolaska Polar Bonni Bear, was the Top Winning bitch in America. She is one of only two bitches in the history of the breed to win the Working Group. She added to this accomplishment by placing in it four other times. Her career was further highlighted by a Regional Specialty win and Best of Opposite Sex at a National Specialty.

On the passing of Bonni in 1975, Carol Kentopp wrote, "She was our beloved house girl. We have a great affection for all our dogs, but there is always that special one, and that was Bonni."

In 1970 the Kentopps acquired Ch. Quibbletown Sock It To Em from Edith Smith. Bred to the offspring of the original pair, "Clyde" made an important contribution to the development of the Karolaska bloodlines. He is the sire of 11 champions to date. Over thirty Karolaska champions trace their pedigrees back to their three foundation dogs.

A Nero litter sister, Ch. Irena Alexandra Baranova, became the first female at the BARANOVA Kennels of Dr. and Mrs. Arthur Shiable in Fairbanks. This was the beginning of several champions and Group placers, including Ch. Karolaska Bolshoi Baranova. "Tuffy" won the National Specialty at Hammond, Indiana, in 1975 under judge Melbourne Downing. On June 26, 1976, he became the fourth Karolaska-bred Great Pyrenees to go Best In Show in Alaska. A brother, Ch. Boris Goudonov Baranova, finished at the National Specialty under Mrs. Crane in 1976.

132

Ch. Karolaska Juan Carlo D. Arctic going Best In Show under judge Dr. R. F. Greathouse at the Alaska Kennel Club show on April 27, 1976. Owned and handled by Carol Kentopp.

Ch. Karolaska Bolshoi Baranov pictured with his owner, Mrs. Carol Kentopp, winning Best In Show at the Kenai Kennel Club Show on May 30, 1976. The Judge is Mrs. Virginia Hampton.

133

The third Karolaska Pyrenees to win a Best In Show in Alaska is Ch. Karolaska Juan Carlo D. Arctic. He is co-owned by Mrs. Joan Pearson of PYRSON PYR KENNEL in Texas. "Carlo" received limited showing in Texas but won several Working Groups and ranked third in 1975.

With the acquisition of their newest stud dog, Ch. El Amor Bruno Balibasque, the future of the Karolaska bloodlines seems well assured. A Bruno daughter, Karolaska Puffin, made quite a sensation by winning BOS from the puppy class at the Golden Gate Specialty in 1976. Shortly thereafter, Puffin continued her winning ways by going BW and BOS at the National Speciality in Anaheim.

In ten years, 11 Karolaska Great Pyrenees have won or placed in the Groups. Several have won at the Specialties and four have won an all-breed Best In Show—a truly remarkable record for any modern Great Pyrenees kennel.

With the increasing popularity of the breed in America, particularly within the last decade, other new stars have risen on the American show scene.

On the East Coast, the Maryland kennels of Frances Glover and Ed Cloud are producing a number of champions who are making distinguished wins for the BARQUEILL prefix. This breeding program began in the middle sixties with the acquisition of three Pyrenees from Mrs. C. Seaver Smith. They are: Ch. Quibbletown Terrible Tyrant who has produced six champions and was the breed's Top Producing Sire in 1969; Ch. Quibbletown Patrician who got the kennel off to a good beginning as a Group placer; and Ch. Quibbletown Wishful Thought who anchored a line of champion-producing bitches.

Several other Pyrenees bearing the Quibbletown prefix are owned by Frances Glover and Ed Cloud. Perhaps the best known of these is Ch. Quibbletown Falstaff. He is a son of Impresario out of Beau-Kay Heidi. Falstaff won or placed in the Working Group consistently during the late sixties and early seventies. He was the Top Winner in the breed for the year 1969, and he twice won the National Specialty.

Falstaff's most famous win came under English judge F. S. Prince at the National in 1971, at Trenton. In choosing Falstaff for his Breed winner, Mr. Prince remarked, "He epitomized for me the ideal of the breed Standard."

Another top winning Great Pyrenees owned by Frankie Glover is Am. Can. Ch. Barqueill Avant Garde who won the Canadian National Specialty in 1975. He was also the second top winning Pyrenees in the United States in that year, with three Group Firsts and 15 Group placings. In 1976 he topped his career to date by winning a Canadian all-breed Best In Show at Kars, in Ontario. Frances Glover and Ed Cloud have owned or produced 25 champions. Four have earned a Canadian championship and others have placed in the Groups.

In Maine, Mrs. Janet Roberts' PYRFECTION Kennels are prominent on the show circuit. Ch. Dar-Jan's Lord Alfred won a Group placement in Ber-

. and Mrs. Arthur Shiable at home in Fairbanks, Alaska. Pictured left to right are Ch. Boris Gou-
nov Baranova; two pups; Ch. Irena Alexandra Baranova, the Shiables' foundation female; and
e of her offspring, Zinnia.

h. Barqueill Status Quo, bred and
wned by Frankie Glover. Here pic-
red winning a Group Second un-
er judge Mrs. Mary W. Crane, at
e Richland County Kennel Club
how, 1975. The handler is James L.
athbun. — *Klein*

muda in 1973. He is the sire of Ch. La Geni de Josette, who went BOS at the National Specialty in 1974. The Roberts' have owned or bred six Pyrenees champions.

The JONRICKER Kennel of Mr. and Mrs. John Thell in Rhode Island has also produced six champions. Ch. Jonricker Mister Magoo is the proud holder of a Group First and a Group Fourth.

Am. Can. Ch. Quibbletown Leo the Lion made an enviable show record for his owner, Mrs. Mildred Miner Moore, in the late sixties. He was 172 times Best of Breed. He was the Top Winner in Canada in the year 1968 and was the second Pyrenees to win a Best In Show in that country, a feat he accomplished in 1969. Mrs. Moore's ZODIAC Kennels lists six Connecticut champions.

The RENAISSANCE Kennels in Bluemont, Virginia, has been actively engaged in breeding and showing for 11 years. The kennel is owned by Mr. and Mrs. David Freedman. Eight of their champions are first or second generation offspring of Castellan Coco and Castellan Chica. The Freedmans have recently become interested in international bloodlines. Several overseas specimens have been imported which embody the bloodlines of France (Pontoise, Comte (de Foix), England (Bergerie, de Fontenay) and Belgium (Val d'Ardennes).

The SHERANDO Kennels of Mr. and Mrs. Robert Eldreth, also in Virginia, have finished five champions.
Mrs. Doris Kemmerlin's YONAH Kennels in Alabama is actively popularizing the breed in the Southeast. Ariel Charm's Cor is a multiple breed winner. Mrs. Kemmerlin has finished five champions.
In Pennsylvania, the PYRSTROM Kennels of Mr. and Mrs. Jack Bostrum have successfully combined the Tip 'N Chip and Soleil bloodlines to produce five champions carrying the kennel prefix. Ch. Pyrstrom's Ringmaster, the previously mentioned Best In Show winner in 1975, is one of the outstanding breeding accomplishments of this kennel.
Mr. and Mrs. Joseph Gentzel of ANETO in Ohio, and Mrs. Gale Armstrong of GALESWAY in New Jersey, are both dedicated breeders who have finished a number of champions. Although newcomers to the breed, the Gentzels finished four in 1975.

In Michigan, interest in the breed was given impetus by Audrey Handwerk, who acquired Ch. Quibbletown Neige Desse and Quibbletown de Blitzard from Edith K. Smith in 1965. Neige was a daughter of Ch. Quibbletown Carlotta by Ch. Quibbletown Impresario. She produced seven champions for the HANDWERK Kennels. In turn a son of Neige Desse out of Ch. Handwerk Hercules, became the founding sire of the ES-PRY-IT Kennels of Al and Patricia Alteri. This was Ch. Esprit Blanc, who distinguished himself by win-

The Top Winning Great Pyrenees brace in America—Ch. Nikris Boule de Neige CD, and his son, Ch. Cumulus de Nikris — winning a Best In Show under the late Hollis Wilson. Owned and handled by Robert Smith. — *Francis*

From left to right: Rhonda Baab with her Ch. Karolaska Klondike Kid, Best of Breed; the judge, Mr. H. Brown; and Anita Baab with Costa Lota's Frosty Snowman, Winners Dog and Best of Winners, at the San Fernando Kennel Club Show, 1974. Both are owned by Ranchita Costa Lota. — *Ludwig*

ning the first Canadian National Specialty in 1972. He also placed in the Groups in the States and sired several champion offspring. Both of these kennels continue to be active supporters of the breed in the Michigan area.

In the middle 1960s Mr. and Mrs. Duncan Wright came to Michigan from California, bringing with them four Pyrenees. Under the affix DE MONT-BLEU, the Wrights bred 15 champions and several Great Pyrenees who earned an Obedience degree. All of these made a strong impression on the show scene during this period. Ch. Prince Andre De Montbleu placed in the Groups. He was among the top Pyrenees in the United States in 1969 and sired 11 champions. Ch. Argenta Juliana De Montbleu whelped six champions. Mr. Wright assumed the presidency of The American Dog Owners Association in the early seventies, and then in 1976 was named national head of the American Society for the Prevention of Cruelty to Animals.

Mr. and Mrs. Paul Turner of WILDWOOD Kennels purchased their first Pyrenees in 1965. They have produced or owned six Michigan champions carrying the Wildwood or Tip 'N Chip prefix.

Mrs. Jean Groves of RIVERGROVES Kennels became interested in the breed in 1967 with the acquisition of Tonya De Montbleu from the Duncan Wrights'. Tonya was shown in Obedience and remains the only Pyrenees in Michigan to claim a CDX title.

In 1970, Mrs. Groves added Am. Can. Ch. Poco Pyrs King Crusher, and later Ch. Tip 'N Chip Sonny's L'Air. Crusher finished his Canadian championship in one weekend with three majors. He was BOB at Westminster in 1975. During the first half of 1976, he earned four Group Firsts and three Group placements.

L'Air is the dam of two champions. She was judged BOS at the 1975 Midwestern Specialty under Mrs. Brenda Judson of England. Mrs. Groves has finished several other champions.

The breed in Minnesota is well represented by Miss Elaine Colberg's PRY-LAYNE Kennels and the ADOUR Kennels of Ron and Judy Hoxmeier. The Hoxmeiers became interested in the breed in 1969 and remain active in the show ring with several champions to their credit.

Miss Colberg obtained her original pair in the mid-sixties. They were Am. Can. Ch. Quibbletown Chesky de Blac and Am. Can. Ch. Joyeuse de Chesky. From these two came two more Am. Can. champions, one of whom, Pry-Layne's Beau de Chesky, went BOB at the Midwest Speciality in 1973. His son, Am. Can. Ch. Pyr-Layne's Alex of Anayobon, won and placed in the Groups and became the fifth American-bred Pry-Layne Pyrenees to also boast a Canadian title.

STARLAXY is the prefix of Dr. and Mrs. Robert Brown of Jackson, Wisconsin. The Browns became interested in Great Pryenees in 1966 and have bred or shown 11 champions to date. Their foundation bitch, Balibasque Touche, was bred to Ch. Tip 'N Chip's Mont-Chanson. This gave them Ch.

Am. Can. Ch. Poco Pyrs King Crusher, owned and handled by Jean Groves. Crusher is pictured winning the Working Group at the Hockomock Kennel Club Show in 1976, under judge Dr. Malcolm E. Phelps. — *William Gilbert*

Ch. Quibbletown Jon Tom, owned and handled by Linda Canfield.
— *E. H. Frank*

Ch. Galaxy Capella O'Shenanvale, Best Winners and Best of Breed at the Bucks County Kennel Club Show, May 6, 1972, under judge Mrs. M. A. Moore. Owned and handled by Dr. Robert Brown.
— *Booth*

139

Galaxy's Bellatrix. She, in turn, was bred to Ch. Tip 'N Chip Sonny's Reflection. From this mating they finished Ch. Starlaxy's Ursa Minor. Ursa was Winners Bitch at the National in 1973. Several fine Starlaxy bred or owned bitches have done well at the Specialties.

Mention must be made of a promising young dog, Ch. Starlaxy Anson de Villevieux, co-owned by the Browns', who was twice BOB at the Chicago International and won the Breed at Westminster in 1976. Anson is the son of Am. Can. Ch. Pyr-Layne's Alex of Anayobon out of Ch. Starlaxy's Ursa Minor. The Browns' have worked tirelessly on behalf of the breed—Dr. Brown in his capacity as the current Secretary of the GPCA and Mrs. Brown, along with John Cobb, as Editor of the *GPCA Titleholders*.

Wisconsin is also the home of COBBERIDGE Kennels owned by Mr. John Cobb. Mr. Cobb acquired several dogs from the Magoffins in the middle 1960s. He is the breeder of Ch. Cobberidge Adam, a top producing sire with 14 champion offspring. In 1971, Mr. Cobb added an outcross, Ch. Bergerie Maria, obtained from Mr. and Mrs. Prince in England. Maria is the dam of Ch. Cobberidge Contessa, who went Winners Bitch at the Detroit Specialty under judge Mrs. Joan Passini-Birkett. Mr. Cobb has owned or bred ten champions.

The RENEFIELD Kennels in Illinois began under the direction of Mrs. Lorene Canfield and her daughter, Linda. Their first breeding pair was acquired in 1967. Ch. Quibbletown Jon Tom and Ch. Quibbletown Ami were both sired by Ch. Quibbletown Jim Dandy out of separate dams. Jon Tom was quite prominent in the Midwest in the late sixties, placing six times in the Working Group.

Ami was bred twice and produced five champions. One of her daughters, Ch. Renefield Glory Hallelujah, sired by Ch. Tip 'N Chip Sonny's Image, went Best of Winners at the Midwest Specialty in 1971. Her full sister, Ch. Renefield Autumn Glory, lived up to her name by going BOS at the National Specialty under judge Mel Downing in 1975.

Ch. Renefield Glory Hallelujah also distinguished herself as a top producer, whelping four champions sired by Ch. Tip 'N Chip Sonny's Reflection. One of these, Ch. Tip 'N Chip Sonny's Sundance Kid, has already been mentioned as the winner of the first Colorado Specialty. The Canfields have finished 15 champions, of which 11 are home-bred.

ELYSEE is the prefix of Dr. and Mrs. James Giffin. They purchased their first Great Pyrenees, Soleil Coquette de Neige, from Jack and Dorothy Magoffin in 1969. Shortly thereafter, Quibbletown Oliver Twist was obtained from Mrs. C. Seaver Smith and shown to his championship at 14 months of age. From these two came a litter of three, one of whom is the foundation bitch at Elysee, Ch. Elysee Racquette Ruff. In turn, she has produced two champions to date, both of whom finished Reserve at a Specialty.

Ch. Karolaska Polar Nero, a Best In Show winning Great Pyrenees. Owned by Dr. and Mrs. James Giffin.

At left, Ch. Elysee Eve, owned by Dr. and Mrs. Robert Brown. Bred by Dr. and Mrs. James Giffin. *At right,* Ch. Elysee Racquette Ruff, winning Best of Breed at the Egyptian Kennel Club Show 1972. Bred and owned by Dr. and Mrs. James Giffin; handled by Paul Hannah. — Photos, *Lane* and *Graham.*

In 1972 Ch. Karolaska Polar Nero joined the Giffin household. He began his career at Elysee by winning BOB at the Chicago International under Mrs. Mary Crane. During the following year he was shown on a limited basis. His lifetime show record includes 16 Working Group placements (in 29 shows). Eight of these were Group Firsts, two of which were followed by a Best In Show. His crowning accomplishment, after which he was retired, was the Best In Show win at the Mississippi Valley Kennel Club show on May 20, 1973, under judge Mrs. Anne Rogers Clark. His handler was William Kramer, to whom much credit must be given for this singular record of achievement. This splendid dog embodies the best qualities to be found in our breed and is responsible, in good part, for the keen interest in the Great Pyrenees which motivates this author. A number of Nero offspring have gone on to fine careers at other kennels in the Midwest.

Don and Nancy Goodwin have been breeding and showing Pyrenees since 1970. Ch. Solomon's Valiant Prince and Ch. Soleil's Pride of Montagne were both handled to their championships. The Goodwins have bred or owned six champions. VALA Kennels is located in Wichita, Kansas.

The BEAU-KAY Kennels of Mr. and Mrs. Ray Ballew in Oklahoma were active in the breed in the early fifties and sixties. Over 15 Pyrenees were owned or handled to a championship. Many of these made a solid contribution to the breed in the Midwest at that time. Several Beau-Kay Obedience titles were also earned. Beau-Kay Wise Zest CD, UT, owned by Suzanne D. Wallace, must be ranked as the most famous of the Obedience winners carrying this prefix.

The Mile High Great Pyrenees Club in Colorado has become the focus of a very active and enthusiastic Pyrenees fancy in the Rocky Mountains. Although composed of relative newcomers to the breed, the Club already lists a number of Speciality and Group winning dogs on its honor roll. Its first President, Robert Smith, is the owner of the top winning Great Pyrenees brace in the breed. One of these dogs, Ch. Nikris Boule de Neige, attained further distinction for the NIKRIS prefix by winning two Specialties: the California in 1974 and the Midwest in 1975. "Bo" has also placed in Groups in both the United States and Canada.

The Club's first Vice President, Mrs. Merry Hauff, is the owner of two Group Specials, one of whom has won two Specialties. Mrs. Hauff's dogs have previously been mentioned in connection with her kennel prefix, BASQUALERO. The Club's first Secretary, Mrs. Carolyn Ferguson, is the owner of DASTEDKE Kennels. Dastedke is the home of Ch. Karolaska Joli Bon Copain, a multiple Group placer in 1975.

The history of the breed in Colorado would not be complete without mention of the DAR-JAN Kennels of Mr. and Mrs. Darrell Brown. This kennel started in 1963 with stock which embodies the bloodlines of Pyr-Haven, Quibbletown and Soleil. Ch. Dar-Jan's Quille de Milieu is a multiple Group placer who won numerous BOBs in the Midwest during the late sixties and seventies. Two other dogs owned by the Browns, Ch. Pyr-Haven Shamrock and Ch. The Willows Prince Albert, left an imprint through the production of ten and seven champions respectively. Dar-Jan lists more than 25 champions, three of whom are also holders of a CD degree and another who has earned a CDX. Dar-Jan has provided stock for kennels in Colorado and elsewhere.

The breed in Utah is well represented by the BASQUAY Kennels of June and Brent Palmer, and CHANTILLI, owned by Ferris and Barbara Hayes. The Palmers began to breed and show in 1967. Their foundation female, Emily Beau-Bali, was bred to Ch. Cobberidge Adam. From this mating came Ch. Basquay's Yogi Bear and Ch. Basquay's Hannibal. Yogi Bear is the sire of Ch. Basquay's Teddy Bear who made a fine show record which included Best of Breed at the Southern California Specialty in 1975, and ranking among the top winners in the breed in that year. Ably handled by Peter Miller, he won 42 BOBs and several Group placements.

Ferris and Barbara Hayes have likewise owned and shown a number of champions carrying the Soleil strain. Ch. Soleil Payaso de Chantilli placed in the Groups and ranked eighth in 1975.

The SKEEL Kennels of Mr. and Mrs. Ned Stuart have been actively engaged in breeding and showing Great Pyrenees since 1960. Located in the heart of the Bitterroot Mountains in Northern Idaho, the dogs soon became an important part of life on the ranch. The Stuarts' first breeding pair was Ch. Soleil Teddy of Skeel and Ch. Soleil Diana of Skeel. They were soon followed by Ch. Soleil Cozann who was in whelp by Ch. Rogue La Rue. From this combination came several distinguished offspring for both kennels: Ch. Soleil Serein Ami, Ch. Skeel's Bonni, Ch. Woodruff of Skeel, and Can. Ch. Skeel's Honey Bee. Cozann was the producer of seven champions and thus ranks among the Top Producing Dams.

Two other important additions to the Skeel bloodlines were Ch. Soleil Winni Too of Skeel and Ch. Soleil Ami Sustenter. Winni was a Rogue daughter out of Ch. Soleil Coquette and a litter sister to Ch. Soleil Pierre de Blu Crest. Ch. Soleil Ami Sustenter was a Rogue son out of Ch. Soleil Milou. Several of the above have placed in the Groups.

Skeel Pyrenees have made important contributions to several other bloodlines, including SNOWMASS, COBBERIDGE, VENTISQUAERO AND MARWELL. Mrs. Stuart lists more than 25 champions on the Skeel honor roll.

On the West Coast, Pyrenees have been on the upswing since the middle fifties. In California, the BARRANCA Kennel of Mr. and Mrs. Dean Williamson became active in 1963. Twelve champions have been produced under the Barranca prefix. The Williamsons based their breeding program on two bitches and one dog, principally of Basquaerie and Quibbletown origin. The first female was out of Ch. Basquaerie Posey by Ch. Rogue La Rue. The other two, Ch. Gunnar Secundo de Barranca and Ch. Tonvaun's Zanette de Barranca, were brother and sister. Their sire was Hendaye Euskalrho Laustan and their dam was Ch. Quibbletown Lee of Ralfrans.

Due to the death of his wife in 1976, Mr. Williamson is disbanding his kennel and moving to Illinois. But several fine Barranca youngsters will remain in California to carry on the kennel tradition.

Among the active kennels in California to make an impression on the current scene is DE FER, owned by Mr. and Mrs. Charles Doran. The Dorans acquired their first pair, a brother and sister, from the SOLOMON Kennels of Mr. and Mrs. Cliff Gregg in 1964. Their first female, Delilah of Solomon, was bred to Hendaye Euskalrho Laustan, himself the sire of 16 champions out of four bitches and one of the top producers in the breed. From this mating came six champions—a feat which has yet to be exceeded in a single Pyrenees litter. The Dorans base their breeding program on Quibbletown bloodlines with an admixture of old California strains. The Dorans, who remain active in the show ring, have currently produced nine champions and three Great Pyrenees with Obedience degrees.

The first breeding pair at the COSTA LOTA Kennel of Allan and Anita Baab, Lakeview Terrace, was Ch. Pyr-Haven Monsieur Montagne CD and Pyr-Haven Billy's Carmelita CD. During the past decade, a number of champions have been produced at Costa Lota—all of whom have been shown in Obedience competition as well.

Today, the Baabs are the proud owners of nine Great Pyrenees, all of whom have won, or are in the process of winning, their CDs. Can Ch. Costa Lota Angila Mia was the second highest Obedience scorer in the United States in 1975 and is the record holder in Canada with 198½ points.

Ch. Karolaska Klondike Kid CD, owned by the Baabs, has won over 60 BOBs. His son, Can. Am. Ch. Costa Lota Frosty Snowman, won a Group second in Canada in 1975.

During the past several years there has been an accelerated interest in the breed in California. There are a number of new kennels actively breeding and showing as of this writing.

Miss Debra DeVita and Miss Joyce Grable have joined forces at WINTERWIND in the San Diego area. The MALEENS Kennels of Elli Pasicznyk have combined Pyr-Haven and The Willows to produce several champions. Mrs. Pasicznyk is the co-owner of Ch. Basquay's Teddy Bear. Mr. and Mrs. John Nordstrum of BEAUCHAN have successfully combined Barranca with De Fer. Kay and Robbin Rodgers in the Lake Tahoe area are the proud owners of AURORE's Ch. Bilbo Baggins, a top winner in Northern California.

Kitty and Norm Carpedus of POSTE DE POMPIER have been successfully breeding and showing Great Pyrenees both in breed and Obedience since 1968. Oroblanco Belle de Pompier is the proud holder of a CD and CDX de-

Ch. Karolaska Joli Bon Copain and Quibbletown Cristal Del Rey—both owned by Carolyn Ferguson of Dastedke Kennels.

Ch. Dar-Jan's Quille de Milieu, a Group placing dog owned by Mr. and Mrs. Darrell Brown. — *Francis*

Ch. Skeel's Bonnie, winning a Group Third under judge Arthur Zane, at Lewiston, Idaho; pictured with her owners Mrs. Evelyn Stuart and Carrie Stuart Wells. — *Roberts*

Am. Can Ch. Nikris Boule de Neige, CD, winning the Great
Pyrenees Club of California Specialty, 1974, under Mrs.
Maynard K. Drury. Owned by Mr. and Mrs. Robert Smith.
— *Bennett*

Ch. Basquay's Teddy Bear, winning the Great Pyrenees
Club of California Specialty in 1975 under judge Vincent
Perry. Number 3 Pyr in '74 and '75. — *Ludwig*

At right, Ch. Starlaxy Anson de Villevieux shown winning the breed at Westminister in 1976. Handled by Mrs. Anne Rapport. The judge is Melbourne T.L. Downing. Co-owned by Anne Rapport and Mrs. Robert Brown. — *Gilbert*

Below, Ch. Starlaxy Anson de Villevieux, gaiting in the Working Group at Westminister. — *Callea Photo*

gree. The Carpedus' daughters, of whom there are three, are active in Junior Handling.

Dr. Betty Hohmann and Mrs. JoAnne Teems have combined their talents at SNOWMASS in the Sacramento area to successfully popularize the Soleil, Skeel and Marwell bloodlines. Dr. Hohmann and Mrs. Teems are co-owners, together with Mrs. Betty A. Wade, of Ch. Cobberidge Adam.

Virginia Barber of EDGINBAR in the Mojave Desert has been actively engaged in raising and showing Great Pyrenees for several years. Mrs. Barber, who merges Tip 'N Chip bloodlines with Pyr-Haven, has produced several champions. Thus the breed is growing in popularity throughout the State.

The CAVALIER Kennel of Mr. and Mrs. Charles McConnell in Seattle has made a significant contribution to the breed in the Northwest. Their foundation male, Ch. Quibbletown Cavalier, must be ranked as one of the top show dogs in America. Kip, who was still active and siring pups at 12 years of age, has a grand total of 139 BOBs, 21 Group placements, and several Group Firsts. Kip recently joined the ranks of the few to win an all-breed Best In Show. He accomplished this feat at the age of ten years at the Pacific National Exhibition in Vancouver under judge Langdon Skarda. Credit for Kip's success must also be given to handler Gene Hahnlen. As Mr. McConnell says, "He was one-half of the dog."

Kip was Top Producer in the United States in 1971, '72 and '74. In Canada, Kip ranked first or second in production from 1965 through 1975. In the United States, Kip has sired 12 champions to date.

A Cavalier female recently won a Best In Show in India. The McConnells have bred or shown over twenty Great Pyrenees champions, including three who have placed in the Working Group and one who has been a Specialty winner. The influence of these will continue to be felt on the West Coast in the years to come.

Two other kennels, recently relocated in the Northwest from California, are EUSKARI, owned by Mimi Cary, and EUZKOTAR, owned by Mrs. Linda Weisser. Both are enthusiastic and dedicated breeders who are actively showing and finishing champions.

In Alaska, the climate and rugged terrain favor the development of the breed. The first breeding pair was brought to Alaska in the early sixties by Charles Bergland of WOLFSONG. These two were Tip 'N Chip Aubisque (a sister to Mrs. Bankus' Luchon) and Tip 'N Chip Matanuska (a brother to her Mont-Chanson.)

Mrs. Ruth Marcey of MARWELL Kennels finished two pups from this breeding: Ch. Wolfsong Skookum Jim and Ch. Wolfsong Tanana Gal. Skookum Jim made several nice wins and placed in the Working Group. Mrs. Marcy has blended Marwell with Skeel to produce some promising youngsters. Marwell's Juneau Nugget went BOS in 1976 at the California Specialty. Two other ranking kennels in America who make their home in Alaska, Karolaska and Baranova, have already been mentioned.

Thus, from coast to coast, the breed is well represented.

Can. Am. Ch. Diro's Abaydos De Pau, the Top Winning Great Pyrenees in Canada, with four all-breed Best In Show wins to his credit as of this writing. Pictured here winning a Best In Show at the Canadian Sportsmen's Dog Show on March 24, 1976, under judge Roy Montague. The handler is Martha Covington Thorne. Owned by Mr. and Mrs. Roy Addie. — *Streeter*

Am. Can. Ch. Esprit Blanc pictured winning the Canadian National Specialty in 1972. Owned by Mr. and Mrs. Al Alteri. — *D.N.H. Ltd*

Can. Am. Ch. Quibbletown Minute Man, the foundation dog at Armil Kennels. Pictured at 11 years of age with his owner, Mrs. Van Osselar, at Ottawa's first Booster Show in 1971. The judge was the late Mr. John Murphy. — *Hodges Photo*

Can. Ch. Armil's Miss Muffet, pictured winning the Working Group as a puppy under the late judge Alva Rosenberg. Owned by Mrs. Van Osselar. — *McNeill*

150

9

The Great Pyrenees in Canada

LEGEND TELLS US that the Great Pyrenees once graced the shores of Canada in the 16th and 17th centuries. Certainly as early as the year 1500, the fisheries off the Coast of Newfoundland were operated by French, Portuguese, Basque and other seafarers. Since the mainland abounded in wolves and other wild animals, it was only natural that the Pyrenean should be brought to Greenland and Newfoundland to fulfill his traditional role—that of protector and companion to the early settlers. Why he did not leave descendants today in Canada remains a mystery, but apparently he did not.

In the early part of this century a French woman, a Mlle. Prevotient, brought back with her from France, to guard her home in Carlisle on the Gaspe Peninsula, five great white dogs from the Pyrenees. This tale was told to Mrs. Francis Crane by a woman who had called and seen the dogs. Unfortunately, she could shed no light as to whether there had been breeding of these dogs or not.

An intrepid Canadian explorer of the early thirties was Basquaerie Marie Blanque, who accompanied her mistress, the wife of Reverend Tom Greenwood, to winthin 30 miles of the Arctic Circle. Reverend Greenwood had been assigned to an Indian outpost in the Northwest Territories. Here Marie thrived in the cold northern winter, living outdoors and making herself useful (as becomes a Pyrenean) by pulling ice and wood on a sled for her mistress.

Great Pyrenees were first exhibited in Canada by Mrs. Crane in 1935. The benching of six Pyreneans at Exhibition Park in Toronto created a sight to stir the admiration of many Canadian visitors.

In 1938 Champion Zayda Van Euskara of Dutch parentage became the first Great Pyrenees to win a Canadian championship. He was owned by Marjorie Butcher.

Then in 1948 came the first Great Pyrenees to win Best in Show in Canada—Basquaerie Edgemere's Rex—scoring at Truro, Nova Scotia, on September 23. In 1952, Cote de Neige Orpheus won a Working Group 3rd at the famous Canadian National Exhibition, but little more was heard from him in Canada. It is believed he returned to the United States with his owner where he completed his American title.

A few Canadian kennels flourished briefly in the late thrities and forties. One of these, Combermere, has already been mentioned. The bloodlines were almost exclusively Basquaerie and Cote de Neige. Breeding was frequently limited to the ownership of a single pair.

In the early fifties only a few scattered specimens were exhibited. These included Laurie 2nd of La Colina (Mrs. Warde); Basquaerie Babillard (Timberly Kennels); Minorduke's Grand Duke (M. Cox); and two specimens from Skahaven Kennels in British Columbia (E. Cardinall).

By the end of the decade, entries at the shows for the year had plummeted to one Great Pyrenees. However, the single entry, Xarine de Fontenay, was destined to become the granddam of the first Canadian-bred Best in Show Great Pyrenees.

Bloodlines in Canada

In 1963, the magazine *Dogs in Canada* instituted a new rating system, the Top Three in each breed. Pyrenees who have won this honor more than once are: Can. Am. Ch. Quibbletown Minute Man (1963, 1964, 1966): Can. Am. Ch. Limberlost Rogue (1970, 1973); and Can. Am. Ch. Quibbletown Val's Heritage (1974, 1975). All three of these outstanding winners made an important contribution in the Canadian bloodlines of the late '60s and '70s.

Quibbletown Minute Man was purchased by Mr. and Mrs. Van Osselaar and, along with Quibbletown Misti Maid, produced a number of very nice progeny, including Champion Armil's Miss Muffet, who was the Top Pyr in Canada in 1967. Another important breeding was Ch. Quibbletown Minute Man to Can. Ch. Rampart House Arete Panda, a daughter of Xarine De Fontenay and Basquarie Bali. This mating produced the dog Can. Ch. Karlston Snowden Kiter.

"Dominic," as he was known, wins a place on the Canadian honor role by being the first home-bred Champion to go Best in Show at the Progressive Kennel Club Show in Ontario, June 7, 1969, under judge Maxwell Riddle. He was bred by Mrs. T.M. Jones and was sold before his win to Mr. and Mrs. O'Dell of Ontario.

The O'Dells continued the bloodlines of ARMIL and KARLSTON under the registered prefix NIMBUS. A number of very nice dogs were produced from Can. Ch. Armil's Amanda and Can. Ch. Karlston Kiri of Nimbus. Through their foundation stock the O'Dells brought together the bloodlines of Quibbletown, Basquaerie and de Fontenay. Through additional purchases later, Tip 'N Chip blood was added.

Can Ch. Rampart House Arete Panda with four of her pups. Panda was the dam of Canada's first homebred Best In Show Great Pyrenees. Owned by Mrs. T.M. Jones.

Can. Am. Ch. Karlston Snowden Kiter, the first Canadian-bred Best in Show winner, at the Progressive Kennel Club Show in Ontario, 1969. "Dominic" ranked in the Top Ten Pyrenees in the U.S.A. in 1969. Pictured with his owner, Mrs. Shirley O'Dell, and judge Maxwell Riddle. — *Stonham*

LIMBERLOST is the prefix of Lois Mackintosh of Ontario. Miss Mackintosh became seriously interested in Great Pyrenees in 1965, and shortly thereafter acquired her foundation female, Quibbletown Valkyrie, from Mrs. Smith. Later a Canadian champion, Quibbletown Valkyrie stamped her quality well on her progreny. Two of her best known offspring, already mentioned, are Can. Am. Champion Quibbletown Val's Heritage and Can. Am. Champion Limberlost Rogue.

Limberlost Rogue, known as "Monty," was Canada's Top Pyr in 1970 and 1973. Val's Heritage, known as "Dennis," was campaigned in 1974 and 1975 and set a breed record for Great Pyrenees in Canda with 26 Group placements and a Best in Show. Dennis also sired the 1976 U.S. Midwest Specialty winner, Limberlost Gold O'Chryshaefen, and the Winners Bitch of the 1976 Canadian Specialty, Simba of Limberlost.

Miss Mackintosh now bases her breeding almost exclusively on Quibbletown bloodlines. Ch. Quibbletown Valkyrie is the top Canadian producer with 14 champion offspring. Limberlost has produced many champions in the past decade and the impact of these will continue to be seen in the future competition.

Mrs. Gisela Fischer of WALBURGA became interested in the breed in 1967 and acquired as her foundation female a sister of Champion Limberlost Rogue (Limberlost Vicki). Later she imported the dog Bergerie Neptune, son of the Crufts Best in Show winner Bergerie Knur. A daughter of Neptune, Walburga's Pandora, was Winners Bitch at the Canadian National Specialty in 1974.

ANAYOBON is the registered prefix of Mrs. Donna Gleeson. Mrs. Gleeson became interested in Greay Pyrenees in 1969 and acquired as her foundation brood matron Nanibijou Teeto O'Limberlost, bred by Miss Mackintosh and Mrs. Fischer. Teeto quickly acquired both a Canadian championship and an Obedience degree. She was bred three times and produced nine Canadian champion offspring, two American champions and three dogs with a CD degree. Two of these dogs, Sir Galahad O'Diro and Lady Guinevere O'Diro, went to Mr. and Mrs. Roy Addie as the foundation pair for the Diro Kennels, of which more will be said later.

Although Anayobon is no longer active as a breeding kennel, it can be counted as the top Obedience kennel in Canada, having four resident Pyrs with CD degrees: Teeto, Can. Am. Ch. Anayobon Eet Too Brutus, Can. Ch. Anayobon's Canook, and Can. Ch. Annie of Anayobon.

DELGADA is the registered prefix of Peter and Dawn Lake. This kennel began with the acquisition of Snow Sonnet Wolfsong CD of Tip N' Chip background. Bred to Ch. Limberlost Marquis de Neige, this female produced Ch. Delgada's All White Pirate. The Lakes have confined their breeding ac-

Can. Am. Ch. Quibbletown Limberlost Rogue was Canada's Top Pyrenees for 1970 and 1973. Owned by Miss Lois Mackintosh. — *Weston*

Can. Ch. Quibbletown Valkyrie is Canada's Top Producing Pyrenees Dam with 14 Champion offspring. The foundation bitch at the Limberlost Kennels of Miss Lois Mackintosh.

Can. Am. Ch. Quibbletown Val's Heritage, the Top Pyrenees in Canada in 1974 and 1975 with one Best In Show and 26 Group placements. He was also Best of Winners at the Midwest Specialty in the U.S., 1975. Owned by Miss Mackintosh. — *Wilbaut*

155

tivities to an occasional litter, and recently have shown some promising offspring, including a group placer, Delgada's Tarascon.

The BARBANN Kennels of Mrs. Barbara Hay Belsito began with the purchase of Ch. Delgada's All White Pirate from the Lakes in 1969. Pirate was shown extensively in 1972, twice winning the Canadian Booster Show. Today, Pirate is the family companion and guardian, fulfilling both roles well.

RUM POINT is the prefix of Mrs. Ruth Cram. The Crams first became interested in the breed in 1964 while living in Harvard, Massachusetts. Mrs. Cram writes, "The name of Rum Point originated in 1970 when we moved to an old farm on a point of land jutting out into the back harbor of Lunenburg, Nova Scotia. In the rum-running days it was the practice of local boats to slip out along our shores and rendezvous with the big vessels engaged in the illegal traffic. Neither we or our dogs have yet found an old cache of the famous liquid, but since the farm is some 70 acres we are still hopeful!"

When the Crams moved to Nova Scotia, the two dogs, Wynken's Ringo Star and Jack Frost, came with them. The Crams' breeding in Canada has so far been confined to this pair. Jack Frost has his Canadian Championship, as does his daughter, Bridget of Rum Point.

Dave and Marty Joos of PYRADISE Kennels in Nova Scotia are the owners of several Canadian champions, two of whom, Ch. Pyradise Zuni and Ch. Quibbletown Moki of Pyradise, have placed in the Groups.

The CHENIL DAUVERNIAC in Quebec Province is the kennel of Jacques Jumelles. In the words of M. Jumelles, "Born in France, I have known Great Pyrenees as watch dogs and have always admired the nobility of the breed. Twenty years ago I immigrated to Canada and thought the Great Pyrenees would adapt well to our country. I imported my first two Great Pyrenees from De La Franche Pierre Kennels in 1970. Both were tall and powerful dogs, with very typy heads and big bone. From their alliance I kept my present champion, Raton Dauverniac."

Raton was presented for the first time in 1974 and completed his title in two weekends with 18 points. Raton has been bred to two Canadian bitches and has produced several promising puppies. Through the importations of M. Jumelles, French bloodlines will continue to be seen in Canada for many years.

Henry and Mary Ellen Hanemaayer of VENTISQUERO Kennels became interested in Great Pyrenees in 1971. Their foundation dogs were Auroja's Mona (of Soleil and Armil background), and Skeel's Benkurion. Mona finished her Canadian Championship in 1973 but Benkurion's career, after a promising start, was abruptly ended by an accident.

Benkurion was bred once to Mona in the fall of 1972 and produced three champions, one of whom is Ventisquero Samson The Great. In April 1976,

156

Can. Ch. Delgada's All White Pirate, winner of the Canadian Booster Show in 1972. Owned by Barbara Belsito. — *Wolf*

Am. Can. Ch. Pyr-Layne's Alex of Anayobon, winning a Group Second under judge Mrs. Winifred Heckmann at 16 months of age. The handler is Willis Hesser. Owned by Elaine Colberg. — *Olson*

Can. Ch. Zuni of Pyradise at home in Nova Scotia. Owned by Mr. and Mrs. David Joos.

Samson went Winners Dog at the California Specialty under English judge Peter Gilbert.

Mr. and Mrs. Hanemaayer have purchased other dogs from Soleil and Skeel. In 1973 they imported a daughter of Chi. Lisblanc Christoph from Mrs. Sheila Ball in England.

DIRO is the registered prefix of Roy and Diana Addie of Carleton Place, Ontario. In 1970 the Addies acquired the previously mentioned foundation pair from Anayoban, Sir Galahad O'Diro and Lady Guinevere O'Diro. These two puppies were shown together as a brace, and at eight months of age achieved their first of four Best in Show brace wins. Both went on to fine show records and attained Canadian championships. Guinevere was honored as Top Dam for 1974 and 1975.

The mating of Ch. Lady Guinevere to Ch. Quibbletown Bonhomme, owned and shown by Angus Morris of Ontario, established the Diro reputation. Six champions were produced, including the home-owned pair, Can. Am. Ch. Diro's Abydos de Pau, and Ch. Diro's Arya D' Aregeles-Gazost. Abydos, in particular, has had a distinguished career in the show ring, winning the Canadian Booster Show three years in succession (1974, 1975, 1976)—the first Great Pyrenees to achieve this distinction.

Abydos is also the top winning Great Pyrenees in Canadian history with four all-breed Bests in Show.

In the second breeding, Lady Guinevere was bred to Am. Can. Ch. Esprit Blanc, owned by Patricia J. Alteri, of Michigan. This mating procued five champions, of which one, Ch. Diro's Banquise, was bred back to Sir Galahad and produced a promising litter which is just beginning to be seen in the show ring.

Diro dogs have gone to some fine young kennels as foundation stock. For Great Pyrenees bred under this prefix, as with the breed elsewhere in Canada, prospects are high.

Thus the Great Pyrenees is well represented in Canada from coast to coast. As with any new enterprise in what Canadians describe as "a developing nation," Canadian breeders are not far enough along to boast their own bloodlines. Instead they have had the advantage of being able to select stock from the established kennels of the world.

The Great Pyrenees Club of Canada came into being in 1971 as the result of the efforts of breeders in Toronto. At about the same time, a group in Ottawa formed a club which amalgamated with the Toronto group. Because of the vast geography of Canada, as the club grew, four divisions were created: The National (Toronto), The Eastern (Ottawa), The Central (Ontario) and The British Columbia Division (which later withdrew to form its own independent club).

Am. Can. Ch. Anayobon's Et Too Brutus CD, pictured winning a Group Fourth at the Mid-Canada Show in 1972 under judge R. W. Nutbeem. Owned by Mrs. Donna Gleeson. — *Mattern's*

Can. Ch. Raton Dauverniac with his master Jacques Jumelle, at their home in Quebec. This dog embodies contemporary French bloodlines.

Can. Am. Ch. Ventisquero Samson The Great, Winners Dog at the California Specialty in 1976, under Eng. judge Peter Gilbert. Owned and handled by Henry Hanemaayer.

At left, Can. Ch. Lady Guinevere O'Diro, winning Best of Breed at the 1973 Canadian Booster S￼
cialty Show under judge J. D. Jones. Owned and handled by Roy Addie. *At right,* Can. Ch. Ana￼
bon Sir Galahad O'Diro, pictured winning a Group Second under the late judge Thomas J￼
Owned and handled by Diana Addie.

The top winning Great Pyrenees brace in Canada, Ch. Anayobon Lady Guinevere O'Diro and
Anayobon Sir Galahad O'Diro, owned and handled by Diana Addie, winning their first Grou￼
Oshawa, in 1971 under judge John Devlin. Four Bests in Show.

160

One of the GPCC's first goals was to hold a Specialty Show. In Canada it is necessary for each new club to prove itself by holding three Booster Shows before being eligible to host a National Speciality . This qualification was met in 1971. However, at least one Booster Show continues to be held each year in Canada.

Four independent Canadian National Specialties have been held since 1972. Canadian Specialty winners have been: Am. Ch. Esprit Blanc (1972), Ch. Limberlost Queen Bess (1973); Can. Am. Champion Quibbletown Val's Heritage (1974); and Am. Ch. Barqueill Avant Garde (1975).

In the field of public relations Canadian Pyrs do a fine job. When dogs were first permitted to participate in the prestigious Ottawa Winter Fair in 1974, it was a Great Pyrenees female who led the procession into the vast arena. The program continued with a demonstration of Obedience work, given by Ch. Diro's Ashtaroth de Vizcana CD, trained by Robert and Judy Thompson. Cart rides were delegated to Ch. Diro's Abydos de Pau, Ch. Anayobon Roi des Montagne and Walburga's Alexander.

In Canadian winter parades it is not unusual to see a Pyr pulling a sled loaded with children. Can. Ch. Delgada's All White Pirate is a true professional at this. He is among Ottawa's most respected "citizens," and his talents have been repeatedly volunteered to raise funds for the city's underprivileged children.

Aside from breeding and exhibiting, Roy and Diana Addie have presented the breed on TV and at demonstrations. Their Pyrs are often written up in the newspapers or pictured at demonstrations which show the dogs at work. The Addies have produced an Audio-Visual history of the breed which has been viewed by over 5,000 people.

CABAS. From a painting by J. M. Joy, discovered by Mrs. C. R. Prince in the Queen's Collection at Windsor Castle. Photograph taken by appointed photographer.
— *A. C. Cooper Ltd.*

GOOD FRIENDS. This pastel print is believed to be of a period with the above painting by J. M. Joy. Discovered at the Phoenix branch of the Royal Wax Museum by members of the Great Pyrenees Club of Southern Arizona. On the back was a number and the word "Bach", possibly a signature. — *Courtesy Karel Armstrong.*

10

The Pyrenean Mountain Dog in Great Britain

by Joyce Stannard

READERS IN AMERICA will be interested to know that in England and the majority of the countries in the British Commonwealth, the title of Champion is earned by winning three Challenge Certificates under three different judges at shows designated as Championship Shows. There are a number of smaller, Open Shows, in which dogs may compete for prize money, but not a C.C. The number of C.C.'s is strictly limited by the Kennel Club, and is linked to the number of dogs registered during the previous three years. A judge awarding a C.C. can do so only to Best of Sex, and only if he is clearly of the opinion that the dog or bitch is worthy of the title of Champion. Recently, in England there were 20 pairs of C.C.'s for the Pyrenean Mountain Dog (as the breed is officially known in this country) and therefore 20 Championship Shows, throughout the year and throughout the country. In Britian champions are entered in the Open Class and so compete against each other and the aspiring champions for the Certificates. Therefore, if a dog is to win his championship, he must do so by defeating those who are already established. The top Pyrenees in Great Britain, in any year, is the dog or bitch who has won the most C.C.'s. It is not uncommon for only a handful of Pyrenees to gain their titles in a given year.

The story of the Pyrenean in England must necessarily begin with mention of the Pyrenean owned by Queen Victoria in 1848. This was "Cabas," a popular dog at Court, who was honored by having his portrait painted by a famous artist of the day. We understand this painting is still in existence at one of the Royal residencies.

In the 1850s, two English explorers returned from the Pyrenees Mountains with several dogs who had faithfully served them as pack animals. But apparently they left no progeny.

In the 1880s we find that our breed was listed under the following names: Pyrenean, Pyrenean Wolfhound, Pyrenean Sheepdog, Pyrenean Mastiff and Pyreanan Wolf Dog. A number of these dogs, all registered with the Kennel Club, were being shown annually at the great Crystal Palace show.

The first attempt to truly establish the breed in England must be credited to Lady Sybil Grant. Lady Sybil first learned of the breed through the pictures of Neron and Diane in de Bylandt's Encyclopedia. This triggered her interest in the dogs, and in 1909 she visited the Pyrenees Mountains in search of foundation stock for her MILANOLLO Kennels. It became readily apparent to her that there were certain difficulties to be met with in purchasing really good specimens; but nonetheless one of her selections, Milanollo Patou, took first place at the Kennel Club Show just one week after leaving his quarantine! Thus began what promised to be a distinguished career for the Pyrenean in England. However, serious food shortages during the first World War and the need to convert her estate into a hospital for the wounded forced Lady Sybil to break up her kennels. And it seems that none of her puppies went to people sufficiently able or interested enough to perpetuate the breed.

The next reference to the Pyrenean Mountain Dog is in connection with the French Duke D' Orleans who took up residence in exile at Wood Norton, Eversham. He brought with him three specimens from France. When he was forced to give up his residence in 1920, the dogs were presented to Lady Milbank of Eaton Place, London; again nothing further is known.

In the 1920s, Sir Cato Worsfold of Mitcham tried to introduce the breed again, but unfortunately five of his imports died in quarantine. By January 1933, he apparently had only two dogs left which had been unsuccessful at stud. Apart from one bitch owned by Mr. A. Croxton Smith, one time Chairman of the Kennel Club, these two were the only Pyreneans in Great Britain—after more than one hundred years!

It was therefore an event of singular importance when Mme. Jeanne Harper Trois-Fontaines opened her distinguished DE FONTENAY Kennels in 1934 with stock imported from France. After several unsuccessful attempts, during which it is said the puppies died in quarantine from sheer loneliness, Madame was able to import a ten-month-old Pyrenean from the de Careil Kennels in Loire. This was Kop de Careil, perhaps the most famous dog in English Pyrenean lore, and in her words, "He was the best I ever had."

After her initial success with Kop de Careil, Madame Harper began a program of importation which spanned many years. In 1934, she returned to the Chateau de Boisy and collected the puppy bitch she had bought the year before—Iannette de Boisy. The first litter at de Fontenay, out of Iannette and Kop de Careil, was born January 4, 1935. Her next import, Iarkotte de Pontoise, was mated in France to the Contesse de Savigny's famous International Champion Estat d' Argeles and had her litter in quarantine.

Milanollo Patou, imported by Lady Sybil Grant from the Pyrenees Mountains in 1909.

A group study of de Fontenay's first Pyrenean family pictured with Mme. Harper in her garden at Moor Park. Left to right: The dam, Ianette de Boisy; her puppy, Monne de Fontenay at the age of eight months; Rip de Fontenay, a litter brother; and the sire, Kop de Careil. — *Courtesy Mrs. C. R. Prince*

Iarkette de Pontoise, *left*, and l'Nethou de Langladure, *right*, comprised de Fontenay's second additions to its breeding stock.

Champion Hubert and Champion Estat de Fontenay, England's first home-bred champic Owned by Madame Harper.

166

Next came Labeda du Mont Picry from Belgium, and l'Nethou de Langladure from France. l'Nethou was later to become the sire of England's first homebred champion, Hubert de Fontenay.

In 1938 the de Fontenay Kennels moved to Hyde Heath, Amersham, Bucks, where they remained to the end of their era.

In 1946 Mme Harper imported Patou de la Montagne from the Du Pic du Jer Kennels of M. Abadie-Toulet at Lac Lourdes. In the following year came Basquaerie Perce Neige II from the United States. Perce Neige became the first American-bred Champion in England, with 15 C.C.'s to his credit.

By a skillful policy of importation and breeding, Mme. Harper built up an array of bloodlines of such strength that her kennels continued throughout the second World War. When hostilities ceased, puppies were shipped to Ireland, Scotland, Norway, Switzerland, Canada, the United States, India, South Africa, Australia and New Zealand, where in many cases they played a major role in establishing the bloodlines of these countries.

Over 30 de Fontenay champions are recorded in England, among them the famous Ch. General de Fontenay and Ch. President de Fontenay (son of Madam's Basquaerie import) who was the winner of 25 C.C.'s.

In 1936 Mme. Harper founded the Pyrenean Mountain Dog Club of Great Britain and remained its President until her death in 1972.

The story of English bloodlines now takes a new turn. In part, this is the story of the issue of one dog, Ch. Bedat de Monda, whose progeny have had a profound influence on the type shown in Great Britain for the past 20 years.

Bedat de Monda, bred by M. Monda of Argeles Gazost in the High Pyrenees, was presented to Field Marshal Lord Alanbrooke in 1947 by the people of his birthplace, Bagneres-de-Bigorre. Later, Bedat was acquired by Mrs. Joan Passini-Birkett of the PONDTAIL prefix. Mrs. Birkett, an untiring worker on behalf of the Pyrenean in England, soon made him up a champion, and to his credit were added a total of nine C.C.'s, numerous Bests of Breed, and three Bests in Show at Open Shows.

Under the expert management of Mrs. Birkett, Bedat de Monda was placed at stud and sired English Champions Pondtail Marechal, Pondtail Niven, Pondtail Nevina, Commander Kip, Tartuffe of Oloron and Am. Ch. Pondtail Rafael.

Another distinguished import of the late forties, also under the direction of Mrs. Birkett, was Basquaerie Louis O'Mont Louis, from the kennels of Mr. and Mrs. Crane. He was shown to his championship and was used at stud, where he was to make an important contribution to the British scene in the years to follow.

Meanwhile, the second World War had left its aftermath in France. Only a few Pyrenean Dogs of quality were to be found in the Pyrenees. For the second time in history the Pyrenees Mountains were combed for the best specimens available, this time by M. Senac-Lagrange and the Doctores Gleises. A

167

Ch. Bedat de Monda, one of England's most influential French imports, pictured here with three of his puppies. Owned by Mrs. Joan Passini-Birkett.

—*Courtesy Mrs. C. R. Prince*

CH. BEDAT de MONDA

1.
2. Ch. Pondtail Niven
3. Ch. Laudley Prettily Natalie
4. Ch. Laudley Lanieve Blanche
5. Ch. Laudley Nito

Princess Ysanne

Ch. Bergerie Charlemagne de Bedous

Ch. Laudley Nevar

Ch. Tartuffe of Oleron

Ch. Bergerie Diable

Ch. Pondtail Zborowski

Ch. Lisblanc Christoph

Ch. Briarghyll Falstaff

Rosalie of Oleron

Am. Ch. Soleil Rayon

Am. Ch. Pondtail Tattoo of Basquaerie

Am. Ch. Soleil Belle Rose

Am. Ch. Pondtail Rafael of Basquaerie

Am. Ch. Soleil Baron

Am. Ch. Soleil Coquette

Am. Ch. Soleil Pierre de Blu-Crest

jointly owned kennel, the Chenil de Pas de L'Ours, was opened in the early fifties.

This kennel, it seems, was to have a greater influence on British bloodlines than on the French. Lady Celia Morris, who was at that time the owner of Ch. Pondtail Marechal, was a yearly visitor to the Pyrenean Mountains. Having the advantage of being able to communicate with the mountaineers in fluent French, and being a perennial visitor, she was finally accorded the privilege of exporting from the Chenil de Pas de L'Ours a Pyrenean puppy bitch who later became known as Ariane of Oloron.

Breeding under the prefix OLORON, Lady Morris mated Ariane to Ch. Bedat de Monda. In 1955 this mating produced the famous Tartuffe of Oloron, a true "dog of the mountains." "Tuffy" quickly followed in his sire's illustrious footsteps and won his championship. In turn, Tuffy sired many famous offspring, including Ch. Bergerie Charlemagne de Bedous, Ch. Bergerie Diable and Ch. Pondtail Zborowski. Lady Morris ceased as a breeder many years ago, but still maintains an avid interest in all aspects of the breed.

The first famous son of Ch. Tartuffe of Oloron was born in 1961 out of Pondtail Laudley Sonata. Owned and bred by Mrs. Birkett, this was Ch. Pondtail Zborowski. "Jason" shattered all previous records held by a Pyrenean in England. He virtually dominated the show scene in the middle sixties, winning a total of 29 Challenge Certificates, 14 Working Groups and 11 Bests in Show at Open Shows. Of the four annual P.M.D.C. Open Shows he attended, he was Best in Show at three, and Reserve at the other.

Ch. Pondtail Zborowski sired many champions during his illustrious career, including Ch. Lisblanc Christoph about whom more will be said later.

A second famous son of Ch. Tartuffe of Oloron was born in 1962 out of Ch. Bergerie Deborah. Owned by Mr. and Mrs. F. S. Prince, this was the dog Ch. Bergerie Charlemagne de Bedous who was destined to become the first Pyrenean ever to win Best in Show at a Championship Show. This distinguished win on behalf of the breed was gained at the largest one day show in the world at that time, the West of England Ladies Kennel Society in 1965.

It was followed in 1968 by another unprecedented victory for BERGERIE and the Princes—a Reserve Best in Show at Crufts by Ch. Bergerie Diable, the third famous son of Ch. Tartuffe of Oloron.

But the crowning achievement of the Bergerie Kennels, and perhaps the most talked-of win of all time, came in 1970 when Bergerie Knur, from a field of 8,000 at Crufts, was named Supreme Best in Show. His breeding will be mentioned later.

As a lasting achievement of the Cruft's victory, *Heredities Ltd.* commissioned Geoffrey Davien to do a sculpture of Bergerie Knur for a limited edition (350) to be cast in bronze. Three of these rare collector's items were given to Mr. and Mrs. Prince, who in turn donated one to the GPCA as an annual trophy to be presented in America to the winner of the National Speciality.

169

Mr. and Mrs. F. S. Prince have judged the breed in England, on the Continent and in the United States. Both are officers of the Pyrenean Mountain Dog Club of Great Britain; Mr. Prince being the current President, and Mrs. Prince the Vice-President, positions they have occupied since the death of its founder, Mme. Harper. Mrs. Prince sent us the following:

"When my husband and I bred Ch. Bergerie Auguste in our first litter, we thereupon formed a partnership and determined to teach the world how to breed champions in one easy lesson! Foundation stock was obtained, as far as possible, from unrelated sources, and breeding began in blissful ignorance of the many years of problems and disappointment which lay ahead.

"We decided to build up a nucleus of both the colored mountain types and the all white show types which we felt would enable Bergerie to keep great size in the breed.

"In practice we found that the accepted techniques of line and inbreeding tended to lose the massive conformation and majestic pressence of the Pyrenean Mountain Dog. The continued mating of all white dogs, although achieving some degree of standardization and improvement in many of the show and breed points, appeared to produce smaller, untypical Pyreneans, and this could ultimately lead to the loss of the Great Dog of the Mountains as we once knew him.

"From time to time Show successes were achieved and up to 30 dogs were kept at one time. A few champions were bred and on one occasion at Birmingham National Championship Show, Bergerie dogs won both the Dog and Bitch Challenge Certificates and the Reserve Best Dog.

"By the judicious use of good dogs and bitches from all available sources, including those imported by Bergerie from France and America, both show and mountain types continued to be bred. Although the dogs were not, of course, highly standardized, they nevertheless were consistent winners in the show ring and were in demand by new breeders requiring healthy and vigorous foundation stock. This was the breeding background that eventually produced the top Bergerie winners."

Mrs. Prince will long be admired for her work on behalf of the Club's displaced Pyrenean program at Bergerie. Countless Pyreneans have been found new homes, and happy new lives—not without its emotional cost.

Bergerie Kennels effectively ceased its breeding operations in 1973 after an unidentified virus of the distemper group killed or severely impaired nearly all the breeding stock, irrespective of age and in spite of full inoculations. The blow was almost a total disaster, but it is to be hoped that the Pyrenean Mountain Dog will return to Bergerie Kennels in the near future.

LISBLANC, the prefix of Mrs. Sheila Ball, began showing and breeding Pyrenean Dogs in 1948, and although this kennel was to produce a constant supply of winning dogs over the ensuing years, the kennel's supreme achievement is to be found in the success of its home-bred champion, Lisblanc Christoph, born in 1964. His sire was the previously mentioned Ch. Pondtail Zborowski and his dam was Ch. Lisblanc Serena.

170

Ch. Tartuffe of Oloron, the sire of many famous English Pyreneans. Owned by Lady Celia Morris. — *Courtesy, I.G.P.R.*

Lady Morris with her French import, Ariane of Oloron, the dam of Tartuffe of Oloron, the fountainhead of England's top winners. — *Courtesy Mrs. R. Prince*

171

In the late sixties, when his sire was at the peak of his career, "Bru" gradually obtained the three C.C.'s required to make him a champion. Then in 1972 he suddenly attained the renown which was to make him the top winning Pyrenees of all time in England.

By the end of the year he had surpassed his sire by winning a total of 33 C.C.'s, including a record 13 in one year alone! Bru finished his career with 120 first prizes; 48 Bests of Breed; 7 Bests in Show at Open Shows and one Championship Show; and three wins of the Working Group.

Lisblanc continues to produce top winning Pyreneans, including Ch. Briarghyll Falstaff and English and Irish Champion Lisblanc the Maverick. South African Champions are also listed among the kennel's accomplishments.

Among the bitches in England, special mention must be given to Ch. Laudley Prettily Natalie. Mrs. Beryl Lord of the LAUDLEY prefix became interested in breeding and showing Pyreneans in 1951. Two years later, Prettily Natalie was born out of Princess Ysanne and Ch. Pondtail Niven.

Prettily Natalie began her show career at 2¼ years of age and quickly obtained her championship. There is little doubt that Natalie dominated the show ring in the late fifties. Her record, which included 23 Challenge Certificates, remained unbeaten for ten years. She was BOB at Crufts four years running and was the first Pyrenean to win a Group at a Championship Show. By great misfortune she was struck down at the peak of her career by a mystery virus.

Natalie bred three litters, all by Ch. Basquaerie Louis O'Mont Louis. The first created a record in any breed with four C.C. winners. The second produced three champions: Laudley Nito, Laudley La Nieve Blanche and Laudley Nevar.

Also during the 1960s came another top winning bitch, who, although not beating the record held by Ch. Laudley Prettily Natalie in the fifties, made her mark indelibly on the show ring. This was Pandora Faymous, born in 1964, out of Andora Fay and sired by Cobber de Bedous. She started her show career at six months and won consistently, soon becoming a champion. She received 18 C.C.'s under 18 different judges, several Reserve C.C.'s, and was Club Pyrenean of the Year in 1967. She won many Bests of Breed and was Group winner at three Championship Shows. Sadly she was never successfully bred and died at just under ten years of age.

The third of the great winning bitches in England was Ch. Briarghyll Camilla. Her dam, Ch. Briarghyll Fleur-de-Lys, was herself a Best in Show winner with many C.C.'s to her credit.

Camilla began a distinguished career by becoming the first Pyrenean to win a Challenge Certificate as a puppy. In the late sixties she was a consistent winner and in the first two years of the seventies she was proclaimed the top C.C. winning bitch of the year. Her record to date, which surpasses all other English bitches, is 24 C.C.'s, six Bests in Shows, and multiple Breed wins.

Ch. Bergerie Charlemagne de Bedous, a son of Tartuffe, and the first Pyrenees to go Best In Show at a Championship Show, in 1965. Owned by Mr. and Mrs. F. S. Prince. — *Courtesy I.G.P.R.*

Ch. Bergerie Diable, another famous son of Ch. Tartuffe of Oloron, won a Reserve Best In Show at Crufts in 1968. Owned by Mr. and Mrs. F. S. Prince.

Ch. Pondtail Zborowski, the third renowned son of Ch. Tartuffe, dominated the show scene in his era. One of England's greatest show winning Pyrenees, with 29 C.C.'s to his credit. Owned by Mrs. Joan Passini-Birkett. — *Courtesy I.G.P.R.*

Ch. Lisblanc Christoph—The greatest show winner in the history of the breed in England, with 33 C.C.'s. Sired by Ch. Pondtail Zborowski. Owned by Mrs. Sheila Ball. (Photo courtesy of Mrs. C. R. Prince.) — *Pearce*

Bergerie Knur—Supreme Best In Show, Crufts, 1970. Pictured in the Princes' garden.

The story of the BRIARGHYLL Kennels of Mr. and Mrs. M. Fielden would not be complete without mention of the outstanding achievements of their current show dog, Ch. Briarghyll Falstaff. Sired by Ch. Lisblanc Christoph out of Ch. Briarghyll Fleur-de-Lys, "Taffy" began his show career at 6½ months of age in 1971. By 1975, fanciers in Great Britain were beginning to revise the record book. He had gone Best in Show at three Championship Shows, including the Club Championship Show; Reserve Best in Show at two other Championship Shows, and winner of a Working Group. It was of singular importance in 1975 when Taffy was named the winner of "Dog of the Year" under the *Vetzym/Our Dogs System*, and Top Dog under the *Dog World System*—the first dog *in any breed* to win both titles outright in the same year!

His record to date is 18 C.C.'s and 19 Bests in Show.

During the past ten years, many other breeders have been making their contribution to the show ring and the breed in general and it is a pity that space is not available to give them all the recognition that is due, but mention can only be made of a few.

First, Miss Peggy Grant-Dalton and her MONCAL Kennels, established in 1958. In 1967 a litter bred out of Moncal Laudley Yaronola and sired by Bergerie Abila de Fontenay produced Ch. Chazen Oscar and Bergerie Knur, the previously mentioned Supreme Best in Show winner at Crufts in 1970.

Moncal Pyrmont Arabella is the dam of two consistently winning champions: Castlenovary Ambassador and Castlenovary The Crusader. Arabella is the daughter of Bergerie Knur out of Ch. Pyrmont Moncal Charmain.

Moncal Pyreneans have been exported to several countries. Their South African Ch. Moncal Erskin de Chateau is a top C.C. winner and is proving a valuable stud in that country.

Then there is the KIPSNO Kennels of Mr. and Mrs. R. Canning. For many years hardly a Championship Show has gone by without a Kipsno being "in the cards". The foundation stock of this kennel came from Mrs. Beryl Lord at Laudley, being Ch. Laudley Seren Arian, and Ch. Kipsno Laudley Gaillard who was Best of Breed and Reserve in the Working Group at Crufts in 1971. Within a few years three more Kipsno Champions were recorded: Ch. Kipsno Trevanion Clairon; Ch. Kipsno Zarahemia's Deb's Beau and Ch. Kipsno Comet.

Another is the CARABRAE Kennels of Mrs. Brenda Judson, located in Sussex. Mrs. Judson bred her first Pyrenean in 1965. During the past ten years she has gradually built up a team of stud dogs of her own breeding who, together with their progeny, are regularly winning in the show ring. Mrs. Judson houses more than 20 Pyreneans at Carabrae, where the facilities are also used as a boarding kennel.

Carabrae Pyreneans have been exported to 15 countries. The pride of this kennel must naturally be Ch. Carabrae Superdocious who was the Best of Breed at Crufts in 1973.

There are many other kennels and many other award winning dogs all over Great Britain today, but these must necessarily be the subject of another chapter and their turn is to come when they can rightfully be cast in the history of the breed.

The Life of a Pyrenean in Britain

For every Pyrenean who graces an English show class, countless others spend their hours in the endless delight of their owners in all those little ways to which only a Pyrenean can lay claim.

To illustrate this we have chosen a few anecdotes from the British Pyrenean Mountain Dog Club's *Newsletter*, reprinted with the permission of its editor, Sqn. Ldr. Peter Gilbert (RAF Retd). The first is by Miss P. M. Foster:

> Sheba (Bergerie Ormonde) is now 4½ years old. Most mornings I take her with our young Golden Retriever, Bess, for a long walk on the hills. Living on the fringe of Exmoor we have endless moorland and wooded walks to choose from, so she is very lucky. When walking on steep rough ground she shows me just how sure-footed a Pyrenean is; when she was younger, she used to frighten me by throwing herself head-over-heels down the steepest bracken slopes and would then stand up unhurt and just laugh at me. Sometimes we see the red deer and I've managed to train Sheba not to chase them. She knows the meaning of the word "stag" and will try to tell me where the deer are, by sniffing the air in a certain way, and then looking back to me as if to say, "They are over that way"—and usually she is right.
>
> On two occasions when walking past a field with two orphan lambs in it, the lambs took one look at Sheba, bleated in excitement and raced down to the gate, where one of them (before I realized what was happening) jumped at the gate and wriggled halfway through the bars to reach Sheba. I had to take hold of the lamb and pull it backwards into the field again. It was convinced that Sheba was its mother and would not calm down until Sheba had touched noses and explained that she was a dog, not a sheep!
>
> After her morning walk she returns home to take on her main task of guarding the family. This is no easy job as she has three humans, Bess (the Golden Retriever), two cats, three donkeys, 46 hens, and Horace the cockerel (a nasty character), to guard—not forgetting our cottage and 1½ acres of land. So you can see she is kept busy!
>
> We have one problem. Most of the door handles here are the kind you push down to open, and Miss Sheba has discovered that all a Pyrenean has to do is to push it down with one's nose and the door is open. This is all right at night, for if she should want to go out urgently she opens the door downstairs and comes up to my bed to awake me, saying that unless I get up at once there will be an accident.
>
> However, in the daytime if we want to keep her in one room for any reason it's not so good. Father has partly solved the problem by fixing little bolts on some of the doors.

176

Ch. Laudley Prettily Natalie, one of the top winning Great Pyrenees bitches in England. Her record of 23 C.C.'s remained unbeaten for ten years. Owned by Mrs. Beryl Lord. — *Courtesy Mrs. C. R. Prince*

Ch. Briarghyll Camilla— England's Top Winning Great Pyrenees bitch, with 24 C.C.'s. Owned by Mr. and Mrs. M. Fielden. — *Courtesy I.G.P.R.*

Ch. Briarghyll Falstaff became the first dog to win both of England's top dog awards in the same year, in 1975. Falstaff has won three Bests In Show at Championship shows. Owned by Mr. and Mrs. M. Fielden. — *Courtesy I.G.P.R.*

177

Once the butcher came and rang the bell but Mother didn't hear him. So Sheba opened the door, let him into the kitchen and helped him unload the meat! When Mother did arrive on the scene the butcher said, "It's all right, Mrs. Foster, Sheba let me in." So Pyreneans do have their uses! Good thing it wasn't the paper boy as she hates him with a passion and would gladly swallow him whole if she had the chance.

Pyreneans in Great Britain are much the same as elsewhere, if this communication from Roy Blatt is any indication:

Carloa (Princess de Fontenay) was one of those Pyreneans who was addicted to bus and train rides. If a gate were ever left unattended, she would await her chance to slip away and join the queue at the nearest bus stop! She always went upstairs. One day I remember racing down to the bus station, shouting her name. She got on and went upstairs, turning to look at me out of one of the rear windows as the bus disappeared down the road. She never learned (and I never taught her) to make a return journey.

Trains were an even greater joy. She would run, dragging me to the platform, and once on the train would yelp with delight at every stop.

What made her likable was a combination of affection and stubbornness. She made firm decisions and stuck by them. A will quite her own. For example, if a walk wasn't long enough on a cold winter's night she would give me the slip about five minutes before she guessed I would turn for home. She disappeared quite noiselessly. I once crept round the corner of a building after bellowing myself hoarse and, for a split second, saw her nose protruding from the opposite corner. In a flash it was gone—and so this idiotic game went on in the dark, round corners of the building.

The memories give me a lot of pleasure. She had a great sense of fun. And yet she had great dignity.

The increasingly popular Fancy Dress Contests, which appeal to the British character, are a favorite pastime in the summer months. Of course, stuffing a Pyrenean into light swimming trunks, tying a hat on his head, hanging a knife, fork, or empty food package round his neck, wrapping him up in newspaper and then parading him before a circle of laughing spectators is certain to produce some interesting comments.

After all, in the words of Mr. Alan Harwood, "Fancy Dressing Up A Dog!"

When I first saw Pyreneas in fancy dress and remembered the old Breed Standard (. . . a dog of great majesty. . . . as serious in play as he is in work . . .) I was embarrased at the affront to the dogs' dignity. But then I recalled feeling much the same at my first sight of adult humans in fancy dress; fine for kids, I thought, but these people are supposed to have grown up! Later it became plain that there was no loss of dignity if the subject felt no loss and my embarrassment was simply that I always felt silly in fancy dress and assumed that everyone else should, too. If it was wrong to project my own feelings on to other people; how much more wrong might it be to project them on to dogs?

Ch. Carabrae Superdocious, pictured after her famous Best of Breed win at Crufts, in 1973. Owned by Mrs. Brenda Judson.
— Peter Gilbert

When (all too seldom now) we see a Pyrenean with that superb bearing which seems to say 'Behold me, for I am a Pyrenean!' we chatter about majesty and dignity and all the other things which we hope distinguish us from our remote ancestors. But the dog has no apes in his pedigree and needs no such face-saving abstractions, nor is his mind devious enough to contain them. He knows nothing of dignity and cares less; he is simply Dog, content in his being, aware of admiration and at peace with his simple world like Adam before the Serpent came.

Neither does he know anything of ridicule of embarrassment. If people laugh unkindly at him he will be uneasy, but at the unkindness, not the laughter. He may well think it odd that Master should require him to wear a funny hat and a tutu, but it seems to give pleasure to many and increases the notice which is taken of him. To the dog it seems no odder than having, on other occasions, to trot backwards and forwards, have his dewclaws and teeth counted and submit to nameless intrusions upon his person, so that Master can pin another colored card on the wall back home.

I suspect that many human objections to dressing-up dogs spring from a feeling that this is not what dogs are for. But what ARE they for? Surely, at least in our urban civilization, we own dogs so that we may have the privilege of giving them a happy life and letting them share such of our pleasures as may please them also. All of us, especially those whose dogs (like mine) live with the family, are tempted to credit them with our own qualities and failings. But the nature of a dog is to be a dog, and part of his goodness is innocent enjoyment of the activities of the pack. If the pack-leader happens to have two legs and trousers and decrees that there shall be fancy dress, few dogs will object so long as the dress is comfortable. Of course, if he doesn't like dressing up, he will let you know and it would be unkind to insist. But most that I have seen seemed to be having a whale of a time playing to the gallery—and I have the photos to prove it.

But don't look for my Minta and Tamber in the Fancy Dress Parades. Their Master looks a right Charlie in a funny hat!

179

Rouky (Picarde de Peoymayou-L'Balaitous) with M. Ducasse, his owner. A dog of contemporary mountain breeding. — *Courtesy I.G.P.R.*

Simoun de Pontoise as a three month-old puppy with Mrs. Virginia Spitzer, Maryland. — *Peter Gilbert*

180

11

The Modern
Pyrenean Mountain Dog
in France

THE PYRENEAN MOUNTAIN DOG is at an all-time high in popularity in France today and many new fanciers have entered the picture. The ever-increasing competition at the shows is having an effect and some evolutionary changes are, inevitably, taking place.

When Senac-Lagrange published the 1927 Standard, he wrote: "As to size we find that it has, unfortunately, been decreasing over the last years. Measurements we took about twenty years ago show that this loss of size amounts to at least three centimeters. It is imperative that fanciers strive to overcome this size degeneration."

That both breeders and judges heeded this plea is apparent in the French show ring today for the smaller dogs are now in the decided minority. In fact, for M. C. Douillard, a modern French authority, the pendulum may well be swinging too far. He writes, "I would caution my friends that what we really must have is a well-balanced subject. It is useless to pursue size and weight to the extreme. When an owner tells me his Pyrenees weighs 175 or 180 pounds, I shudder."

Guy J. Mensencal, Secretary of the French Pyr Club, describes Rouky, a winner at recent shows, as about ideal at 32 inches and 140 pounds. He also finds Rouky close to perfect in type as well:

> This dog presents an imposing figure of elegance. He has a good coat and a well-plumed tail, carried low in repose and wheeled over the back when the dog is at attention. Though the rear is a bit straight, the bone structure is strong. He has an excellent temperament. And he is siring excellent puppies.

Alex de Fontenay, imported from England in the mid-sixties by M. Andre Delattre, as an outcross for Pontoise bloodlines.

Vallire du Comte de Foix — a typical French head of the better type. — *Courtesy I.G.P.R.*

Champions Drex and Dallia of Pontoise, a dog and bitch owned by M. Andre Delattre. — *Courtesy Mr. C. R. Prince*

182

The excellence of his puppies stems, in part, from the perfection of type found in Rouky's head. The ears are not too large or heavy and they lie close to the skull, almost hidden in the dog's ruff. We should never tolerate big heavy ears set on above the level of the eyes.

Rouky's eyes are rather small, slightly oblique, rimmed with black and they have the true Pyrenean expression. His muzzle is of proper length and proceeds from the forehead without an abrupt stop. Lips are tight and they have full black pigment. We must remember that an abrupt stop, a loose-lipped drooling mouth and lack of pigment are all very serious faults.

Senac-Lagrange also mentioned in 1927 that many of the Pyreneans of that day were "often too straight behind." For the most part French breeders have been able to overcome this, and most of today's winners are sufficiently angulated. But the fact that Mansencal mentions this defect in Rouky points out that it is a problem to which breeders continue to give attention.

Monsieurs Douillard, Mansencal, and such prominent breeders as Delattre (PONTOISE), Docquin (DU GRAND BAOU), Giralt (DU COMTE DE FOIX) and Mme. H. Gimenz (DU CLOS D'ARGENT), all attach great importance to what is considered the correct head. In 1907 when the French Pyr Clubs were attempting to draw up a standard, the correct head was one of the primary causes of dissension. Some thought it should be described as "wolf-like," with a good length of muzzle. Others violently disagreed, preferring "Mastiff-like," indicating a broadly rounded skull.

Senac-Lagrange solved the problem, temporarily, by declaring that the head approached that of the Pyrenean brown bear, possessing both breadth of skull and a tapering muzzle.

At the Cauterets Pyrenean Speciality in 1938, this writer found that after ten years of experience with the Senac-Lagrange standard most of the mountaineers had come to accept it, though many were unhappy with the description of the head in that no mention had been made regarding what the shepherds believed to be a cardinal point . . . the slight protrusion of the occipital bone at the rear of the skull.

Pierre Houert, breeder of the de Barzet Pyreneans, was most voluble on the point, explaining that his father and grandfather before him had always insisted on the bump. When asked why the bump was so important, he explained it had always been considered a sure sign of a keen nose, a superior intelligence and a tractable disposition.

Pierre's dogs did not win many prizes at the show and I had nearly forgotten his comments but in 1970, when the new French standard became official, lo and behold, I found the bump had at last been incorporated into the description of the head. When I asked why, I was told breeding for the breadth of skull called for in the previous description (without the bump) had led, gradually, to a shorter, squarer, untypical muzzle; while the dogs possessing the slightly protruding occipital bone were usually found to possess the correct tapering muzzle.

V'Izoure du Comte de Foix, an all-breed Best in Show winning bitch at Auch, in the Pyrenees mountains. Note the emphasis that mountain breeders place on the head. Owned by M. and Mme. Giralt, Foix. — *Alpy. Tarbes, France*

Pauchka de la Franche Pierre, an international show winning bitch (Luxembourg and Belgium), showing a strongly boned French type.

The wording in the 1970 standard (which is given in an earlier chapter) is explicit: *"The peak of the occipital bone, being visible, gives the posterior portion of the skull an ogival, vaulted, form."* And also, incidentally, serves to accentuate the muzzle length.

Pierre Houert, and the other Pyrenean breeders who believed as he did, are at last vindicated, at least as far as the head description is concerned. But still to be determined is whether or not the genetic pattern governing the shape of the skull is also responsible for passing on mental and psychological qualities as well.

Probably the most visible evidence the writer noted on seeing the French dogs in the show ring at the Paris Exposition in 1974 was that indeed the skull does not fall away abruptly at the back and the ears and muzzles are slightly longer than we see commonly in our own show rings. It should be noted that while the ears are somewhat longer they are not at all thick or heavy, but rather thin and fine-textured.

Formerly most Pyrenees in the kennels of France were first and second generation descendants of stock purchased directly in the mountains. Today this is no longer true and there is a constant interchange of bloodlines between fanciers throughout France that is many generations removed from the mountains. Contact is also maintained with kennels in Switzerland, Holland, England, Belgium, Norway, Sweden, North Africa, Italy and the Middle East. Some dogs have also been imported from the United States.

The modern European show scene is, then, quite active and growing ever stronger. The upstanding French dogs tend to be taller than some of their foreign counterparts with more depth of skull and somewhat less angulation in the rear. And although many of the dogs are now being bred outside of the mountain region, the old mountaineers have been able to write into the standard a point they consider essential.

Irish Ch. Perenvay Fincarra, the Top Winning Irish Pyrenean, owned by Mrs. Renee Millington. — *Courtesy I.G.P.R.*

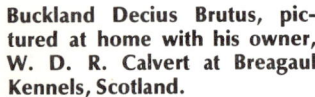

Buckland Decius Brutus, pictured at home with his owner, W. D. R. Calvert at Breagaul Kennels, Scotland.

Ch. Elegant Man of the Mountains with Ruth Nicholson, Australia, 1954. — *Courtesy Ranee Van Eck*

12

The Breed
Around the World

DURING the past two decades, the Great Pyrenees has made noteworthy advances around the world. Specimens from some of the finest bloodlines are to be found in such far-flung places as Holland, Belgium, Finland, Italy, India, Korea, Japan, Mexico and South America, to name but a few. In Ireland, Scotland, Australia, New Zealand and South Africa the breed is fast becoming a well recognized and popular addition to the world of dogs.

Ireland

The popularity of the Pyrenean Mountain Dog in Ireland is certainly on the increase if one considers that ten years ago there were but a dozen Pyreneans in the "Emerald Isle," whereas today the number is over one thousand. The majority are family pets. Only a few Irish owners are actively engaged in breeding and showing Pyreneans.

Canine activities in Ireland come under two separate authorities. In the North the Kennel Club (England) guides the affairs, whereas in the South the Irish Kennel Club has jurisdiction.

Under Irish K.C. rules, Green Stars are awarded in place of Challenge Certificates. They have different point values according to the number of dogs presented for judging. To become a Champion, a dog must win 16 points made up of at least one four-pointer or two three-pointers, the balance as they come.

The first Pyrenean known in Ireland was the dog "France," imported by Mrs. Georgina McMahon in 1898. Vacationing in the High Pyrenees, Mrs. McMahon returned via England with her puppy dog—quite unaware that she was breaking the quarantine. However, the customs officials were said to have "turned a blind eye" (this would never be heard of today) and so she continued merrily to her destination in Dublin. At the age of seven, France was struck by pleurisy.

In 1932 Mr. and Mrs. Brown-Clayton of Carlow purchased two Pyrenees Mountain Dog puppies from Mme. Harper. The Claytons gave up the breed in 1940, possibly because of the difficulties imposed by World War II.

In 1951 the family of Mrs. Brighid O'hEigeartaigh imported a puppy called Barcelona Brumas. On the death of his master he refused to eat and became so wasted that he had to be put to sleep. Having learned the wonders of owning (or being owned by) a Pyrenean, a new puppy, Xillian de Fontenay, was quickly acquired from Mme. Harper. He lived for 12 happy years as the family companion. On his passing the O'hEigeartaighs came to the aid of displaced Pyreneans and thus, over a 25 year period, they must be ranked as the oldest Pyrenean family in Ireland.

Today's Irish Pyreneans trace their bloodlines to five imports of the late fifties: Yaan of Pondtail, Bergerie Bertha, Mount Louis Shepherdess, Laudley Yanason and Caruso de Fontenay.

Mrs. Renee Millington of PERENVAY Kennels is the leading Pyrenean breeder in Ireland. To her Ch. Vanessa of Parenvay goes the honor of being the first Irish-bred champion.

Mrs. Millington's foundation bitch, Ch. Clarissa de Bedous, bred by Mrs. Alcock out of Ch. Laudley La Nieve Blanche and Ch. Tartuffe of Oloron, was the first Pyrenean to win an International Championship. Clarissa's son, Ch. Perenvay Fincarra, sired by Bergerie Kennard, is the top winning Irish Pyrenean with 23 Green Stars to his credit at the last counting. He is also the winner of two Bests In Show, including a Championship Show in 1974.

The top winning bitch in Ireland is Ch. Perenvay Goolagong, owned by Mr. Michael Coad.

Lisblanc The Maverick, owned by Mr. and Mrs. Tonk and bred by Mrs. Shiela Ball, became the second English/Irish Champion, an honor he attained in 1975.

Other champions to make an impression on the show scene in Ireland include Croftside Centaur, Renean Atgos, Andres of Drumbuoy, Davdier O'Doda, Belinda of Siffin, and most recently Mrs. Pat Brown's Karlina of Perenvay.

Scotland

The first reference to the Pyrenean Mountain Dog in Scotland is given by Robert Leighton who, in *The New Book of the Dog* tells of the use of Pyrenean blood to restore quality and strength among several breeds, with special reference to the Scottish Deerhound.

The next Pyrenean "influence" in Scotland must be credited to the activities of Lady Sybil Grant's Pyreneans in the 1920s.

188

Lady Sybil's family had an estate in Wester Ross. Mrs. Ena Calvert tells us that to this day there are dogs in this area with many Pyrenean characteristics—obviously part descendants of Lady Sybil's early Pyreneans.

In 1948 Mme. Harper exhibited her dogs at the Championship Shows in Scotland. Miss Lockhart, a member of a well-known family in the linen trade in Kirkcaldy, Fife, owned a Pyrenean who is pictured carrying its mistress' golf clubs over its shoulder.

Little more is heard of the Pyrenean in Scotland until the late fifties. At this time Mr. and Mrs. Calvert started their famous BRAEGAUL Kennels with their foundation bitch, Vivienne de Fontenay, purchased from Mme. Harper.

To complicate matters, the day after the Calverts arrived in Scotland, with Vivienne in full season, Mr. Calvert departed once more for England, leaving Mrs. Calvert in a sea of furniture and boxes to mate Vivienne with Ch. Colas of Hi-dene. Two months later Vivienne presented the Calverts with a litter of ten, from which they had their famous Ch. Braegaul Chicot—the first, and currently the only, Scottish-bred Pyrenean to attain a championship.

At the Scottish Kennel Club's Championship Show the next year, Vivienne was benched among the Obedience dogs (apparently the organizers didn't quite know what to do with a Pyrenean). All day the Calverts listened to those passing remarks which are so familiar to owners to Pyreneans: "A white St. Bernard", or "Alsatian" being the favorite speculations. Finally, a Mr. Know-It-All arrived and, with his head cocked quizzically to the side, declared to one and all, "Aye, that one's mother went a bit wrong. There's a fair mixture there." Mr. Calvert had to be forcibly restrained by his better half. Such an insult to his wonderful Pyrenean!

With only a few shows available in Scotland, the formation of a Scottish Club was proposed. This actually came about when Mrs. Margaret Cairns, a very good friend of Pyreneans, suddenly turned to Mrs. Calvert at the Championship Show in Edinburg and said, "Ena, I will give you 100 pounds if you can get a Scottish Pyrenean Club started!" The club was formally established in 1970 and currently lists over 200 members. It organizes two shows each year.

Mrs. Calvert writes, "We now have quite a number of breeders, with well-known prefixes, including Mishow, Braegaul, Choucoune, and more recently Chendimer, Zilken, Millchase and Ashley. New blood has been brought in from selected puppies from well-known bloodlines in England and Ireland, and every effort is made to encourage owners to breed dogs to the requirements of the standard and with excellent dispositions."

There can be little doubt that breeding in Ireland throughout the sixties was dominated by the dogs at Braegaul. Braegaul Zender, winner of a Scottish Challenge Certificate, is hale and hearty at 11½ years of age, sire of 217 Pyreneans at last counting. In addition to Zender, the Braegaul Kennels offer four dogs at stud: Buckland Decius Brutus, son of the renowned Ch. Pondtail Zborowski; Braegaul Gay Stuart, winner of Best in Show; Royal Apollo of Berg-

189

erie, a young dog already a leading winner in the show ring; and Braegaul Gaskoigne, also a Best In Show winner. There are 13 bitches, including stock from Bergerie, Laudley, Millchase and de Fontenay.

The esprit de corps found in today's Scottish Pyrenean Club can be seen in the following passage, sent to us in 1974 by Mrs. Calvert:

> "As we had a record number of Scottish dogs qualified for Crufts this year, the Scottish Pyrenean Club hired a private coach to convey our contingent 400 miles to Crufts, taking seats out so that the dogs had plenty of room. So it was a comfortable journey for all concerned. We were amply rewarded as, with the exception of one bitch, all the Scottish dogs were in the prize tickets. Our President had gifted bottles of champagne to be presented to any Scottish winning dogs and these were split in the coach. So it was a very, very happy, cheerful party on the way home!"

The Calverts are past officers of the Scottish Pyrenean Club and the authors of an attractive booklet on the breed. Success of the breed in Scotland has been the result of a lot of hard work, not to mention the constant encouragement of new members to show and breed to a standard of perfection. Although both Mr. and Mrs. Calvert have, as they say, "reached their allotted span of three score years and ten," they still hope to keep Braegaul to the fore for many years to come.

Australia

Credit for bringing the first pair of Pyrenean Mountain Dogs to Australia must be given to Mr. and Mrs. J. Gatehouse. Their first two Pyreneans, from the de Fontenay kennels of Mme. Harper, were to provide one of the more unusual happenings in Pyrenean lore. As Madame tells the story in *My Traveling and My Dogs*:

> "A young dog made history in 1939 (Costaud de Fontenay). Having never seen the London docks, my husband and I decided to see the dogs off to their new home in Australia. There was a young bitch going too, Contesse de Fontenay.
> "'Let them play together', we said. 'The bitch is not yet eight months old and the dog less than a year old.' But that was on the 15th of August. War was declared a few days later and the ship on which the dogs were traveling took three months instead of six weeks to make the voyage to Australia. When it arrived in Melbourne, Mr. and Mrs. Gatehouse received the following urgent message: 'Do come and fetch your menagerie!' Little did they understand what this meant, until they came to collect their dogs—along with six lovely puppies."

And so Australia had its first litter born at sea!

For the next several years Mrs. Gatehouse controlled the breeding of Pyreneans in Australia quite effectively. She sold only the *dogs* from any given litter. All bore the kennel affix OF THE MOUNTAINS.

From a litter whelped in 1943, came the well known Dando of the Mountains. During the War, Dando became famous in Melbourne by conscripting for the Red Cross. He would be found sitting outside an exclusive store on Collins Street where, by a strange coincidence, Mme. Harper aiso displayed her high fashion clothing; and for each hand he shook, he received a donation and enlisted a volunteer. Quoting from an article which appeared in the Melbourne newspaper,

> Affable and dignified throughout the day, Dando didn't seem to tire of shaking hands with the adults and children who answered Red Cross roll call. Last year Dando enrolled more than 1400 members. He will be on duty again today at the Tourist Bureau, Collins Street.

After the Armistice was signed, Dando's owners, Mr. and Mrs. W. Woodward, sailed to England and brought back with them two females from de Fontenay, Kamila and Kedah. With the acquisition of these two females, the second breeding kennel in Australia came into being. Under the prefix WALWOOD, a litter out of Dando and Kamila was registered in 1947. A few months later, Mr. Woodward ordered a male, L'Admiral de Fontenay, from Mme. Harper and received the following letter:

> I have arranged for the puppy, L'Admiral de Fontenay, a son of Imperatice de Mont Blanc by Patou de la Montagne, my imported dog, to leave England on the 17th January on the S.S. Port of Quebec, which is sailing for Melbourne. Thomas Cook and Son are taking care of the transport arrangements and I will supply biscuit, etc. for the journey. I hope he will arrive safely. He is a real mountain type which will be good for your breeding as the all-white dogs are in danger of becoming a sitting-room pet.

But while the dog was still in quarantine, tragedy struck the Woodward family. The sudden death of Mrs. Woodward left the kennel without a mistress. All breeding under the prefix "Walwood" came to a stop.

The early de Fontenay bloodlines of Australia were now to continue under the care of Mr. and Mrs. Keith Nicholson. The Nicholsons were the owners of Ch. Elegant Man of the Mountains. To their foundation dog they now added Ch. Walwood Annette, and took over the care of L'Admiral de Fontenay. Through television, newspaper and magazine articles, the Nicholsons widely popularized the breed in the middle fifties. Six litters were bred under the prefix CHATEAU. Their breeding ceased in the sixties, but the Nicholsons' continue to own and show Pyreneans in Australia today. Mrs. Nicholson has retained an abiding interest in the breed and serves as the current President of the PMDC of Victoria.

In the middle sixties only a few litters were bred in Australia. The two which are best known were bred by Mr. R. Williams under the prefix NIDAROS. By 1968, there were only eight Pyreneans registered with the Kennel Control Council. All were too closely related for sound breeding, but Wynne

Henderson of Sydney brought new blood into the picture by importing Laudley Yarran Nuncio from Mrs. Beryl Lord of England. The dog was a son of Basquaerie Nuvolari of Pondtail out of Laudley Yaronde.

A mating between the imported Laudley Yarran Nuncio and the resident founding female of the ANDORRA Kennels of Mr. and Mrs. Van Eck, Ch. Nidaros Pastourie, gave the kennel its first litter in 1968. From this breeding came Andorra Tania, first of a long line of Andorra champions. More imports were greatly desired, but owing to a case of rabies in 1969, the Australian government placed a two-year ban on the importation of dogs.

As soon as the ban was lifted in 1971, the two dogs, Juno and Juliette de Fontenay, were on the first ship to leave England for the Andorra Kennels in Victoria.

Juno proved to be an outstanding sire with five champions to his record. One, Ch. Andorra Ramesus (Juno and Juliette), won the title of Best Pyrenean Exhibited in 1974. He also took the Challenge and Best of Breed at the Royal Melbourne Show.

In 1975 the Van Ecks, in partnership with Mrs. Jenni Werner, imported the dog Ch. Briarghyll Kelso from Mrs. M. Fielden. Kelso was the Best Pyrenean Exhibited in 1975, won his championship in short order and went Best In Show at the first Championship Show held by the PMDC of Victoria.

Mrs. Van Eck writes, "It is hoped that English and Australian Ch. Briarghyll Kelso (Ch. Briarghyll Falstaff—Bergerie-Pomona) will strengthen the breed in Australia."

The history of the Pyrenean in Australia would not be complete without mention of two other contemporary kennels: First is BREAN, the prefix of Mrs. Barbara Luck. Her foundation bitches, Nidaros Astrid and Nidaros Andora, were acquired from Mr. R. Williams. Astrid was mated to Laudley Yarran Nuncio. The first champion to carry the kennel prefix was Ch. Brean Captain Cook, followed by Ch. Brean Conchita, Ch. Brean Matilda, and in 1975 by Ch. Brean Kathleen. The last two are owned by Ruth and Keith Nicholson. Ch. Brean Matilda went Best of Opposite Sex at the PMDC of Victoria Championship Show.

The second is SANITAE, owned by E. O. Bright. Mr. Bright acquired his first Pyrenean in 1969 from Mrs. Van Eck; his second, a few months later, from Mrs. Luck. From these two a litter was whelped in 1971. His first champion was Sanitae Oswin Lord. A little brother, Ch. Sanitae Chasa Prince, was equal Best Pyrenean for the year 1973, along with Andorra Anastasia, owned by Colin Smith. Mr. Bright is also the breeder of Ch. Sanitae Janine Neti, owned by Mrs. V. James. In 1974 he imported Lawndown Sycin Ap Meredydd (Ch. Lisblanc Cristoph-Meredydd Creoso Menna) who has sired three litters, still youngsters.

There are a number of other breeders in Australia, all of whom have bred one or two litters, several with promising careers in the show ring before them. Today there are several hundred Pyreneans in Australia with the major-

Ch. Bastien del Aprisco, Best of Breed, and Ch. Cherryglen Elizabeth, Best Opposite Sex, at the National Dog Show, New Zealand, '75. Both are owned by Mrs. Lynlie Watson. — *Courtesy I.G.P.R.*

The First Open South African Pyrenean Specialty, 1976. Pictured left to right: Sancho de la Neige, bred by Ivan and Marie Cooper and owned and handled by Mrs. P. Robbins, Best Opposite Sex; judge Paul D. Strang; and Princesse Sur La Montagne, bred by M. Shana and owned and handled by Mr. D. Fuller-Peterson, Best of Breed.

ity residing in Victoria. The interest is slowly growing as the breed is now represented in every state except the Northern Territory, where it would be far too hot. 1975 and early 1976 saw more imports into Australia than ever before. These will no doubt have a significant impact on the growth and development of the Pyrenean in Australia.

The first Pyreneans to come to New Zealand appear to have been Kappel and Lolette de Fontenay in 1947 and 1948. Unfortunately, this is of historical interest only as the dogs were never mated and little is known of their activities in New Zealand.

In the mid-fifties, Tarba and Tosca, a breeding pair from de Fontenay, were imported by Mr. and Mrs. Rhodes of Reporoa. Four litters were produced, and under the prefix ALAMAR the Rhodes became the first serious Pyrenean breeders in New Zealand. A puppy bitch, Alamar's Rose, was sold to Mrs. Weaver of Havelock North.

Mrs. Weaver's interest in the breed caused her to import yet another of Mme. Harper's dogs, Cirano de Fontenay. He was the son of Madame's own French import, Irving de Pontoise. Mrs. Weaver chose the prefix BELLAIRE. Cirano de Fontenay and Almar's Rose bred three litters which unfortunately had a rather low survival rate. In the mid-sixties, one of these puppies, Carlos de Bellaire, was acquired by Mrs. Allison Wood of Waimauku.

Carlos was to become a valuable asset to the emerging bloodlines of New Zealand. He carried in his veins the blood of the first imports—going back into de Fontenay and Pontoise. Interest in the breed began to fade in the late sixties. By 1969 only seven Pyreneans were alive in New Zealand. All the bitches were spayed family pets. Only the dog Carlos de Bellaire was in his prime.

Credit for the revitalization of the breed in New Zealand must be given almost exclusively to Mrs. Lynlie Watson of Tauranga and her DEL APRISCO Kennels. As her first step, Mrs. Watson went to England and personally selected a promising daughter of Ch. Pondtail Zborowski as foundation matron for her kennel. This female, Cherryglen Elizabeth, quickly fulfilled her expectations by becoming New Zealand's first Pyrenean Champion.

In 1971 Cherryglen Elizabeth was bred to Carlos de Bellaire and gave the country its first pair of home-bred Pyrenees champions: Michelle and Candida del Aprisco.

In July 1972 Mrs. Watson added still another dimension to the New Zealand scene by importing from Mrs. M. Fielden the English dog, Briarghyll Excelsior. Excelsior, sired by Ch. Pondtail Zborowski out of Ch. Briarghyll Lisblanc Fleur de Lys, won his championship in short order. Doubling up on the Zborowski line, Mrs. Watson bred Ch. Excelsior to Ch. Cherryglen Elizabeth. This mating gave Mrs. Watson three more Champions: Benedict, Bastien and Bonita del Aprisco.

A number of recent imports to New Zealand include Andorra el Dorado, a de Fontenay-sired male owned by Miss Karen Harrison; Notsuch Cassiopiea, a bitch obtained by Miss D. Harris from Brenda Judson; Shiloonas Joanna and her little brother, Ronan, (offspring of Ch. Lisblanc Christoph), owned by Miss Betty Foster; and Briarghyll Paragon, a son of Meredydd-y-Myndd sent from England by Mrs. Fielden to Mrs. Ann Downing.

The Pyrenean Mountain Dog Club of New Zealand was formed in 1972. Its aims are to popularize the breed, improve the standard of breeding, and insure the general welfare of the country's Pyrenean dogs.

South Africa

Mrs. Denise Tudhope's successful introduction of the breed to South Africa, and her generous and unstinting devotion to its well-being, parallel to a striking degree the accomplishments of Mrs. Crane in America and Mme. Harper in England.

Mrs. Tudhope was born in France but emigrated to Africa before World War II to become a school teacher. Her posts were deep in the rugged interior of the veldt where the ranchers required semi-private instruction for their children. As a result she developed the extraordinary self-reliance that characterizes her personality today. Her school-teaching days are vividly portrayed in Eileen Bigland's novel *The Lake of the Royal Crocodiles* in which Denise is the Mademoiselle.

After marrying a South African and rearing a fine family of five children she was widowed and subsequently became involved with dogs.

Her first breeds were St. Bernards and Bernese Mountain Dogs. One of her Saints became the leading show-winner in South Africa. But always in the back of her mind was an early love affair with a Pyrenean bitch named Cora, her childhood playmate.

And so in 1967 Mrs. Tudhope made contact with Mme. Harper and imported her first pair of puppies, Freddy and Fidelia de Fontenay. The media had been alerted for this intriguing event and as a result press photographers and reporters gave the arrival of the puppies unprecedented coverage. Pictures and stories about the great white dogs appeared in dozens of South African newspapers and magazines. The Pyreneans had achieved instant fame, but a lot of hard work remained to be done.

As no Pyreneans had ever been shown in South Africa it took two years of constant effort. Dogs were shown all over the country; others were encouraged to show their puppies from Mrs. Tudhopes' AYLWARD Kennels; more dogs were imported for new owners; a Pyrenean Mountain Dog Club was formed in April, 1969. The breed was finally recognized and became eligible for the award of Championship Certificates.

Although Freddy de Fontenay had throughout this time collected 9 C.C.'s and 9 Bests of Breed, they all counted for nothing. Mrs. Tudhope had to start again from scratch in order to make him the first Champion Pyrenean dog in Southern Africa.

As President of the Eastern Transvaal Pyrenean Mountain Dog Club, Mrs. Tudhope was a tireless correspondent, keeping in touch with overseas clubs and journals as well as the leading breeders in England, France and America. She contacted isolated owners from Capetown on the Indian Ocean to Salisbury in Rhodesia. More puppies and dogs were imported for interested fanciers from the kennels of Mme. Harper, Mrs. Pledge, Graham Alcock, Mrs. Prince Captain Grant-Dalton and Sheila Ball in England; Ena Calvert in Scotland; and M. Andre Delattre in France. These imports, coupled with the puppies raised by South African breeders, led to a rapid increase in the country's numbers. The population grew from the two original imports in 1967 to 1500 dogs in 1976—all in nine short years.

While a great measure of this success story is due to the dogged determination of Mrs. Tudhope, we should also note that most of the imports she chose were of very high quality and came from established bloodlines. Then, too, the climate of South Africa seems to suit the Pyrenean. The high central plateau with its backdrop of towering mountains, coupled with its sunny days and cooling breezes, seems to remind the dogs of their homeland in the Pyrenees Mountains.

Visiting South Africa in May 1976, the writer discovered that the Pyrenean success story is broadly based and that there are a number of gifted and enthusiastic fanciers actively engaged in breeding and showing. A partial list would include:

DE LA NEIGE of Ivan and Marie Cooper. The Coopers obtained Ch. Ramos de Pontoise from Mrs. Tudhope, who had imported him from M. Delattre. Their foundation bitches are Goya de Fontenay, and Blanche—a bitch Mr. E. Von Gericke brought out from England. Blanche is a daughter of Longdorham Bernard, a linebred grandson of Eng. Ch. Bergerie Charlemagne de Bedous. A number of De La Neige champions have served as foundation stock for other breeders.

The BASQUE Kennels of Robin and Kathleen De Kock obtained Noble Seigneur de la Neige from the Coopers. This dog became the first South African-bred champion. Sired by Ch. Freddy de Fontenay out of Ch. Goya de Fontenay, Ch. Basque's Noble Seigneur died of stomach torsion but left a number of notable offspring. Basque-bred youngsters are doing well at all the shows.

The PENDRAGON Kennels of Peter and Joan Wilkins bought their stud dog Ch. Pendragon's Fairbanks of Aylward from Mrs. Tudhope. The Wilkins are quite dedicated and have just finished their home-bred female Ch. Pendragon Katinka.

Mr. and Mrs. G. Elliott of ROY DE BLICQUY imported their first breeding pair, Fidele and Fleur de Fontenay, from Mme. Harper in 1967, just a few months after Mrs. Tudhopes' original pair came to South Africa. However this pair had puppies first, making the Elliotts the breeders of the first litter born in South Africa.

196

h. Freddy de Fontenay, the first South African import, with his
grandson, in 1973. Owner, Mrs. Denise Tudhope, Aylward Kennels.

Ch. Lisblanc the Xebec Du Chateau has won four
Bests In Show at Championship Shows in South
Africa. Owned by Mrs. Inge A. Briechle.

Crown Princess Mahendra Kumari of
Alwar with her Best in Show winner,
Cavalier Snow Princess. — *Courtesy
Charles McConnell*

197

Mr. John Matthews of CRAIG DUNE owns Pendragon's Pretty Please, Pendragon's Nevar Bein of Craig Dune and Kipsno Carnation (an English import). He lives near Capetown.

Mr. and Mrs. Douglas Pitchford are the owners of HIGH ERCALL. Mr. Pitchford is the current President of the Pyrenean Club. Although very active in business he has found the time to show their male, Ch. Oloron de la Neige of High Ercall, bred by the Coopers, to one of the greatest show records in the country.

Mr. and Mrs. J. Smith of CAUTERETS edit the Club Journal with a great deal of flair. While building a new kennel, a new house, and raising a family, they are also breeding beautiful dogs.

Mr. Ronnie Watt and his father have assembled a kennel of very fine South African Pyreneans at MONTRACHET. Many of their young puppies show great promise. They intend to import more bloodlines from England, France and America.

There are many distinguished South African Pyrenees at the DE CHATEAU breeding establishment of Inge and Josef Briechle. Ch. Moncal Erskine de Chateau, called "Grant" after his breeder, Captain Grant-Dalton in the United Kingdom, is one of South Africa's top winning Pyreneans with 33 C.C.'s and about as many Bests of Breed. He was sold to the Briechles' by Mrs. Tudhope, his importer. From the United States the Briechles' imported Ch. Balibasque Teddy Bear. He is another of their great winners.

The undoubted star of this kennel is the young dog Ch. Lisblanc the Xebec du Chateau, imported from Sheila Ball, and called "Cristoph" after his famous English sire. Mr. D. Becker, who gave Cristoph Best In Show at the Northern Natal Kennel Club Show in August, 1975, had this to say: "A beautiful Pyrenean with lovely head and good pigmentation . . . sound in movement. Without a doubt a worthy Best in Show winner." And, as a matter of fact, Cristoph has since repeated a number of times as a Best in Show winner.

Mrs. Zilberman (ZILBERMAN Kennels) is primarily a breeder of the little, tousled Pyrenean Sheepdogs which she hopes to popularize in South Africa. However, at the instigation of Mrs. Tudhope, she is bringing out from France a young Pyrenean Mountain Dog, Lancelot du Comte de Foix, bred by the Giralts'. The Giralts' U'Yzoure is the dam of this dog and Iceberg du Grand Baou the sire. Iceberg is a son of World Champion Tempo du Grand Baou. This combination of France's leading bloodlines—the Comte de Foix of the Giralts and the du Grand Baou of Madame Docquin—makes Lancelot one of the most interesting stud dogs yet to arrive in South Africa.

From the foregoing quick glance at the South African kennels we see that the best bloodlines of England, France and the United States are represented. Most of the dogs are big. Males average about 30 inches at the shoulder and bitches around 28. Type is generally excellent and the heads and expression reflect the true attributes of the breed.

It is interesting to note that Mr. and Mrs. Huvard of Falls Church, Virginia, have recently imported a South African bitch and two puppies.

"September", the lioness, and Cavalier Snow Princess—"benched" in India. — *Courtesy Charles McConnell*

A very proud moment in the life of a young Pyrenean. Paula de Laudez, a mascot in the 1st Battalion of the Jamaica Regiment, has just been presented to the Queen Mother on her visit to Jamaica in 1965. In the background is Princess Alice of Athlone, Grand Aunt to Queen Elizabeth II. Very shortly after this event, Paula was promoted to the rank of Lance-Corporal. — *Courtesy I.G.P.R.*

199

Mme. Harper Trois-Fontaines at 87 years of age, with one of her favorites, Edis de Fontenay. — *Thomas Fall Ltd.*

13

Breeding the
Great Pyrenees

WHEN CHOOSING YOUR STOCK, it is important to begin
with a mental grasp of what it is you are trying to accomplish. The object of
any breeding program is to preserve the essential qualities and physical characteristics of the breed. Put aside any thoughts of "doing your own thing" in
so far as trying to improve on basic type and conformation. The French judge,
M. Douillard, recently wrote in a French canine review, "It is both ignorant
and presumptuous to try to improve the Pyrenean Mountain Dog. One only
succeeds in making the dog ugly." To this we can only add a fervent
"Amen!"

A thorough understanding of the breed standard is a basic requirement for
anyone planning to breed dogs. Beyond the standard, however, there is an il-
lusive something extra: a certain almost extra-sensory perception which gives
to those who have it a kind of success which others, perhaps more knowledgeable but less wise, never seem quite able to grasp.

A successful breeder is one who knows what he likes and is willing to stick
by it. Knowledge of this sort does not come spontaneously. An eye for a good
dog is something you can be born with, but an eye without a mind behind it is
just an eye. You need to learn everything you can about the breed, and especially the bloodlines from which you plan to choose your stock. Visit as many
kennels as you can, talk to the owners, see the tried and true producers, the
retired dogs and the up and coming ones.

Attend dog shows and make mental notes on the different types you find in
the ring. Read McDowell Lyon's *The Dog in Action*, the "bible" on balance
and gait. Study pedigrees for at least three generations.

A successful breeder is one who sees the faults in his own dogs as readily as
he sees those in his rival's. Perhaps that little "extra" is the good sense to
breed with the *whole* dog in mind, and not to put emphasis on any one single
attribute at the expense of the overall dog.

Keep these thoughts at the front: The Great Pyrenees is a large and powerful working dog, his *soundness* arising out of his correct proportions and well-knit morphology. *Type* is in the head. *Beauty* is a combination of type, coat and bearing. And most important, a *sound disposition* in a Pyrenees leads to a spirited, intelligent self-confident, outgoing and dependable companion and protector.

Pedigrees are important because they are the means to study the bloodlines and learn the relationships between the various dogs. They are of greatest value when the dogs are known, or have actually been seen.

Champions do indicate merit and do give some indication of quality. However, they are not always completely informative as to the overall superiority of the individuals listed. Some championships are won through the accident of less than normal quality in the competition. And the opposite is also true—some dogs do not win their medals simply because of lack of exposure.

Count the championships, but also study the patterns of inheritance. Look for qualities which have endured from generation to generation. Familiarize yourself with the individual dogs. This will give you a sound perspective on the assets of the bloodlines in question.

In any plan for mating there must be a positive and systematic approach. Broadly speaking, any litter which has the same Great Pyrenees on each side of the pedigree is an *inbred* one. However, this term is usually applied only to those matings which are in the order of parent to offspring or brother to sister. Interbreeding among common dogs further removed is *linebreeding*.

When one breeds two dogs with a common ancestry, their litter inherits some of the same genes from each side of the pedigree. This allows for the statistical possibility that genes will "double-up" at the same locus. The result is two-fold: the expression of all traits is more uniform, but recessive genes may come to the surface, thereby giving rise to serious or lethal problems.

Linebreeding is the safest and best method to preserve type and conformation provided that the foundation dogs are well chosen and one has the judgment and experience to pick the best puppies.

Inbreeding, on the other hand, requires a genetically clean stock, a knowledge of the faults and virtues of all the common dogs for at least three generations, and the willingness to cull ruthlessly when it becomes necessary.

Most breeders prefer to avoid frank inbreeding. Instead, they keep the overall relationship to common dogs rather high by using them several times farther back in the pedigree. After having linebred for three or four generations, most breeders have found from experience that it is wise to bring in new blood. The use of a stud from a totally different bloodline may be considered. This produces an *outcrossed* litter and "reshuffles" the genes that have tended to become fixed, in a more or less predictable manner, through previous linebreeding. Many times, particularly with an overly refined bitch, an outcross will give surprisingly good results. An improvement in the health and vigor of the resulting pups is apparent from the time they are born. The process is known as "nicking." While the litter will sometimes lack uniformity, nevertheless some really good Pyrenees show dogs have been produced in this manner.

When two strains have nicked successfully, other crosses between them may work as well. Pups from such matings are usually bred back into one of the two strains, thereby providing a basis for a new line.

One final method is to breed a dog and a bitch who are both of mixed ancestry. Neither has a linebred background. When using this approach, it is essential that one have a definite goal in mind.

One dog may carry an attribute or quality totally lacking in the other. Or it may be a matter of breeding a good sound bitch to the best stud dog available. But if the mating is a "back yard" one, chosen only because the two dogs are readily at hand for breeding, then in most cases the pups will be no better than their parents.

Temperament and Disposition

In striving to breed dogs of superior type, one simply cannot overlook the importance of character. When you consider that guarding is ingrained, it is somewhat remarkable that viciousness and aggression have never been a problem in our breed. In part, this is due to the fact that the breed has not achieved instant popularity. And in part because those who maintained the bloodlines of the past appear to have understood the supreme importance of using only dogs of sound disposition for breeding.

Aggression in dogs is not always due to inheritance. But at times a dog, like a person, may be born with an unstable personality. In a powerful guard dog, this would be a frank disaster. A Pyrenees, if it has once attacked and injured anyone, for whatever reason, would have to be classified as a potentially dangerous animal. You simply cannot adjust your life to live with a nervous, aggressive or unstable giant dog. In most cases the only acceptable solution would be to put the dog down.

The "soft" or shy dog is another serious behavioral problem which also shows a high rate of inheritance. A Pyrenees who panics at the approach of a stranger could be dangerous and should be kept under observation until some solution can be arranged. A shy dog is not dependable and cannot be relied upon to overcome it under all circumstances.

Do not confuse fear with aloofness. Some Pyrenees retain a standoffish attitude toward strangers, but do not display any sign of fear when approached. They are aloof but remain steadfast.

Close linebreeding is said to be responsible for causing high-strung, nervous and aggressive dogs. In point of fact, the statement is a false one, relying as it does on the unfounded assumption that just because two individuals are closely related their offspring are going to be shy or aggressive. Obviously, it is the genetic potential in the background of the pair which determines the outcome. A fundamentally sound strain remains fundamentally sound, and one which uses a mentally unstable dog as a pillar of its program is eventually going to produce nervous and aggressive animals.

Therefore the prime consideration, when breeding the Great Pyrenees—or any guarding breed for that matter—is to select only the most self-assured, intelligent and discriminating individuals to carry on the bloodline.

Markings and Pigmentation

The coloring matter found in the coat and skin of mammals is due to a pigment called melanin. Melanin, in the Great Pyrenees, acts to turn the skin black in those areas where pigmentation is required (eyelids, eye-rims, lips, nose and palate), and to impart the necessary color to the coat patches as well. For a more detailed discussion of pigment inheritance, the reader is advised to consult Little's *Inheritance of Coat Color in Dogs.*

There is unquestionably a correlation, although a general one, between a well-marked blaireau Great Pyrenees and one which also carries black pigmentation. Therefore, the value of the blaireau dog is, in the mind of a breeder, further enhanced by his reputation for producing well-pigmented offspring.

When all-white dogs are mated to all-white bitches, there is a grave danger that pigmentation will break down. If this is carried for several generations, missing pigment is almost a certainty. In addition, one approaches the problem of albinism, including deafness and impaired vision. Accordingly, only the most knowledgeable breeder who is familiar with the markings and pigmentation of all the dogs on both sides of the pedigree for at least three generations will attempt to breed two pure-white Pyrenees.

Pedigrees, unfortunately, do not provide information on markings and pigmentation. But most breeders will be happy to provide this information. It is extremely useful.

Breeding an all-white to a blaireau is the safest and best method to use for the typical mating. About half the puppies will be blaireau and the others white. The marked pups will usually have even patches of color on the head, often a patch at the base of the tail, and perhaps an occasional spot on the body.

Mating two blaireau dogs will often produce very strong pigmentation, but sometimes a number of color patches on the coat. Nevertheless, some beautifully marked puppies sometimes result from such matings.

The late Marjorie Butcher, addressing a dinner gathering in 1971, observed that in her experience it was the dog with asymmetrical markings, those with a half-mask on the head and ear of one side only, which gave the first indication of pigment breakdown. "What I really preferred were those perfectly lovely puppies with badger markings—nice even ones which fade into just a light

204

shading. This is what will give you the good pigmentation. So you don't have to look for the heavily marked dog.''

When picking a stud dog, choosing a brood bitch or simply buying a puppy, go over the individual carefully for evidence of strong pigment. Rarely, you may find that heavy markings on the coat are still accompanied by weak pigment, or yellow eyes. So don't rely upon the fact that the dog is known to be blaireau. Look for yourself. A black palate is a better indication of genetically sound pigment than heavy coat markings. And some Pyrenees carry black nails, which is another prized finding. Finally, part the hair on the undersurface of the belly. If you find patches of dark skin, you have a well-pigmented dog.

Finally, in choosing your stud dog and brood bitch, never make the mistake of assuming that extra-strong pigment in one of your producers will automatically overcome poor pigment in the other. Too often it is the one with the poor pigment who dominates the litter.

The Brood Bitch

Before you decide to breed your Great Pyrenees bitch, give careful thought to the effort and expense which goes into producing a litter of healthy and active puppies. It can be both time-consuming and expensive. A Pyrenees litter can seldom be sold locally. This means added cost in advertising and added work in finding the right sort of home in which to place them. In all, there is no profit to be made from breeding the Pyrenees.

Many people are inclined to believe that a Pyrenees bitch needs to have a litter to be psychologically fulfilled. This is another of those ''old wives' tales.'' A spayed female makes an outstanding house pet!

There are certain special qualities to look for in a female who is likely to be a good breeding prospect. They are:

* *Type* is of paramount importance. The head and the true Pyrenean expression stamp this breed apart from all others. We cannot expect a bitch with a poor head to whelp puppies that will be an asset to the breed.

* *Balance* and *Soundness*. Size and strength are also necessary, but in a bitch we should give greatest consideration to correct proportions. Over-refinement must be avoided, but most breeders agree that a very feminine bitch makes the best brood matron.

* A bitch must have *character*. The calm, intelligent self-assurance that is part and parcel of the breed. A nervous, hare-brained or otherwise unreliable female can easily pass these undesirable traits on to her offspring.

* Look for *the imperfections*. No bitch is perfect and even the best have some imperfection, however slight. Whatever the fault may be, remember the cardinal dictum: NEVER BREED A FAULT TO A FAULT. Specifically, if your bitch has long flat feet and after examining on the spot all the possible choices for a stud dog you choose, in the end, a dog that also has flat feet, the chances are that you will produce a litter of long, flat-footed puppies.

A Great Pyrenees bitch may be mated after she is a year old. Most breeders prefer to wait until the second or third season at which time she is emotionally mature and well able to adjust to the role of a brood matron. But one should not wait until the bitch is three or four years old before mating her for the first time. Her pelvic ligaments are no longer elastic and this could give her trouble whelping.

It goes without saying that a prospective brood matron should be kept in top physical condition. An overweight bitch, lacking in exercise tolerance, is difficult to mate and many times will not come into season regularly.

Her physical check-up should be as complete as possible and should include a test for heartworms. A maiden bitch should be examined by the Vet to be sure that her vaginal orifice is of normal size. There should be no constricting ring which would prevent normal entry. A heavy membrane, or hymen, is common in our breed. This can be removed by simple surgery well in advance of breeding—not during the heat season when you plan to mate her.

Due to the increase in the incidence of brucellosis in dogs in the United States, a serum agglutination test should always be done on both the bitch and stud dog before mating. This test is now available in veterinarian clinics and can be run from a blood sample in a few minutes.

Absence of clinical symptoms is no guarantee that the animal does not harbor a subclinical infection. Once the disease is contracted, it quickly passes by oral or genital contact throughout an entire kennel. There is no satisfactory cure and all infected animals must be eliminated. The stud's owner should therefore request a vet's certificate showing that the visiting bitch has been tested for and found free of brucellosis.

Chronic vaginal or uterine infection is a common problem in the Great Pyrenees, as it is in many of the large breeds. During estrus, the vulva of a Pyrenees female becomes quite enlarged. At the same time, the protective plug of mucus is discharged from the cervix, opening the path for ascending bacterial infection. The result may well be a subclinical metritis. Unsuspected metritis may be the underlying problem when a bitch (a) refuses to accept the male, (b) is bred at the right time but fails to conceive, or (c) delivers stillborn pups or pups which sicken and die during the first few days.

Because of this, many breeders routinely culture the vaginal secretions of every bitch early in the heat cycle. If the culture is positive, the Vet will recommend a course of antibiotics.

Before you mate your Pyrenees bitch, have the Vet X-ray her pelvis. This should be done after one year of age. If the X-ray indicates actual bone changes of hip dysplasia, *do not breed her.* By the same token, the bitch should be bred only to a stud with excellent hips. Certification by the O.F.A. or other highly reliable authority is desirable.

Also prior to breeding, the bitch and the stud should be checked for worms. Roundworms are difficult to avoid in puppies, but their number can be greatly reduced by having the bitch wormed before breeding. Any other parasites, if found, should be vigorously treated.

A beautiful head study of Ch. Cote de Neige Pataud. Owned by Paul Strang.

Champion Cote de Neige Ariette II—The classic head and expression to be looked for in an outstanding brood bitch. Owned by Mr. and Mrs. C. Seaver Smith, Jr.

207

A Great Pyrenees bitch is usually at her best as a brood matron from 18 months to five or six years. Generally, she should not be bred from more often than once a year. However, a strong bitch who has raised only two or three pups and who has lost no condition can safely be bred from on her next season.

In Pyreneans, it would appear that at about six or seven years of age the breeding capacity of bitches is in decline. The possibility of complications increases and one must be prepared to take the risks involved.

The Stud Dog

If your bitch came from a breeding kennel, it is clearly a good idea to talk to your breeder before making a final decision on the right stud dog. Your breeder is thoroughly familiar with the strengths and weaknesses which lie behind your bitch. This knowledge can be vitally important in choosing a compatible stud.

Some breeding kennels also offer stud service. If you have an outstanding bitch from that bloodline, you might want to give serious thought to using a stud from that same strain to reinforce the best qualities in your bitch. If your breeder does not offer this service, he or she will be able to tell you where to find a suitable mate for your female.

The special qualities to look for in a Pyrenean male who is likely to be an outstanding stud prospect are:

* *Overall size, bone, and a rugged constitution,* tell us that the male is a sound and purposeful working dog. Being a Great Pyrenees, he must be a virile animal with an air of masculinity and a bold temperament. He should be well-knit without appearing too refined, and yet he should possess in good measure all the essential points required by the Standard. Moreover, he should be strong in the qualities lacking in the bitch.

* His *manner* should be open, assured and self-confident; his eyes bright, clear and expressive; his bearing alert and friendly. Should the male appear timid, you would be well advised to look elsewhere. Overall, he should give the impression of being a dog you would want to own yourself, and one you would trust implicitly. An Obedience title would demonstrate a dog's willingness to accept and execute the wishes and commands of his master. A championship plus an Obedience degree is an added bonus. Beauty and brains are always a good combination.

* His *production record.* If a Pyrenean sire has had a career as a producer, his record becomes a matter of considerable importance. If he has sired the type of Pyrenees you like, particularly if several different bitches were used, you have strong evidence in favor of his potency. The number of champions produced is not always as meaningful as you may think. There is usually a lapse of several years between a mating and a championship. The top Pyrenean producers are often recognized well after they have stopped producing. But their offspring may also retain their sire's prepotency.

Ch. Rogue La Rue—The Top Producer in the breed with 28 champions, including the Best in Show winner Ch. Soleil Pierre de Blu Crest. Owned by Mr. and Mrs. Jack Magoffin. — *Courtesy I.G.P.R.*

Ch. Quibbletown Impresario, a son of Lorvaso de la Colina. The second most prolific stud in the breed's history, he sired 18 champions, and lists among his progeny the greatest number of top winners in recent years. Owned by Mr. and Mrs. C. Seaver Smith, Jr. — *Gilbert*

Ch. Tip 'N Chip's Roxanne has produced eight champions—the second most prolific dam in the breed. Owned by Mrs. Judy Bankus.

209

The show record of a prospective stud dog may include a championship, multiple Breed wins, Group placings, or even a Best in Show. Unfortunately, not all great show dogs are outstanding producers. By the same token, some of the top producers have not been particularly distinguished in the ring.

If you have to choose between production and wins, choose production.

Part of the breeding preparation is to see that the stud dog has been chosen well in advance. It is the responsibility of the breeder (who is the owner of the bitch) to come to a clear understanding with the owner of the stud dog concerning the breeding terms.

Usually a stud fee is paid in cash at the time of the mating. Often the stud's owner will agree to take, instead, "pick of the litter", which is a puppy of his own choosing. The age of the puppy should be agreed upon. If the bitch does not conceive, the stud's owner may offer a return service at no extra charge. But this is not obligatory in any way. Terms vary with the circumstances and the policies of the kennel. If these are in writing, there will be no misunderstandings at a later date.

A male offered at stud should at all times be kept in top physical condition with regular exercise, routine health checkups, and a sound diet. Excess weight is a severe handicap to a stud dog. A fat dog is apathetic. He could even be so heavy as to lack the stamina to mount a bitch. A poorly kept or rundown dog is obviously unsatisfactory.

Before a Great Pyrenees is offered at stud to the public, a pelvic X-ray should be made and, if the results are less than perfect, the degree of imperfection should be taken into consideration before deciding whether to use him. If actual bone changes of hip dysplasia are diagnosed, he *should not*, in all good conscience, be offered at stud.

A Pyrenean male should ordinarily be used at stud for the first time at about one to two years of age. If an older dog is not a known producer, a sperm count, as well as a culture of the prostatic secretions (if the count is low) should be done. A chronic infection can severely depress sperm formation, or even render the dog sterile. This can often be improved with corrective measures.

A sound and healthy Great Pyrenees male remains fertile for at least eight or nine years. Many are able to sire litters throughout their entire life. This depends to some extent on how often the dog is used and how well he is cared for in his older age. In many cases, however, a Pyrenees older than nine years must be considered on the decline.

Breeding a Great Pyrenees does not make him aggressive, or inclined to fight other dogs. One drawback, however, to keeping a stud dog in the house is that his territorial "marking" instinct may become uninhibited. This could be a problem, especially if the dog were previously housebroken. If there are top stud dogs available, one might consider not owning a stud dog at all. The temptation is always there to use him, whether he suits your bitch's bloodlines or not.

210

Finally, we should not forget that years ago, in the Pyrenees mountains, our dogs led a very different life. Their days, as well as nights were filled with action, excitement and challenge. The terrain was rough and it toughened their muscles. Purpose and resolve built character. As working dogs, our Great Pyrenees used to get more exercise in a week than many, today, get in a month. Weaklings fell by the wayside. Only the strong and fit were left to perpetuate the race.

So in choosing the ideal stud dog or brood bitch to carry on the tradition, we should be concerned not only with bloodlines, pedigrees and show wins, but also with past history. And, even more importantly, with a vision of what lies ahead. Our litters will be, hopefully, of show quality. But they must also possess, to a marked degree, the strength and the vitality that will guarantee us future titans of the breed.

Mating

Once the foregoing considerations have been met—that is, the bitch is found worthy to be bred and the right stud dog has been chosen—the only barrier to a successful breeding is the mating itself.

This should provide few difficulties providing that both animals are healthy, keen and receptive. A mating will usually take place very quickly and conception will result.

Much has been written about the mating cycle in bitches. The important thing to remember is that a female, of any species, is unpredictable.

As a generality, estrus, the season of heat, lasts 21 days. The onset is signaled by a bloody discharge. The vulva begins to swell. By ten days it is two to three times normal size. When the color changes to straw or watermelon, the bitch is ovulating. This is usually seen from the 10th to the 14th day. This is the textbook time to breed.

After that, the discharge becomes creamy due to the presence of white cells. This signals the end of ovulation. The bitch will now refuse to stand for the male.

There are recorded instances of a Great Pyrenees bitch being bred as early as the fourth day and as late as the 21st day—and yet conceiving a litter! So practically speaking, a certain amount of trial and error is necessary. The best time to breed a female is any time she will accept the stud.

If the bitch flirts and plays coyly, if she switches her tail, "flags" and stands firm—these are all good signs that she is ovulating and ready to be bred.

An experienced stud will make his own investigations. Some have become so knowledgeable that they actually ignore the bitch until they "know" she is ready. Young ones, however, are inclined to act foolishly and cannot be relied upon at all.

211

When the bitch is due in season (six months after her last one) she should be watched carefully. As soon as she shows color, the owner of the stud dog should be notified. He will probably want the bitch at once. This has the advantage of letting her settle into the new routine after a nerve-wracking trip. And the owner of the stud is less likely to miss her ovulatory period.

Neither animal should be fed for several hours before the mating. Avoid the heat of day. In summer, bring both dogs into the house, or the kennel room, where it is relatively cool. Otherwise, the bitch should be taken to the enclosure of the dog as the male is often more confident and assertive in his own surroundings.

Keep the number of people to a minimum. The fewer the distractions, the better.

If the female has a heavy or matted coat, it is a good idea to trim the pants away to expose the vulva.

Both dogs are introduced to each other on leads. Once it is seen that the bitch is friendly and receptive, the dogs may be let off lead to romp for a short period. This must be kept to a minimum because it is taxing on the male and reduces his stamina.

A good Pyrenees stud seldom needs or welcomes assistance. Some prefer to have the bitch held; others do not.

If the mating does not proceed within a few minutes, i.e., either the stud is disinterested or the female flies at the male, it usually means that the bitch hasn't begun to ovulate. Separate the dogs and try again in 48 hours.

Specifically, *do not* insist that the male attempt to breed an unwilling bitch. This will almost never "put off" a vigorous male, but it does confuse and frighten the female, thereby making future attempts more difficult if not impossible.

A slightly nervous bitch, or one who would rather frolic than get down to the business at hand, may have to be held.

Infrequently one encounters the bitch who, despite all efforts to get her to breed willingly, becomes frantic and throws herself to the ground. This bitch has to be classified as totally unmanageable. If a bitch of sound disposition consistently refuses to receive a stud, it is a good idea to have her examined for hormonal imbalance, vaginal abnormalities, and chronic metritis.

When the bitch is ready to be mated she will switch her tail and stand quietly for the dog while he mounts. As the male penetrates he begins to tread up and down rather than thrusting forward. The knot at the base of the penis swells and is clasped by the vulva. This produces the "tie." The dogs are joined and will remain so for ten to thirty minutes. During this time it is wise to have someone posted at the head of the bitch to steady her. If she attempts to jerk away, the male may be injured.

After the tie is accomplished, the male unclasps his forelegs and places both on the ground on the same side of the bitch. He may lift his hindleg over the back of the bitch, and the two dogs will stand back to back.

212

A basket of puppies from Basquaerie. — *E. Morgan Savage*

A court of law will accept "no tie" as proof of no impregnation. Laws are governed by practicality and not exceptions. In rare cases there can be a pregnancy without a tie. But only an actual pregnancy can prove this.

For practical purposes, a bitch will accept a male only during the period when she is fertile. One good tie is therefore usually sufficient. Some breeders, however, prefer to breed twice during the receptive period. This should be done with a 48 hour interval in between.

A mating between a tall dog and a short bitch can present a mechanical problem. The answer is to stand the male in a ditch (or breed on a slope), to equalize the difference.

Finally nervous or apprehensive owners will almost always communicate this to the dogs. A calm, collected approach is the best. If one of the dogs is a housepet, or if for any other reason the mating is difficult for the owners, the entire matter should be put in the hands of a capable Vet.

A mother and her pups.

14

Whelping and
Care of the Litter

THE PERIOD OF GESTATION, the time during which the
Pyrenean bitch carries her litter, as reckoned from the day of the first successful mating, is 63 days. It is not uncommon, however, to find a bitch who
whelps on the 59th or the 66th day. However, if she whelps before the 57th
day, the pups are going to be too young to survive.

Because the Great Pyrenees carries her litters well up under her rib cage, it
is not always possible to tell whether she is pregnant. Often, by 40 days of
gestation, one can see a darkening and enlargement of the nipples. Shortly
thereafter, an experienced breeder may be able to palpate puppies in an enlarging uterus. Occasionally, however, one or two pups can be carried to maturity without anyone even suspecting that the bitch is pregnant.

A brood matron should be lean and well-conditioned, neither run down and
depleted from an earlier litter nor allowed to become obese. To this end, routine daily exercise of a moderate nature is advisable. However, pregnant
bitches should not climb fences, rough-house with other dogs, leap down long
flights of stairs, or engage in otherwise violent pursuits. Supplemental feedings and vitamins are advisable in certain cases, especially if a bitch is older,
below par from an earlier litter, or recovering from an illness. However,
excessive weight gain should be avoided at all costs. An overnourished bitch
is apt to carry overnourished puppies and this can contribute to difficult labor.

Whelping quarters to house the dam and her puppies should be provided
well in advance. Such quarters are best located in a quiet, out-of-the-way
spot, free from the comings and goings of children and visitors. Another important consideration is that the whelping area must be clean, dry, draft-free
and warm. When the pups are born, floor temperature should be kept near 80
degrees—at least for the first two weeks.

An adequate whelping box for a Great Pyrenees is at least four by five feet
in size. The sides should be 12 to 18 inches tall on three sides, and eight

inches on the side where the bitch goes in and out. This side can be replaced by a taller board when the puppies are older. The sides should not be nailed to the floor board. Instead, they are held in grooves made by nailing one by two inch molding around the margins. The sides are then joined together, and held in place, by hook-and-eye latches. The floor is much easier to clean when the sides can be removed. The box is then lined with clean newspapers.

Before the construction of the box is finished, a ledge around the inside, six inches from the floor, should be made by nailing six-inch boards to all four sides. In this manner, puppies can crawl under the ledges, which they will do instinctively and thus will be protected from being accidentally smothered by the dam.

Some thought should be given to keeping the puppies warm when the mother is away from the nest. For example, if the room temperature were only 68 degrees, below the recommended temperature, when the dam is absent and her body heat is no longer available to keep the puppies warm, in about 30 minutes a puppy's core temperature drops to 94 degrees. Metabolism and the feeding urge slow down. This is a chilled and fading pup. If ambient temperature cannot be well maintained, supplemental heat can.be supplied by using 250 watt infra-red heat bulbs, either suspended above the floor of the litter box or mounted in photographer's flood light reflectors (plant lights) and directed into the box from each side, to provide a surface temperature of 80 degrees.

The bitch should be introduced to her litter box about two weeks before she is due, and required to sleep in it. By the time she whelps she will understand that she is to do so in the box, and not in her master's bed.

Further accessories include a small box with a towel-covered hot water bottle or a heating pad in the bottom of it, in which pups can be placed and kept warm while new ones are being born; a bulb syringe to aspirate secretions from the mouth of the new-born pup; sterile artery forceps to clamp a bleeding cord; cotton or silk thread for ties; and an antiseptic to apply to the stump. Scissors, clean-laundrered towels and plenty of fresh newspapers complete the whelping preparations.

Whelping

Several days before the bitch gives birth to her litter, one can observe a loss of appetite and increased restlessness. She seeks the seclusion of a dark, sheltered spot, may be given to digging in the garden, and goes about in a flurry of activity which is the ritual of preparing her nest. Several hours prior to delivery, the rectal temperature falls from a normal 101 degrees to 100 degrees or below. This can easily be missed. A normal temperature does not mean she won't whelp that day.

Whelping begins with rapid panting, general uneasiness and straining. The canine uterus is composed of a central body and two horns. The fetus develops in the horns. First the horn contracts and the fetus is pushed into the central cavity. Next the body of the uterus contracts and throws the presenting part against the cervix, which gradually dilates, allowing the puppy to be passed into the vagina. Its head then appears at the vulva, often surrounded by the bag of water. If the bag ruptures in transit a variable amount of straw-colored fluid is passed.

After the head is delivered, the rest of the puppy slides out easily. The bitch chews the water bag, if this is still intact, then severs the cord, and eats the membranes together with the attached placenta when it is delivered.

The usual Pyrenean bitch will have her puppies easily and take care of them well, as her mountain ancestors have done for thousands of years. The less one interferes, the better. A novice bitch, however, may require help. If she should fail to remove the membranes enclosing the puppy, these should be removed and the puppy stimulated by rubbing it vigorously with a dry towel, while removing any secretions from the nose and mouth with a bulb syringe, and then presenting it to the dam to sniff, lick and cuddle.

The bitch will usually *shred* the umbilical cord, and in so doing the vessels will contract and no bleeding will be encountered. But if the cord is cut cleanly, or too close to the belly wall, it may bleed, and you should be ready to clamp the cord and tie a thread around the stump below the clamp. Stumps should then be cauterized with iodine or some other suitable disinfectant.

The dam will try to eat some of the placentas as they appear. No attempt should be made to prevent this as a placenta supplies hormones which aid normal labor. Puppies should be allowed to nurse in between births. The sucking action helps to bring on the colostrum and appears to stimulate contractions.

If it is necessary to assist a puppy which is partially delivered from the vagina, grip it with a sterile towel and maintain a gentle pull—but only when the bitch is straining. Never probe the birth canal with unsterile instruments or fingers. This only invites a post-partum infection.

An attempt should be made to account for all the placentas. A retained placenta, or placental fragment, can cause a potentially fatal metritis. For this reason, it is advisable to ask your vet to examine a dam after whelp. He may prescribe an injection to clear the uterus. This injection also stimulates the let-down of milk.

A Great Pyrenees bitch with six puppies will usually take six to eight hours to whelp, but a large litter may take considerably longer. Although pups usually appear at regular intervals, it is not a matter of concern if a pup does not arrive for one or two hours. On the other hand, if the interval between births is unduly long, and if at the same time the bitch is straining and appears in distress, there is possible cause for concern. Similarly, the passage of green fluid, which signifies separation of the placenta, should be followed by the birth of a puppy within two hours.

The prolongation of any phase of labor is called "dystocia." This is due either to a birth canal which is too narrow in relation to the size of the part, or to the failure of the uterine muscle to develop enough strength to expel the fetus. Often these two are interrelated, a difficult birth being followed by arrested labor due to uterine fatigue.

Abnormal presentations all have the effect of increasing the width of the presenting part of the fetus to a point where exit from the pelvis is impossible. The "breach," or posterior presentation, occurs so frequently that it may be inaccurate to classify it as a malpresentation. It usually causes dystocia only when it occurs in the first puppy.

When difficult labor is suspected, the veterinarian should be called at once. It is certainly better to call the vet on a "false alarm," even if only to gain reassurance, then to delay in the hope that in time the problem will correct itself without outside help. Often the problem can be dealt with by the vet rather simply—if attended to in good time. However, the same problem, if neglected, becomes more complicated, perhaps leading to Cesarean Section under trying circumstances.

New-born Puppies

A good mother instinctively keeps her nest and puppies clean. By licking the belly and rectum of each pup, the dam stimulates the elimination reflex. During the first four weeks, do not handle the puppies more than necessary (and little handling is necessary). A constant nervous fuss is upsetting to the dam and disturbs the pups' rhythm of eating and sleeping. The puppies sleep 90% of the time and eat 10%. They jerk, kick and whimper. This is "activated sleep." It develops the muscles which will be used later.

The average Pyrenees puppy begins to open its eyes and its ears at about two weeks of age. It begins to stand at three, and is ready to socialize with people, and can even begin to tell the differences between them, by about one month. Also at about this time it will begin to eat from a dish—although this can be accomplished earlier in the case of an orphan.

After the puppies are about two to three weeks old their nails should be trimmed every week so they do not scratch the skin of the dam. When they begin to walk, it is advisable to change the lining of the box from newspapers to indoor-outdoor carpeting, which gives better traction for the feet. A Pyrenees puppy should never be kept on a slick surface as its hind feet will slip apart and this can be bad for the development of its hip joints. When carrying a pup from place to place, slide one hand between the forelegs and the other beneath the stomach or hindlegs. Put the puppy down with all four feet firmly on the ground before releasing its weight. NEVER lift a puppy by its front legs alone as this will weaken or dislocate the shoulder joints.

PUPPYHOOD
The first twelve weeks.

Heavily marked puppy at one week. Eyes are still tightly shut; the pigment is not completely set on the nose. Good rate of growth apparent: Pup weighed a little over a pound at birth and now weighs close to two pounds.

By two weeks the eyes are open, though bleary. On this pup, the nose is now completely black. Occasionally a bit of sticky matter prevents the eyelids from opening properly and help is required.

By three weeks the eyes are open alertly. Early signs of good bone, as well as coats, are visible. Sharp toenails should be trimmed. Many breeders give the first worming now.

Individual character and personality turn on strongly at four weeks. Pup weighs six pounds.

At five weeks the leggy stage begins.

The excellent angulation of this eight-week-old pup shows clearly here. Generally, the good and bad structural faults seen at this age are retained in adulthood.

Note the characteristically large ears at two months of age. A high ear-set, shown here, may improve with time. The pup weighs 17 pounds.

An appealing puppy, but observe the east-west front and weak pasterns.

At three months, a cobby puppy with good bone and tight feet. The ears are well placed. The muzzle is beginning to lengthen. A knobby wrist joint is characteristic at this age. The pup now weighs about 30 pounds.

The Fading Puppy

For the first 48 hours, a puppy has a tendency to curl with its head under its chest. After that, it lies with its head up. A puppy which continues to lie with its head curled under its chest may be sick. Listen for a piercing cry which continues for several minutes. A healthy pup is "round, firm, and fully packed." A sick one is apathetic, wrinkled, cold, and lies apart from the pile. Rectal temperature is below 96 degrees. Respiratory rate is low, and the pulse or heartbeat is below 80. When the puppy is put on a nipple, it nurses apathetically, drops the nipple, cries and eventually falls asleep. One of the best ways to monitor the progress of a litter is to record the daily weight gain. A Pyrenean puppy should gain 1 to 2 ounces per day at this stage. A puppy failing to gain weight, or one which is losing, is in serious trouble.

A puppy may start to fade for a variety of reasons. Once it becomes chilled, and misses one or two meals, it loses the competitive edge. It could be septic as a complication of intrauterine infection (metritis) or an infected umbilical stump; or because of a contagious disease, either bacterial or viral; or it may have received an injury; or it may not be competitive due to constitutional inforiority.

Treatment of a fading puppy must begin at once. Otherwise too much valuable time will be lost. The first thing to do is to WARM the puppy—not by putting it in an oven—but by holding it close to your chest, beneath a fur-lined jacket, where human warmth and movement stimulate it. DON'T FEED A CHILLED PUP. Instead give it a solution of 10% glucose (or honey) in water by means of an eye-dropper. Meet the large water requirements of a new-born pup by giving three ounces per-pound of body weight per-day. Next, increase the humidity of the whelping area to at least 50% and be sure that the temperature on the floor of the litter box is at least 80 degrees. Then ask your veterinarian to examine the litter. He may want to advise further precautionary measures.

Orphan Puppies

A dam could be unable to raise her litter because of post-partum metritis, acute mastitis or breast infection, "acid-milk" syndrome, eclampsia, or inadequate milk supply. In such cases the pups may have to be supplemented or hand -fed.

This is not the chore it used to be because of the ready availability of dried reconstituted bitch's milk, from your vet or a commcercial source, which has replaced the need for special formulas, goat's milk, and foster mothers.

Puppies may be fed by eye-dropper, small animal nursing bottles, and gastric tubes. The latter are preferred by those who have had experience with their use.

A puppy nurser holds four ounces of formula. These can be purchased from agricultural stores, pet shops, and through veterinarians. Complete instructions are provided for the preparation of the formula and for the use of the nurser. Formula should be offered six times in 24 hours, bearing in mind that a Pyr puppy needs three ounces of formula for each pound of weight per-day.

If the pups were unable to receive the colostrum, the first milk of the bitch, they lack passive immunity and are susceptible to a variety of diseases including distemper. In such cases, shots containing passive antibodies should be given at three weeks of age. The regular vaccinations are then given at eight to ten weeks. Orphan pups should be kept in separate compartments, such as shoe-boxes, because having no mother to suckle they tend to suckle each other. A hand-fed pup will also need to be "burped." For the first week, massage the abdomen and genitalia of each puppy to stimulate elimination. A wad of cotton soaked in warm water can be used for this purpose.

A dirty puppy should be cleaned with a damp cloth. A light application of baby oil may be applied to its coat. As soon as the eyes open, encourage the pups to drink milk from a dish.

Weaning

Weaning time depends upon several factors which include the size of the litter, the condition of the dam, the availability of mother's milk, and the inclinations of the breeder. Large breeds, such as the Great Pyrenees, seem to wean early and to do well. Weaning can usually begin by three to six weeks of age, and takes about two weeks to complete.

Puppies should be weaned on basically a milk diet. Start with a mixture of evaporated milk mixed half-and-half with water, add baby cereal to make it sloppy, and give one raw raw egg yolk a day (for iron). As the pups begin to eat the mixture well, increase the number of feedings. Feed in a low-rimmed metal dish (pie pan) and push the pup's nose into the mixture.

After several days the diet can be advanced to a high quality puppy kibble with raw hamburger and cottage cheese mixed in equal proportions, with enough water to make it sloppy and soft. One or two feedings each day should still be milk alone. Remember to provide WATER at all times. Water deprivation can cause serious kidney problems which may not appear until later in life.

Separate the dam a few hours before each feeding so that the pups will be hungry. After they have finished the meal, let the dam back in so that the pups can nurse. This progressively decreases the demand on mother's milk, and helps to dry her up. Finally, the pups will be eating four meals a day. Now the dam can be removed completely. At this time withhold all food from the dam and give her only small amounts of water, After 24 hours, her breasts should be inspected to be sure there is no engorgement. If all is well, she can be returned to a normal maintenance diet.

Worming and Puppy Shots

Almost all puppies have adult round worms in the intestinal tract by two or three weeks of age. Because this parasite is so ubiquituous, often transferred from dam to fetus, it is almost impossible to prevent it. Accordingly, most breeders worm their puppies before they send them to their new homes. A stool check should always be made before giving any worm medication. Other parasites may need to be attended to at the same time. A follow-up stool check should be made at three months of age and a second course prescribed if more parasites are found. Puppy shots are given when the litter is about eight to ten weeks old. These shots pretect against distemper, leptospirosis and hepatitis. A rabies shot is given at six months of age. If interstate health regulations require a rabies certificate to ship a puppy, a rabies vaccination can be given before six months. Booster shots are required at regular intervals.

Socialization

The period between four and sixteen weeks of age has been identified by canine psychologists as THE critical period in the life of a puppy from the point of view of sociability. An undersocialized puppy is at a severe disadvantage later in life, when it is forced to meet strange people, sights and sounds. Try to give the young puppy as wide an exposure as possible to the types of experience which will make up his later life. Obedience classes, and confirmation classes, even for a young puppy, are heartily recommended for their socializing influence. Classes are sponsored by community 4-H Clubs, Scouts, the YMCA and local kennel clubs.

15

Choosing a
Great Pyrenees Puppy

ONCE YOU HAVE your heart set on owning a Great Pyrenees, the question becomes whether to purchase a male or female puppy. At what age? And from whom?

The male dog is certainly more impressive. He may be a little less easy to housebreak and more inclined to roam if not confined. When mature, he seeks the company of females. His exuberance could present a problem for an elderly owner. Should you already own another male of a large breed, a female is by far the wiser choice. Two adult males of any large breed seldom, if ever, learn to live together peaceably.

A female, while somewhat less impressive, is more refined in every way than her male counterpart. Quick to sense the moods of her master, she is often more openly affectionate. A female goes into season at about one year of age and every six months thereafter. During this period she attracts males and must be closely confined.

A spayed female makes an outstanding house pet. Having no puppies of her own, she remains attentive and devoted to her family. She is subject to fewer health problems; she will probably eat less and live longer than her unspayed-sisters, or brothers. A spayed female cannot, of course, be shown. The operation should be considered only after her first season.

The best age at which to buy a Great Pyrenees puppy is when the individual is about eight to twelve weeks old. At this age you can usually tell whether the pup is going to be a show or breeding prospect. This is also the best age at which to ship. Puppies younger than four months, in particular, are formative. Most new owners prefer to take charge of the care and training of their puppy while it is still young and impressionable. But most of all, if they buy an older dog they miss all the fun of watching their puppy grow up.

In the matter of selecting a kennel and picking your puppy, most of the leading dog publications, including the *AKC Gazette*, carry kennel advertisements for Great Pyrenees. The American Kennel Club (51 Madison Avenue,

New York, N.Y. 10010—Tel. 212–481–9200) can provide you with the name and address of the current Secretary of the Great Pyrenees Club of America who, in turn, will mail you a listing of breeders.

After you locate several breeders who appear to have the kind of puppy you are looking for, write to each one and explain whether you are interested in a male or female, plan to show or breed, or are looking for a family companion and pet. A sincere inquiry, providing the breeder with some information about the prospective buyer, is much more likely to elicit the type of information you are looking for than a hastily scribbled inquiry.

Ask about prices. A Great Pyrenees is not an inexpensive dog. It's generally true that you get what you pay for. Try to purchase the best puppy you can afford. Inquire about kennel policies for warranting unsound puppies or guaranteeing quality. If you buy a pup as a show and breeding prospect, this guarantee should include some provision for the correct "bite" and pigmentation; a stable disposition; and sound hips and bone structure. Of course, no breeder should be expected to offer you a guarantee that the pup will win in the show ring. Picking a future champion at eight weeks of age is extremely difficult, even for breeders with considerable personal experience. Then, too, the care, training, feeding, medical care and socialization of the pup after the purchase are every bit as important as is the genetic background of the parents.

At times, the bloodlines you esteem most highly may be found a long distance away. This need not deter you because, thanks to the improved airlines' standards, transportation of dogs has become a commonplace and safe procedure. To many buyers, however, this mail order service is abhorrent. They feel that to miss the personal exhilaration of making their own selection is to miss all the fun.

There is no need to panic when, on the appointed day, you find yourself standing before a litter of bouncing puppies and find that all appear to be, at first glance, equally loveable. Take your time and go over them in every detail. Common sense will prevent any serious mistakes.

At this age they should be active, alert, playful and full of vitality. Any that shrink away when spoken to, or that attempt to run away and hide, can be classified as shy. They may possibly overcome this later, but taking the chance is not worthwhile.

Examine them first head-on. The pigment should be strong; the nose black and shining; and the lips and eyerims the same. Staining below the inner corner of the eye indicates weeping. This may only be a passing phase, but it can also be a danger signal of future troubles such as blocked tear glands, loose lids, allergy or inverted eyelashes.

Raise the lips and check the gums; they should be bright and pink. Puppies with pale gums often become listless, weak or pallid—either because they need worming or because of a more serious problem.

226

Picking a puppy is a simple matter.

"We'll take one of each."
Mrs. Denise Tudhope's first litter in South Africa.

227

Look at the teeth. The upper and lower front teeth should meet edge to edge (an even bite), or overlap slightly as do the blades of a scissors. A gap between the upper and lower teeth indicates that the bite is undershot or overshot. This would be unacceptable in a show or breeding prospect.

Check inside the ears. They should be clean, sweet-smelling, pink and free of accumulated dirt or wax. The position of the ears—set at a level with the eyes, held low and close to the head—can usually be appreciated at this age. High-set ears may drop when the pup is older, but all other things being equal, pick the puppy with low set ears.

Next part the hair and look at the skin. It should be bright and clean and free of rash, eczema and fleas. The coat itself should be thick, furry, have a good live feel to it and show some gloss or sheen. The skin should also be loose; so much so that you can gather up a handful without disturbing the pup. A tight-skinned pup is in poor condition, often from worms, and should not be considered until the condition is corrected.

As the pups move about and play, watch especially for those with wide, well-angulated rears and good strong pumping action in *both* hind legs. It may be apparent that some are pushing more with one rear leg than the other. The weaker leg may also have a slight swiveling motion. This may disappear, but unfortunately it often remains with the individual for life.

A blocky pup, one of those broad-chested, four-square pups built like a tank, is a better prospect than a lanky one. Pay attention, too, to the front legs. They should be strong, well-boned and straight when viewed from the front and side. Toeing out (east-west front), out at the elbows, weak pasterns and splay feet are faults that are quite visible, even at this age. The tail should reach to the hocks, with perhaps a little to spare.

And don't select a pup with long toes. Choose instead an individual with the shorter, slightly arched toe structure that indicates a close-cupped foot, rather than a hare-foot, in the adult.

Dewclaws should be present on all legs: double on the rear, single on the front. Inspect the rear dewclaws carefully. Single dewclaws, or misshapen dewclaws, are not uncommon. A malformed or an absent rear dewclaw would be a real liability to a dog in the show ring.

The back should be straight, level, broad and strong. It is relatively easy to spot the pup with either a roached or sway back. Others may have backs which are nearly level but seem hunched up in the rear. This could be a danger sign. Dysplasia is something of a problem in any large breed. Ask if the parents have been certified clear of this ailment (by appropriately taken hip X-rays).

Palpate the male pups to see if both testicles are descended. At this age, testicles can retract, which can make this a somewhat difficult exercise which requires patience. Occasionally, one testicle does not descend until the dog is 16 weeks old. However, one that does not descend by 16 weeks may never de-

An evenly badger-marked puppy with an engaging expression. Markings of this type fade as the puppy matures, leaving grey fringes on the ears. The pigment around the eyes and on the nose of this eight-week-old pup is complete.

A promising youngster—still an adolescent at five months. Note the position of the ears, the root being set at a level with the eyes.

scend. A dog without two fully descended testicles is automatically disqualified in the show ring under American Kennel Club rules.

A sweet disposition is essential to most breeds and this is certainly the case with the Pyrenees whose adult size and weight are impressive. As good health and a good disposition so often go hand in hand, it is perhaps wise, in making the final selection, to pick the individual that appears to be really bursting with vitality and self-confidence.

After you have made your purchase, you will want, and should receive, advice and counsel in the future weeks. Any guarantees concerning the puppy should be discussed and agreed upon *before* the check is signed.

Before leaving the kennel be sure to ask for and receive the pup's registration papers, pedigree, health certificate, information on when puppy shots (DHL) were given, and a diet sheet. You may want to change his diet later on, but when moving a young animal into new surroundings it is important that his food at least be recognizable.

"Pick of the litter." A Parisian tourist has purchased a pup from a shepherd in the village, and has been told to go out to the farm and help himself. — Eugene Gayot, *Le Chien*, Paris, 1867.

16

Care and Upbringing of the Great Pyrenees

DESPITE HIS LARGE SIZE, the Great Pyrenees is an ideal house pet. He is not clumsy or awkward in any way. He is naturally fastidious and therefore easy to house train. He can live outside in almost any weather. There is no climate too cold—so long as shelter is provided. He is able to adapt to hot weather as well, if he is given shade and plenty of fresh water at all times.

Unlike the coat of some short-haired breeds who seem to shed continuously, the Pryenees' coat is neat and tidy. The double coat insulates against dirt, which brushes right out instead of working into the skin. A dog will shed his coat once a year. A female, however, may shed after each heat season; and again after whelping a litter. A thorough coat brushing once or twice a week will keep a Pyrenees in sparkling condition.

The New Puppy

A Great Pyrenees puppy is usually weaned by four to six weeks of age. Shortly thereafter he will be ready to join his new family. A pup who arrives at his new home is often tired, thirsty, and most of all unhappy at not finding his brothers and sisters. For the first night or two, confine him in a room with a loud ticking clock or a radio for company—and perhaps a blanket to pull and tug. Some pups howl and bark. This should be anticipated and ignored if possible. A pup will adjust more quickly if left alone. Pyrenees puppies love to slap and play in their water. Water bowls may have to be put down at frequent intervals if spillage is to be avoided.

A constant nervous fuss is upsetting to a puppy. Respect his sleep periods; let him spend some time by himself.

During the first six months in particular, bones are soft and growing rapidly. Strenuous play on slick surfaces, such as kitchen linoleum and wet cement, can cause the feet to slip and slide, potentially damaging growth cartilages. Jumping from sofas, or down several stairs at a time, is to be discouraged.

Most breeders supply a diet sheet with a new puppy. It should be followed for the first few weeks, at least, since an abrupt change in diet can cause digestive disturbances. The Pyrenees is not a heavy eater. This often comes as a surprise, since it is usually assumed that a large dog will eat a great deal of food. Then, too, he is not active for long periods at a time. As a consequence, he eats no more than dogs of medium weight.

Modern dog products supply all the protein, carbohydrate and minerals needed to raise a healthy Pyrenean puppy—provided he eats it well. Vitamin and mineral supplements need not be given to the average eater. A poor eater may need supplements. This decision should be left up to your veterinarian. Giving calcium and vitamins to a pup who doesn't need them is not only foolish economy, but may actually be harmful to his growth.

After three months of age, a puppy can be fed any of a number of high quality modern kibble preparations. Meats, cottage cheese, milk or table scraps may be added. This does *not* include pastry, candy, potatoes, greasy foods, splintery bones and other indigestible morsels.

Older puppies should be fed twice a day, as much as they will eat in 20 minutes. Then pick up the dish. As a rule of thumb, feed the puppy up to his appetite. The only thing to avoid, and it doesn't happen often at this age, is feeding a puppy too much. An overweight puppy is in danger of developing structural defects.

An older dog will be kept trim by feeding once a day. Calorie requirements differ from dog to dog, are less as the dog grows old, and are less in warm weather. In our experience, the amounts suggested by the product manufacturers are usually grossly over-estimated in Pyrenees.

Obesity in the adult dog is usually due to feeding ''snacks'' and ''treats'' between meals. Most of these are high in sugar and therefore very palatable! Common sense will aid the owner in keeping his dog in trim condition.

A pen or fenced-in yard is an absolute necessity. There are times when you have to leave your puppy alone. It is best to leave him in a safe enclosure out of doors, rather than in the house where he can get into mischief. A Pyrenees should not be allowed to run free in a neighborhood. He could be hit by a car or stolen. Dogs will roam out of a natural curiosity, or in search of a breeding mate. Bitches, of course, MUST be confined for the full 21 days of their seasons.

A pen ten feet long by five feet wide is adequate for a house pet. A kennel dog should have one twice this size. The fence must be six feet tall and made of chain link. The pen should be surfaced with ½ inch gravel to a depth of several inches. If your Pyrenees is a digger, line the pen beneath the gravel with chicken wire. The gate should be made to latch securely. Pyrenees are quite adept at lifting latches with their noses.

For sanitary reasons, dirt is a poor surface on which to kennel a dog. Cement is undesirable also. It can cause splayed feet and broken down pasterns.

A good practice is to put your puppy in his pen for an hour or two each day. Make it a pleasurable experience by feeding him in it.

Dogs can harbor a number of intestinal parasites. The appropriate antihelmenthic can be chosen only after a microscopic examination of stool showing the parasite, its eggs or larvae. This requires the skills of a veterinarian. There are a number of patent worm preparations available at pet shops and dog shows. Some of these are not only ineffective against the parasite in question, but may be harmful if used too often. Avoid over-worming with harsh or unsound preparations.

Obtain your puppy's immunization record and be sure to keep it current.

Training

Begin to train your Great Pyrenees puppy in ordinary household manners as soon as he arrives. He is, by nature, eager to win his master's approval at all times. Use this important attribute to its greatest advantage. Reinforce his desire to respond to praise and affection—not to punishment.

Never strike a Pyrenees. In a sensitive breed such as ours, striking with the open hand makes a dog shy and distrustful of people. If a Pyrenees needs to be severely disciplined, give him a verbal tongue-lashing and take him to his pen via choke collar and leash—not by seizing and dragging him by the scruff of the neck!

A mature Great Pyrenees is an animal with a definite sense of independence. Accordingly, he must be shown, while still a puppy and easy to dominate, that he has a circumscribed place in the family hierarchy. Don't allow your puppy liberties you don't intend to give him when he grows up. Dogs have wonderful memories! A successful relationship between dog and master is based on firmness and consistency.

Housebreaking may be started as soon as the pup moves in. But don't begin to punish him for his mistakes until he is old enough to understand—usually not before four months of age. Instead, take your puppy out of doors several times during the day, immediately after meals and long naps, the last thing at night and the first thing in the morning. If you lead him to the same area each time, it helps to inspire the desired action. After he has done what he came to do, praise him excessively. If the pup is not consistent at night, confine him to a small area. A Pyr pup will not soil his bed or his sleeping quarters.

Your puppy should be taught to walk freely on a leash and have good manners, especially if you are planning to show him. After all, no judge is amused by a dog who cuts capers in the show ring.

Start first with a soft nylon or leather collar and switch later to a light choke collar. Leave a collar on for short periods only. Then attach a leash which can be dragged along behind. Next, pick up the leash and begin to lead the puppy with occasional firm tugs, interspersed with lots of pats and "well-dones". Accustom your pup to walk on the left side, to move out smartly and stay abreast—neither lunging ahead or dragging behind. As the exercise progresses, exert a little more force with each tug—then stop and adjust the pup in a show pose. This is good discipline, whether or not you intend to show. But if you do, be sure your pup always stands (never sits) when you come to a stop.

A choke collar should always be removed after an exercise. A dog running loose with a choke collar is in grave danger. A foot could get caught between the collar and his neck, or the collar could become snagged on a fence. Collars, in general, are best left off, especially if you plan to show. They may break the coat and stain the hair. In communities where collars and tags are required, use a well-fitting, soft, round leather collar. It is least likely to damage the coat, and is certainly the safest.

For those interested in showing in conformation, begin your pup at once with the daily routine of "stacking." The pup should learn to stand easily, without moving, as a person grooms and handles him. Put the pup on a raised table about a foot or so high. It affords better exposure for grooming and saves an aching back.

Another important exercise is to teach the pup to come promptly when called. This is basically an extension of the leash training exercise. Let your pup out to the end of a long rope and, as you call him by his NAME, give the rope a quick tug. When he moves toward you, shorten the rope. He will eventually have no choice but to come to you all the way. Respond by giving him lavish praise and a choice tidbit. Repeat this exercise over and over until your pup is letter perfect before removing the rope.

Never call your dog to you to receive punishment. If he refused to obey a command to COME, show your displeasure by catching him and leading him to his pen. He must learn that obedience is inevitable. Whenever you give a command, be sure to make it stick!

Pyrenees puppies chew in order to develop strong teeth and powerful jaws. A pup should be given a hard rubber ball or a rawhide toy to gnaw. He should not be allowed to start working on the furniture. If you catch him in the act, give him his toy and point out in no uncertain terms that you would much prefer he chew on it instead. Various spray-on products leave an unpleasant scent which will effectively discourage chewing on such items. They work well if you take the time to apply them.

Chronic or neurotic barking is a sign of boredom or lack of attention. Chaining a dog is not only conducive to barking but is an open invitation to a bad disposition and poor physical development.

Barking in the house often can be controlled by confining the dog where he can't see or hear what's going on outside.

A Pyrenees puppy is, to say the least, an exuberant animal. He is more than a match for the average child, and likes nothing better than a good chase and a tussle. If allowed to become overly excited in play, he may unintentionally nip, scratch, or even knock over a small child. Accidents such as these can be avoided by careful supervision. As he grows older he will automatically begin to play with a soft mouth.

A well-behaved Pyrenees is a source of pride and joy; a tremendous asset to any family; and a notable deterrent to any would-be thief or vandal. He instinctively feels that his home and family are the center of his universe and that he is duty bound to guard and protect them against all trespassers. All the kindness and affection which you show to your puppy will return to you measure for measure, with love and devotion, in the years that follow.

Some DO's and DON'T's

DO take your Pyrenees to the veterinarian for periodic check-ups. Worm only when indicated and under medical supervision. Keep all vaccinations current.

DO register your dog with the Kennel Club. An owner who is proud of his dog is proud to have it registered with the official organization. It enhances the dog's value.

DON'T clip your dog's coat in summer. This ruins the coat and exposes the skin to sunburn.

DON'T force your Pyrenees to take violent exercise in hot weather. This can lead to heat stroke.

DON'T remove the dewclaws. They are a necessary breed characteristic. Their removal will eliminate your dog in the show ring.

DO provide plenty of fresh water. A Pyrenees requires much more water than other breeds of comparable size—especially in warm weather.

DO give your pup plenty of daily exercise. This is the best way to insure that he grows into a sound healthy dog.

DON'T leave a choke collar on your Pyrenees.

DO plan to take your dog to obedience class. Consult a good book, such as *The Koehler Method of Dog Training*

Finally, DO teach your children to respect the puppy in his routine. This is excellent training for children, as well as being good for the dog.

Accustom the puppy to a thorough grooming once a week. Like a good surgical operation, this requires adequate exposure and a competent assistant. Note the "experts" at work. — *J. Clawson*

17

How to Groom
Your Great Pyrenees

THE GREAT PYRENEES is one of the easiest of all breeds to maintain properly. Because he is a real working dog, he has been endowed by nature with a coat which is self-cleaning and mat and tangle resistant. Whereas there are many different methods to keep him snowy white and in top condition, thee there is only one goal—to enhance his centuries-old beauty and not to alter his appearance by artificial man-made means.

This natural look is a combination of a relatively coarse yet supple outercoat of long guard hair which contains natural oils and is weather resistant; and a dense woolly undercoat which adds body and insulating properties. The top coat lies almost flat.

This magnificent coat can be kept magically white and free from mats and tangles and loose dead hair by a thorough brushing at least once a week with a wire carding or pin brush. Take special care to see that the soft woolly hair behind the ears is completely brushed out. This is the one area where lumps of fur do form if neglected. If such lumps are present, use sharp scissors and *carefully* cut downward towards the skin into the fur ball in narrow strips; then tease these out with your fingers.

Groom under the ear flaps after the dog has been in tall grass, weeds and brush. Foreign material, mostly plant matter, can enter the ear canal by first clinging to the hair surrounding the external orifice. To remove dirt and debris, use a cotton swab saturated with 70% alcohol. This dries quickly without leaving moisture, which predisposes to ear canal infection.

A regular inspection of the teeth will tell you if there is any build-up of tartar. This can be removed with a dental instrument; or by your veterinarian at the dog's routine check-up.

If the toenails are not worn down by activity, they should be filed or trimmed. Pay special attention to the front and rear dewclaws which don't make surface contact. The rear dewclaws can rather quickly grow around into the pad if they are not regularly trimmed.

Bathing is best restricted to an occasional bath for a specific purpose. During shedding, for example, a bath will help to loosen the dead undercoat.

At all times, make grooming a pleasurable experience for your Pyrenees. If he grows to dislike the basic routine, or if he becomes restive, a simple procedure is made most difficult.

If this seems overly brief, it is because there is little, other than common sense, involved. Only if you wish to show your Pyrenees will he require additional grooming.

To take any Pyrenees into the show ring poorly groomed is to do the breed a great injustice.

It is not necessary or advisable to bathe before every show. There are certain risks with bathing. If, for example, the dog is due to shed, the bath will hasten shedding and loss of coat. Over-bathing also deprives the coat of its natural oils, leaving it dull and brittle, And a wet undercoat next to the skin can begin a cycle of dermatitis. However, when the coat is badly stained or has a strong odor, when it appears lumpy in spite of thorough brushings, the only solution is a complete bath.

The Bath

All bathing and trimming should be done at home several days prior to the show. Heavily built dogs with an abundant coat should be bathed about a week before the show to give the coat time to quiet down. Slender dogs, or dogs losing coat, should be washed the day before the show so that the coat can be fluffed as much as possible during the drying process.

First, brush out the coat, removing any knots or mats, and plug the ears with cotton. Wet the head and body thoroughly. Use a good commercial dog shampoo made especially for white-coated breeds. Lather and rinse the head carefully, keeping soap and water out of the eyes. After the whole dog has been lathered and rinsed, re-lather and re-rinse the legs, feet, and those areas of stubborn stain again.The secret of getting a white and lustrous coat, one with "silver tips" shining at the ends of the hairs, is to rinse, rinse and rinse again! Soap left in the coat yellows it. It will also cause it to turn green if you should happen to use a bluing in the final rinse. And then the whole process will have to begin again from scratch.

Next, dry the coat gently using either towels, a professional groomer's hair dryer, or a vacuum cleaner adjusted to blow. Whatever the means, handle the coat carefully to preserve the integrity of every hair possible. While the coat is still damp, a firm holding hair spray or lacquer can be worked into the hair of the hock, ruff or topline—wherever more body is desired. Finish this phase by thoroughly drying the entire coat.

238

To Hold Condition

In between baths, a means of drycleaning the show dog is necessary. There are a number of good commercial drycleaning preparations (such as *Foo Foo*). Besides being expensive for use on a large, white-coated dog, they can cut the coat if used as often as would be necessary in campaigning a Pyrenees. Calcium carbonate, talcum or baby power, Fuller's earth, and corn starch are all effective and can be used frequently without danger of injury to a healthy coat. Various mixtures of any of the above whiteners often lead to good success. If you decide to experiment, use a dog other than the one you are exhibiting. When you have found a combination which whitens and can be completely brushed out, you will know it is a good one.

A day or two before the show, dampen the coat with water, a section at a time, using a trigger-sprayer such as a clean Windex bottle. Sprinkle a large amount of the cleaning agent onto the coat, and work this in well with your hands and a soft bristle brush.

Pin brushes are fine to remove dead hair, but they can do damage to the healthy coat. Do the whole dog and allow the coat to dry completely. For obvious reasons, work outside on a grooming table.

When the coat is dry, *remove all the excess powder!* Cleaning substances remaining on the coat are clearly against American Kennel Club rules. Moreover, if the dog, judge and handler vanish in a white cloud during the examination or the gaiting of the dog, it leaves a very poor impression.

To remove excess powder, start at the bottom of the dog with a soft bristle brush. Brush against the lay of the hair, being careful to get down to the skin. Brush the whole dog. Do this again and again until all traces of the powder are removed. If your Pry doesn't object, a vacuum cleaner simplifies this task.

Trimming

Trimming should be done on a clean, thoroughly brushed dog. The novice should practice and perfect his techniques well in advance of actual exhibiting. The tools needed for trimming are thinning shears, sharp scissors, a steel comb and a stripping tool. A steel file, a grinding appliance, or a standard dog nail clipper may be used to manicure the nails. In trimming the nails, make sure you do not cut or file into the quick. Filing of course, is safer. The nails should be filed back because if the dog stands on his nails the toes will spread.

One principle to remember in trimming is to trim only the undercoat—never the top coat. An exception to this are the feet. The hair on the bottom of the paws should be cut flush with the pads. This also helps to keep the feet from splaying. Using sharp scissors, shape the front and sides of the paw, following the natural curve of the foot. The stray hairs are cut—not chopped.

The Pyrenees foot is not a mop! Your goal is to give the paw a round, compact, close-cupped appearance.

Trim the eyebrows, whiskers, and stray hairs around the mouth to give a neat appearance, as shown on the right. — *Bridget Olerenshaw*

To trim the hocks, brush the hair straight out and settle it down gently with a slicker brush. With sharp scissors held parallel to the leg, trim the hair on the back of the front pastern close at the heel pad and tapering into the feathering of the upper leg. On the back leg, the contour should not be so severe as to spoil the impression of a vertical drop from the hock to the ground. Remove as little hair as possible—just the ragged edges.

On the face, carefully remove the whiskers, stray hairs around the mouth, and the eyebrows to give a neat appearance. A pair of straight manicure scissors with a blunt end is ideal for this job.

Some trimming of the topline and head may also be considered. Occasionally an over-abundance of undercoat, in one part of another, spoils a perfect silhouette. This trimming is difficult and requires skill and patience, if it is to be attempted at all. A quick, rough job will call attention to the area you are attempting to blend.

To level the topline of a dog who appears too high in the rear, thin hair from the rump. Use a comb to lay back the topcoat while exposing the woolly undercoat. With thinning shears, make a few cuts into the wool. Comb this out completely, take a good look, and repeat. The procedure is tedious because only small amounts of hair are removed with each cutting. A fast job with too much hair removed will give the rump a lumpy look.

The day of the show you may want to back brush the rump hair and dampen it with water or a super hold hair spray. Brush it flat and weigh it down with a folded terry towel until dry.

To achieve the appearance of ears set close to the head and level with the eye, thin or strip the woolly hair behind and on top of the ears. Puppies often have large tufts of hair which can spoil a good ear look. Always cut with the

240

Trimming the dewclaws. Clip in front of the quick to avoid pain and bleeding. — *J. Clawson*

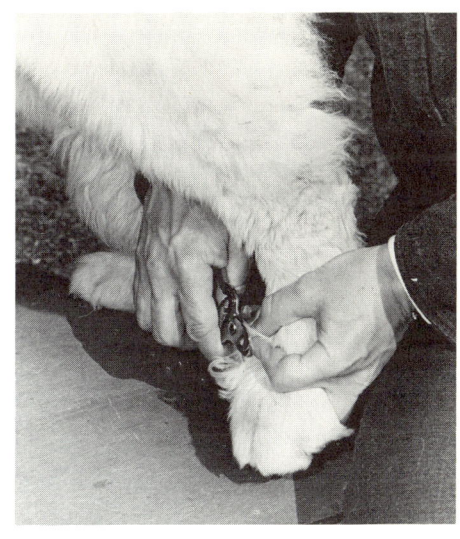

The front feet. Shape the front and sides of the paws by following the natural curve of the foot and blending the back of the pastern into the feathering of the leg. Remove only enough hair to get an even border.

A well-groomed hock and rear pastern achieving a natural look. Not too much hair has been removed.

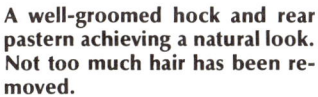

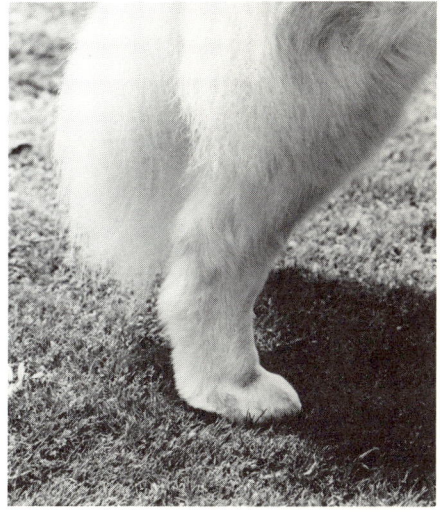

241

Ready for show!

lay of the hair. Remove small amounts and comb out thoroughly to see the result before proceeding further. Too much "doctoring" is readily visible and results in a rough, chopped appearance.

Having now arrived at the show with a clean, trimmed, and thoroughly brushed Pyrenees, it is time to put on the finishing touches. Use chalk on any areas that have picked up dirt. Wipe it off with a damp terry cloth towel or a Show Coat pad. Alcohol will remove every bit of chalk and restore shine, but it is very drying to the hair.

If there is much dry brushing to be done, spray the parts needing further attention lightly with water as you work them over. The water will reduce static electricity and breakage of hair. It won't take long to dry if you spray lightly, using just enough moisture to "stand" the coat up.

Back brush the tail and the neck ruff gently and thoroughly with a pin brush. Brush the feathering and hocks straight out and the hair on the front legs up. Take the dog off the grooming table and let him shake to settle the coat in place. Smooth the rump hair gently with your hands.

Use a white lipstick covered with a bit of chalk to cover eye stain if any is visible. Lastly, put a small amount of vaseline on your finger and apply it to the nose to make it shine. If your dog does not, by nature, have jet black nostrils, do not attempt to conceal this artificially with blackening agents. The result always looks "faked" and the penalty, if caught, is suspension of your showing privileges.

242

18

Showing Your
Great Pyrenees

by Mary W. A. Crane

LET ME SAY right at the outset that showing is *hard work.* If you are not prepared to take the time to train your dog, right from the start, in good manners, etiquette and behavior in the ring; if you are not willing to spend the hours on the grooming; if you are of a disposition that cannot stand DISAPPOINTMENT when you lose (and NO DOG will ever win all the time); and if you are too sensitive to take fault-finding and gossip—then, but only then, DON'T THINK OF SHOWING YOUR DOG. For unfortunately, all these things are bound to happen to you, first or last, in the dog-show game.

Competition can be harsh. Feelings can rise to the surface and words or looks can seem to convey disapproval, criticism and even ill-will among competitors. A loss today for the same dog that won only yesterday calls for a broad philosophical outlook, as well as faith and devotion to the dog, and an optimistic hope for the future! This observation is true with ALL breeds—it is not meant as a criticism of Great Pyrenees' owners alone, of course.

Now that we have eliminated the weak at heart, let us proceed with the positive, brave souls who have the great desire to show their dog. We shall assume, therefore, that you have trained him from puppyhood to WALK freely on a leash; to let people handle him and feel him all over; and to learn not to shy away from or fear the presence of other dogs nearby.

Before you consider taking the fatal step, I earnestly suggest that you attend at least one dog show to observe the procedure and see how it appeals to you. If, having been subjected to it, you have caught the bug, I then suggest that you take your puppy to a MATCH SHOW in your vicinity. These are often called FUN MATCHES. They are informal and instructive, often being more in the nature of picnic get-togethers. One can usually find side classes for all sorts of humorous points from costumes to "the most endearing puppy", to

243

Ch. Cote de Neige Symphonie, winner of over 100 Bests of Breed, and the first American-bred Great Pyrenees to win a Best In Show, at the Tonawanda Valley Kennel Club Show in 1947. Owned by Mrs. Frank C. Butcher.

Ch. Cote de Neige Pastourette was considered a nearly perfect bitch. Note the head and expression. Owned by Mr. and Mrs. C. Seaver Smith, Jr.

Ch. Basquaerie Beau Estagel, three times Best In Show winner in the 1940s. Pictured here winning the Breed under judge Mrs. Sherman R. Hoyt at the '49 National Specialty. Owned and handled by Mrs. Francis V. Crane. — *Evelyn Shafer*

cart pulling, and others. While held under Kennel Club rules, they remain informal in every respect and do not count for championship points.

At these matches you will have the opportunity to meet other "doggy people," although not necessarily in the Great Pyrenees breed; and they, in turn, can advise you how and where to write the show superintendents for listings and entry blanks. Notice particularly the closing date for entries. They close well in advance of the actual day of the show. You alone are responsible for getting your entry in on time. This is STEP NUMBER ONE. Now you are ready to enter a championship show.

If your dog is a puppy (under one year of age) enter in the PUPPY CLASS. If he is over one year, but purely a novice, I would suggest the AMERICAN-BRED CLASS. The OPEN is usually considered the class for older and more experienced dogs. However, if your dog is an import from a foreign country, OPEN is the *only class* for which he is eligible.

Assuming that your dog is now entered, proceed to STEP NUMBER TWO. this is to GROOM well, so that when you appear in the ring you will have a dog of whom you can be justifiably proud. A dog clean and white, well brushed, with whiskers and eyebrows trimmed and with the excess hair around the dewclaws and back of the leg from hock to pad, as well as around the perimeter of the foot, trimmed to a neat line. (This is purely in the interest of tidiness).

I might add that your own appearance should be one of neatness, good grooming and conservatism in dress. In this you will complement your dog to the fullest!

STEP NUMBER THREE is to have your entry on a suitable leash attached to a loose choke collar. The collar should be applied so that the weight of the chain slackens the loop when the lead is held loosely. One keeps the dog alert, and attentive to one's commands, through gentle but firm tugs on the leash, and under control at all times. Do *not* "string" your dog up too tight under the chin as this forces his ears too high and alters his expression. Always move the dog in the ring on a loose leash.

Having your dog thus prepared for his ring debut, be sure that you are at ringside well before the designated time to enter the ring. This is wholly the responsibility of the exhibitor. You will be given an arm-band by the ring steward which is your designated number for this show and is so recorded in the judge's book. The judge is not allowed to see a show catalogue before he judges, so neither you nor your dog is known to him in advance.

Now is the time for you to COLLECT YOURSELF, for when your class and number are called you must walk into the ring. Always remember that the best help you can give your dog is assurance of your faith in him. Convey this confidence to him by a kindly pat. But if your hand is shaking and you are continually fussing over him, resetting his legs, etc., you are only going to make him react nervously as well. This is also annoying to the judge who, wherever he may be, is always conscious of movement in his ring.

Now a word about "baiting" your dog to get an alert expression. Even professional handlers, on occasion, can overdo this gesture. It consists of holding a tempting morsel, a bit of cooked liver, in front of the dog's nose just out of his reach. A handler knows when to lower or remove it for the judge to examine the dog's expression. In a Pyrenees, expression is VERY IMPORTANT. It consists of a tight-lipped mouth with an even bite, a strong rather lengthy and adequate muzzle, slanted oblique eyes, a medium ear set on a level with the eyes, and a broad flat skull. All too frequently the novice exhibitor does not know when to remove the bait, thus keeping the dog off balance and continually stretching out to grab the morsel. This can prevent the judge from properly appraising the animal's head.

Ring procedure is usually pretty stylized. The entries are first moved around the ring, counterclockwise, one behind the other. As they line up, the judge looks them over in a general way and then goes over each dog individually for conformation points (and this is a detailed examination from the mouth to the tail and dewclaws). Each exhibitor is then asked to move his entry up and down in a straight line on a loose lead, often both at a trot and a *walk*. Nothing shows up gait—its action and faults—more quickly than a walk. As the dog approaches the judge he is asked to stop and stand just as he is for the judge's inspection. After these examinations have been completed, the dogs are posed again, one behind the other, while the judge picks his winners down to fourth place (if the class is large enough to boast that many entries).

Am. Can. Ch. Quibbletown Cavalier was shown extensively in the United States and Canada from 1965 to 1975. His record includes 139 Bests of Breed and 21 Group placings. Pictured here winning a Best In Show at the Pacific National Exhibition, B.C., under judge Langdon Skarda. Handled by Gene Hahnlen. Owned by Mr. and Mrs. Charles McConnell. — *Hodges*

Ch. Soleil Pierre de Blu Crest opened the doors for the breed in the 1970s with five Bests In Show. One of the breed's greatest winners, pictured here going Best In Show at the Bucks County Kennel Club Show in 1971. Owned and handled by Vic Capone.

What the Judge is Looking For

Since there has been considerable interest in the matter of what constitutes a good gait, a few words from the judge's viewpoint may be timely. As the judge looks at the entries moving about the ring, he is watching the reach of the legs, both fore and aft; to see that they are of good length and stride. He is looking at the topline, especially at the withers, to see if it bobs up or down, or remains smooth and level as it should. When he moves the dog straight away and back toward him on a loose leash it is to see if the dog travels straight and true in front, or whether the dog is "out at the shoulder", is throwing its legs or feet inward or outward instead of straight ahead, or raising them in a hackney gait. From the rear he looks to see if the legs and feet toe-out (implying cowhocks), inward (bowed legs), move too narrow or too wide (faulty structure), or whether the stride is true and straight ahead at a walk while converging toward the center line as speed increases. When a dog is told to stand naturally his leg structure shows immediately. The front legs should be straight. The stance behind should be well angulated and wide with feet pointing straight ahead, the weight evenly distributed. Movement and stance, as described, often reveal the presence of hip dysplasia, certainly when of a severe nature, and other anatomical faults as well.

The judge will prefer the well-balanced dog, whose height at the withers is as long as its body, who is well proportioned, sound in gait, and TRUE to TYPE.

When all the individual classes have been judged and the winners of each selected, the first place contestants in each sex enter the ring for the judging of *Winners Dog* followed by *Winners Bitch.* The second best is designated *Reserve Winners.* Eligible for this competition is the entry who was second in the same class as the winners, who thus competes against the remaining winners of all the classes in each sex, for the Reserve titles.

The final breed competition then moves into the ring. It includes Winners Dog, Winners Bitch, and those Champions in the breed, irrespective of sex, who have been entered as Specials. It is from this final array that Best of Breed is chosen, as well as Best of Opposite Sex to Best of Breed, and Best of Winners (competition between Winners Dog and Winners Bitch). Later, the Best of Breed will be called to enter the Working Group which, in turn, is composed of the Best of Breed winners in the 30 or so breeds found in this Group.

The final progression is the judging for Best in Show which brings together the winners of the six Groups: Sporting, Hound, Working, Terrier, Non-Sporting and Toy.

Ch. Quibbletown Cinderella U.D., the first Great Pyrenees
to earn the Utility Degree, in 1960. Owned by Mrs. Silbert.
— *Schley*

Ch. Barqueill Avant Garde winning the Working Group
at the Shawnee Kennel Club Show in 1975, under judge
Mrs. Maynard Drury. The handler is James L. Rathbun.
Owned by Frankie Glover. — *Gilbert*

249

Ch. Karolaska Polar Nero, winner of two Bests In Show, pictured winning the Working Group under judge Robert Waters, at the Mississippi Valley Kennel Club Show on May 20, 1973. The handler is William T. Kramer. Owned by Dr. and Mrs. James Giffin. — *Ritter*

Ch. Pyrstrom's Ringmaster, winning a Working Group First at Longview, Texas, under judge J. Harry James Thomas, in 1976. The handler is Dick Cooper. Ringmaster's record to date is 48 Group placements, of which 13 are Group Firsts; one Best In Show. The breed's Top Winner in 1975 and 1976. Owned by Miss Nan Hall Hamilton and Mrs. Judith G. Bankus. — *Twomey*

In closing, let me again emphasize five pertinent facts:

1. The judge is looking at *your dog*, not you—so don't be self-conscious.
2. The perfect dog has yet to be born! So the ultimate selection comes down to each judge's personal appraisal of the merits of the dogs under him on that day.
3. A win depends upon the competition present. A dog that wins one day may not win the next under another judge, or against different competition. Dogs vary in their actions from day to day. After all, we all have our good days and our bad—and so do our dogs. It always helps to have a dog who exudes personality and is animated in the ring. You can usually depend upon him to do his best at all times. Shyness, timidity and viciousness are always severely penalized and condemned.
4. Try to watch the techniques of the professional handlers. You can learn many valuable and helpful points by watching how they present their dogs, for their expertise brings out the *best points* in any dog they handle. If they seem to win much of the time (and this is something the perennial "kicker" is apt to complain about), look again and you will see how well their dogs are "put down" (groomed), how well the dogs are moved and posed. These all help the judge to form an opinion of the dog.
5. AND LAST, remember always that the dog you come out of the ring with is the one you took in. If you loved him then, love him now! Enjoy the show—it should not be a chore. Above all, *always be a good sport*—win, lose or draw. Congratulate your opponent and don't argue with the judge!

Bazen de Soum in Massachusetts, just prior to his departure for Labrador in 1932.

Three Alaskan pioneers—hauling the family's fuel. On the far side is Balibasque Beau of Karolaska, CD; on the near side is Quibbletown Queeka Bear. In front, pictured at six months of age in this 1968 photo, is their daughter, Ch. Karolaska Polar Bonnie Bear, who became the top winning bitch in America.

19

The Great Pyrenees
as a Working Dog

A GREAT PYRENEES named Bazen de Soum lived in North Newfoundland in the 1930s. He loved to do sled-work. Here is his story in "his own" words:

> One winter day my mistress, Anna Kivimaki and I decided to show the New-foundlanders that a sled pulled by a Great Pyrenees and two huskies could make the difficult trip from St. Anthony to Canada Bay, a distance of 80 miles, and return. Of course, in those days dog sleds were the chief form of transportation. And if you had business in Canada Bay, you really didn't have much choice.
>
> The morning broke bright and clear, but the going was sort of rough for us at the start because the two huskies were young and inexperienced. As a matter of course, the heaviest dog is usually hitched to the shortest trace as his weight is more effective well to the rear. But when our team finally hit its stride, I was in the lead, the other two milling around on equal length traces behind.
>
> Weather changes with lightning rapidity in northern Newfoundland. On the second day out the temperature dropped and the snow began to fall in a thick blanket. Visibility was down to 50 yards. It was time to think about shelter. The Green Wood *tilt* (log cabin) was five miles away but in the wrong direction.
>
> However, there was an island called Hare Island in the arm of the coastal bay. My mistress had heard that men went there in the seal season to hunt and live in a little shack on the island.
>
> Although she had not actually seen the shack, she decided that this was to be our destination. The sun the day before had broken up the ice, so there was water between the shore and the arm. We crawled along the winding trail among the scrub trees for an exhausting mile before we could finally get out onto the ice.
>
> At this point, my two helpers attempted a mild revolt. Driven back by the blizzard, the huskies tried to get at the seal meat which was tied on top of the komatik in a burlap sack. However, I would allow no such insubordination.

With bared fangs I warned the huskies in no uncertain terms that the meat was forbidden! One crack of my mistress' whip settled the matter. Two huskies thought better of their rascally attempt to sneak the food.

We were all nearly exhausted when we sighted the island. After a bit of searching, we found a very small log cabin complete with a rusty stove for warmth. We knew if the huskies were allowed loose they would high tail it back to civilization. So after we were all fed, I crowded the two huskies under a bunk and stretched out in front. When one stirred the least bit, I growled a warning.

That night we were joined by a party of six men who had come to hunt seals. The blizzard continued for three days, during which time my mistress and the hunters swapped yarns and played a card game called Auction. This was particularly hard on her knuckles, which wrapped the table every time she put down the card that took the trick.

As the third morning dawned clear and cold, I led the team off to a fine start. At one point while crossing the ice a gleam of water suddenly appeared. But by cutting quickly to shore the danger was averted. The next day we were again in good form and my mistress rode part of the way on the sled. And on the third day the wind died and we arrived in Canada Bay well before nightfall.

After a four day rest, during which my mistress looked into the affairs of the Mission sawmill, we prepared for the return journey. On the first day it rained and so we were all exhausted by the time we got to the first *tilt*. The next day was bitter cold. But by now we were in top form. Toward evening we sighted Hare Island. Our friends, the sealers, had seen us coming and had begun to heat tea on the roaring stove.

The next day was ideal. The sun was bright; the snow was hard, and we fairly flew as our mistress shouted the magic words: "Home, home, home!"

My mistress told me we held a record for being the smallest team to make this journey. I was very proud because she said to everyone, "The success was all due to Bazen, our leader, and a real companion on any trip."

Draft Dog

You may wonder if today's Great Pyrenees are the workers they used to be in days gone by. Actually, today's Pyrenees are often given the chance to prove they have the capabilities they once had in the past.

A Pyrenees has done guard duty in the 4-H Dairy Barn at the Sonoma County Fair in California for the past several years. During the day he wanders about the barn, sleeping atop the tack box or happily playing with the children who come by. There is a sign fixed to a stall with the words, "Guard Dog On Duty—Keep Away!" Adults read and believe. Small children ignore the sign and stop to pet the fluffy dog and are greeted with a wet tongue instead of bared teeth.

Nighttime is a different story, though. Here Barbo has the run of the barn and challenges every visitor with a fierce bark. He admits only those who belong. Despite security problems and thefts from other barns, the dairy barn has never been molested.

254

The entertainment between games at Dodger Stadium. Allan and Randy Baab with four of their Companion Dogs.

Barbo is an example of the working Pyrenees at the Poste de Pompier Ranch of Kitty and Norm Carpedus. Kitty and Norm believe that the way to bring out the best in a Pyrenees is to give him the chance to work at his traditional European tasks, guarding livestock and pulling carts. And they have proven it, not only with their own dogs, but with many from unhappy homes who are given to them as a last resort.

Thousands of visitors to the Renaissance Pleasure Faire in Northern California, Mrs. Carpedus tells us, enjoy the sight of Pyrenees pulling children in colorful carts. Few realize that these are not "Sunday cart-pulling Pyrs," but dogs who make their living at this, or similar work, the year around.

One of these dogs, named Snow, is used regularly around his owner's ranch as a draft animal. One wet winter a number of small trees had floated down the creek during a flood and lodged against the fence. To make the field usable, the trees had to be removed, but the ground was too wet for a tractor. With a heavy chain attached to his work harness, Snow half-floated, half-pulled the trees and branches from the field, then snaked them up a small hill and along a gravel road for a total of more than 300 yards.

On his fifth trip out of the field, his 16-year-old owner looked up to see an SPCA truck on the road. The Humane Officer watched as Snow approached off lead, tail wagging, doing what he loved best. The officer grinned and shook his head. "I got a call that a dog was being abused. If you see one, let me know." Turning to leave he remarked, "Now that's what I'd call a *real* working dog!"

255

Pack Dog

It could well be that the demand for the Great Pyrenees as a working dog, and a pack-dog in particular, will increase in the next few years. If so, this could be due, in part, to Rod Perry's soon-to-be released movie about Alaska, entitled "Sourdough." With the rugged beauty of the Alaskan Wilderness as its background, the courage and individuality of both man and dog are seen at their finest. Rod Perry wrote in the *Alaskan Magazine* (Feb., 1976): "Wendy and Goblin, our two Great Pyrenees dogs, are co-stars of "Sourdough" and only their great strength and that of my father (who portrays the Sourdough) made it possible to reach the back country." Here is Rod Perry's account of back-packing with a Pyrenees, written in 1970 and published in the *Pyr-Alaskan:*

My brother, Al, and I are photographers and we own a Great Pyrenees who not only works almost daily, but is a veritable necessity to the continuation of our professional activities. A company that we formed is involved in the production of nature, adventure and travel motion pictures. Our packs containing food and gear for extended bush forays were back-breaking enough before we cast our hats into the cinematography business. But the addition of 50 odd pounds of camera equipment and film soon led to the realization that we had to find a gimmick.

We began to consider all possibilities in the realm of mountain transportation—from mechanical conveyances to mules, llamas to yaks. One idea after another was discarded. Reasons for this ranged from mechanical breakdown to difficulty in providing feed. Many of the wilderness routes we take will stop a goat and bog a snipe. Nothing we could think of could follow us over these courses.

Then we considered dogs. Perhaps our answer lay somewhere within the canine fraternity. But they'd have to meet several requirements. They must be able to haul sizeable payloads for long distances over difficult terrain. Prerequisites for this would be great size, strength, endurance and willingness to work. Obviously, we could not tolerate a dog that tended to give chase or bark at the sight of game. Thus, an animal of calm disposition and trainability was needed. Could any dog measure up? We investigated the various breeds to see if any fitted our needs. We finally purchased a year-old Pyrenees bitch named "Sugar" from Ted Rumsey of Eagle River.

After a period during which Sugar received strict Obedience training from Al, we decided it was time for her to make her first trip into the mountains. Al strapped a pack to her back and they were off on a forty mile jaunt. Many dogs, new to the game, take time to adjust to the weight and swing of the load. Sugar just fell into the job as if she'd done it all her life. No hesitation, not even as much as a wondering glance at the strange encumbrance on her back. Al had placed it there and to her that was reason enough to pack it.

At first the load collided with a log here or a rock there and caught on a protruding branch. But she has since learned just how far the bags protrude and now seldom experiences any difficulty. She discovered that if she jumped over a

Ch. Cavalier Michel—a modern undercover agent. What precious contraband do you carry?

downed log she would high center on the pack bottoms. Now she jumps on top of the log with all four feet before she continues over. She sizes up other difficult situations at a glance and has become very adept at picking her own way around places that would hang her up.

By late Fall she had packed about 500 miles. Not many Pyr owners have the opportunity to see what really hard work will do for their dogs' muscle tone. To witness her corded muscles methodically sauntering over the mountain under more than half her weight in moose meat makes one shake his head in disbelief. But when a grueling day is done and her pack is finally removed, to watch her romp and beg for a game of tag is worthy of a Charlie Chaplin double take!

While on one filming jaunt, Al and Sugar located a mineral lick that attracted about a hundred white Dall Sheep. While filming them Al frequently left Sugar for long periods on "Stay" as he searched for interesting camera angles. Not once did she show any inclination to rush the animals. Perhaps their similarity to domestic sheep awakened age-old instincts.

As Al and Sugar left the mountain near dusk one day, they jumped a black bear at fifteen yards. Sugar growled a warning and showed some willingness to mix it with the bruin. A sharp command from Al kept her at heel.

We feel that Sugar would tackle a bear if one of us were charged while filming. It is hoped that we never require these services of her. I'm sure that with its lightning quickness and great strength, an average-sized black bear would be a match for more than one Pyrenees in a fight to the death. A lone dog burdened with a heavy pack would give a bear little trouble but the distraction might just give us time to make a getaway.

Most breeds constitute a health hazard in Bear Country. Bowser as readily chases the bruin as he would the neighbor's cat. The big difference in comparing bear and cat chases is that when the very irate she grizzly is pounding after Bowser, he runs to you for protection! A downright unsanitary situation.

257

However, the Great Pyrenees is usually content to mind his own business. If trouble comes his way, he is not one to back down; but he doesn't go out and look it up. So Sugar is a real advantage in Bear Country.

Sugar adapts well to new and unusual situations. The first time we introduced her to a canoe she came aboard as if she were an old voyager. She has since canoed over 200 miles and has never given us any trouble. One time after we upset the canoe in the rapids, she even brought Al's down jacket ashore.

The Great Pyrenees has other advantages that make the breed an asset to an operation like ours. Low metabolism is one. Even carrying up to a two-week supply of dry dog food, Sugar still packs a good share of our camping equipment. Another advantage is the beautifully photogenic quality of these animals.

Lately, Al has been preparing Sugar for the Anchorage Fur Rendezvous weight-pulling contest. She has taken to the sled work readily. After only ten days of pulling in our firewood, she is breaking loose and pulling over four times her weight.

Incidentally, Sugar did indeed enter the weight-pulling contest and finished second among 23 entries, pulling the fantastic weight of 1325 pounds! Most of her competition came from the Saint Bernards, weighing 150 to 200 pounds. The winner was a part Pyr and part Husky who pulled 1375 pounds. From the reports we received, it appears that most of the weight was pulled by the Pyr part.

For the lover of winter sports, the Great Pyrenees has other unique and interesting uses. A French breeder tells of his experience in crossing the Alps on skiis from Nice to Lake Leman with eight Pyrenees. Some of these were dog-porters and others served as guides, forging ahead but stopping with infallible instinct at dangerous snow, thereby finding the safe paths. When the slopes become too gradual for downhill skiing, the dogs served as horses, pulling their master through the glistening powder at nothing less than a gallop. His dogs were also used for life-saving work. They were trained to bring back a piece of clothing from the lost traveler and then lead the rescue party back to the scene.

A delightful story of the intelligence of a Great Pyrenees comes from Mrs. Crane:

"Frenchmen of all walks of life seem to be in complete agreement on the fact that the Pyrenees is the most intelligent dog in the world. As an illustration let me cite a tale that may be hard for most of you to believe. Some years ago a personal friend of mine, living in southern France, told of an instance that she herself witnessed. It is, therefore, told with the utmost sincerity. One of the dogs was trained to fetch water from the village square. He would carry a bucket in his mouth, go to the trough, turn on the spigot, fill the pail, turn off the spigot, and carry the brimming pail home.

"When I told this to my veterinarian he laughed and said, 'That's all right, but you better leave out the part about turning off the spigot.' And the rest of you may feel the same."

258

Two early Cote de Neige Pyrenees—at home in the mountains. — *Press Pictures*

Guard Dog

The amazing intelligence of the Pyrenees dogs, as well as their capacity to act with prudent foresight, is shown by two incidents narrated by Dr. Edmond S. Bordeaux (*Messengers from Ancient Civilizations*). Both are delightful examples of the traits we look for in our present day Pyreneans:

My summers of childhood were spent on my family's estate in Dordogne, France. And inextricably linked with my memories of the hundreds of acres of giant walnut trees, apple orchards, the centuries-old stone buildings, and the stern matriarchial figure of my grandmother, were the magnificent Pyrenean Mountain Dogs which guarded our estate.

All of the dogs were of breathtaking beauty and immense size—their snow-white coats covering lean muscles, toned to perfection by their daily romps with the small shepherd boys. These boisterous games of wrestling, hide and seek and tag, were welcome diversions from their daily schedule of hard work. For these dogs were, first and foremost, guardians of the highest caliber, using their amazing intelligence in feats of strategy that would shame a general.

One example I will always remember was the "incident of the apple thieves," an event which made a peculiar impression on my young mind. Toward the end of every summer, our hundreds of huge apple trees were loaded down with dark red, juicy beauties waiting to be harvested and sent to market,

Leading his master's flock to summer pasturage.

all protected from greedy view by a high stone wall which surrounded the entire estate. But the determination of small boys is a powerful thing, and on this day, two clever little entrepreneurs had spirited away from their father's tool shed a stepladder, letting their common sense be overruled by the thought of how sweet that first bite of stolen apple would taste. They found a likely spot and hoisted one side of the stepladder over the wall. Then they climbed up merrily, all prepared to come down the other side. However, their well-laid plans did not materialize! The boys did not know that the five Pyreneans had heard them long before they had the ladder in place. But, intelligent strategists that they were, they did nothing—only came to a spot near the plotted crime and waited and watched, silent and unmoving. One of them stationed himself near one of the many dog-size openings that were to be found all along the perimeter of the stone wall, clever little doors which allowed a dog to get out, but which could not be re-entered. And the moment that both little criminals were on top of the wall, ACTION! One dog rushed through the wall opening and got to the ladder in time to prevent either of them escaping as they had come, three dogs stayed at their post to prevent the culprits from descending into the orchard, and the fifth dog ran for the gardener. Such teamwork!

The end was woefully predictable. The good gardener arrived, removed the stepladder and thanked the boys for bringing him such a fine one which he could certainly use. He also told them that to steal from one's neighbors is a very bad thing, and if they had come to the front gate and asked, he would have given them each a bag of apples. Then he went outside, let the Pyrenean back in through the gate, and left the boys to jump off the wall, go home without a step-ladder, and meditate on the sorrows of a life of crime.

Another example of the amazing intelligence and teamwork shown by the Pyreneans concerned again a small boy—this time, the son of a houseguest who wandered where he was warned not to go. The forbidden spot was a large cistern full of water, just a small swimming pool to an adult, but dangerous for a small child who did not know how to swim. But hanging over the cistern was a very large pear tree, and at this time of year its branches were heavy with juicy golden pears, made all the more tempting by their forbidden location. The worst happened: The little boy reached for a pear and fell into the water, but luckily his howls were heard by the five Pyreneans before he had a chance to take a breath and howl again. When the dogs reached the cistern, one jumped in im-mediately and grabbed the child's jacket in his teeth, holding the screaming boy afloat. The others stayed where they were and waited until the dog in the water had dragged his protesting charge to the side. Then all four, scrambling and pushing, managed to pull the child out of the cistern and on to the ground (fortu-nately, the water level was high). The boy's clothes were in shreds after this over-enthusiastic rescue, but he was safe and whole—though it was a long time before he went pear-hunting again!

National magazines for sheep breeders carry ads for Great Pyrenees under the listing: Sheep-Dogs—Guard. A Washington State sheepman reported that his first Pyrenees saved him $1500. The year before, he had lost nearly a hun-dred lambs to coyotes and feral dogs. In 1969 the University of Wyoming sponsored a project to test the use of Pyrenees on sheep ranches. The project is still in progress.

In fact, today's Pyrenees, like his mountain ancestor, needs no training or special instruction to attack wolves, coyotes or other predators. This is not a learned response, it is a breed instinct—stronger than fear or regard for per-sonal safety.

Two examples serve to illustrate this characteristic trait. The first concerns a spayed Pyrenees bitch, Elysee Pollyanna. It is based on a story which ap-peared three years ago in the *Marshfield News*:

The predators referred to in Missouri as "wolves" are actually both coyotes and coy-dogs, the latter being hybrid crosses with feral dogs, often at-taining greater size than their wild canine cousins. Some time ago, a pack of these animals fell upon T. H. Macdonnell's sundry stock dogs, killing one and mangling several others. The dogs lost all spirit for fighting and, at the howl of the pack, would always turn tail and flee to the security of the house or barn. Macdonnell is a serious rancher and raises a fine strain of Herefords. At calving time, predator losses were seriously undermining his breeding pro-gram. After trying several different breeds and finding none suited to the work of protecting his calves, Macdonnell acquired a Pyrenees named Polly. She proved her worth, at least as far as Mrs. Macdonnell was concerned, by showing the cattle that the family garden was not the proper place to take their evening snack!

Polly needed no special instructions to size up the situation as far as the wolves were concerned. One late afternoon when icy sleet was falling, a wild pack was heard in the lower pasture. Polly and a stock dog sped down to the quarter-mile fence, but the Collie, smelling the wolves and recalling his recent encounter, turned and ran back to crouch trembling between the rancher's legs. The Pyrenees continued on to the half-mile gate and turned into the woods. As Macdonnell arrived he saw a large silver animal (at first he thought it was his Pyrenees) lunge from behind a bush and grab his bitch by the throat, throwing her to the ground. But she tore free and the two animals met head to head, rearing high and snarling in the heat of combat. The outcome was obvious—the pack leader was no match for the Pyrenees, and turning tail he fled with Polly in close pursuit. The leaves were scraped bare where the animals fought. As the rancher went on he eventually came upon three newborn calves with Polly standing guard, open-mouthed, smiling, and breathing heavily. There wasn't a mark on her!

Unfortunately, this was not to be the case after the next encounter. The coyotes, having superior numbers, fought as a pack. Some of them worked behind her and tore at her tail and hindquarters. As she crawled back to the ranch, her tail was dangling from a four-inch stub. After two operations and an inevitable tail amputation, Polly returned to her family with a sorely wounded dignity. For weeks she hid herself under the bushes so nobody could make fun of her sorry appearance.

Interestingly, the loss of her tail never affected her balance or agility.

One might forgive a dog for losing its spirit after such an experience, but in Polly's case such sympathy would have been wasted. Rather than diminishing her courage it made her only the more determined to hold her supremacy in her own territory. The cattleman quickly availed himself of the chance to acquire a companion for her—this time a mature male. Today, no four-footed interloper sets foot on this cattle ranch!

The second account appeared in the *GPCA Bulletin* in 1972, and starred Suki and Yukon, a bitch and a dog, belonging to Jack and Carolyn Nix of rural New Mexico:

One summer afternoon the barking of Suki was heard from the ranch and peering through binoculars it was apparent that she was being attacked by a pack of coyotes. As Jack searched for his rifle, Yukon sped to the rescue. Hackles up in rage, he joined his mate and scattered the coyotes who beat a hasty retreat. As Jack arrived, the reason for the fracas became apparent. There before them was the carcass of a calf, its throat a gaping hole. Both dogs immediately lay down beside the calf, and although implored repeatedly to return to the ranch, they simply would not budge until collars and leashes were sent for.

Thus the Great Pyrenees—guard and fighting dog extraordinaire when the need arises—retains his ancient heritage.

The Great Pyrenees as a Soldier

The association of our Great Pyrenees with the Armed Forces is another subject which bears mentioning. As a War Dog his practical value has always been somewhat restricted because of his coat color. At night, or against a green background, he stands out as an easy target for enemy fire.

But in an arctic or alpine campaign he is the ideal dog for pack-work or messenger service. Here his white coat blends with the snow and ice. It also provides protection against the sleet, snow, and the extremes of cold. No other breed can lay claim to so many advantages to an army operating in the Nordic climes.

Luz and Pastoure of the de Loubonniers Kennels both saw action with the Alpine Chasseurs in the Italian Campaign in the Second World War. Both were wounded in action and lost their lives. They were buried on the scene of battle, high in the Alps, and will long be remembered for the gallant service which they gave to their native France.

In 1942, ten Great Pyrenees were shipped from Framingham, Massachusetts, to Front Royal in Virginia to begin training for the Arctic Campaign. A second and larger contingent was dispensed to Camp Rimini in Montana where they were later joined by the first. The dogs were trained to work in rotation, three dogs assigned to one man. They were taught to carry 40 pound packs of ammunition, machine guns weighing up to 60 pounds; and lastly, to pull a toboggan laden with Red Cross supplies. On the success of the program, the Defense Department reported, "Of all breeds tried out for pack work, the Great Pyrenees are proving themselves most satisfactory."

Although the progress of the War led to the cancellation of the proposed Arctic Campaign, several dogs were dispatched to active duty in Greenland and Newfoundland. Returning servicemen brought reports of their success. But by August 1943, the last had been returned to his owner.

Ch. Basquaerie Brinker was one of those who had been away for about a year. His dewclaws had been removed "to prevent their catching and tearing in deep snow" according to the Army report! He received both an honorable discharge, as well as a Certificate of Honor "in recognition of his loyal service to our nation during this great War."

Reports of the use of Pyrenees as War Dogs antedate the above. The French Army before the turn of the century was said to favor a cross with a Pyrenean dog for ammunition portage "on account of his strength which enables him to carry as many as five hundred cartridges." And there are documented reports of Pyreneans serving as First Aid Dogs in World War I.

An intelligent and obedient class, in New Mexico. From left to right: Ch. Andre El Encantado de la Lux, CDX, owned by Nancy Wood; Cynthis Lyon, owned by Richard Davison; Diane's Frosty Bear, owned by Diane Thomas; Ch. Skeel's Juliet of Corrales, owned by Doris Thomas; Valle del Oso Yeti, owned by Carla Greth; Dar-Jan's Bright Angel, owned by Doris Thomas; Ha-Bou-Scha, owned by Bob Jones. The long sit and the long down. — *Courtesy I.G.P.R.*

Quibbletown Mighty Peer CDX, owned and trained by Frances H. Pavey. — *Courtesy I.G.P.R.*

The Great Pyrenees in Obedience

The ever-rising interest in Obedience training and showing, as reflected by the entries at American Kennel Club Obedience trials held in conjunction with the all-breed shows, has focused new attention on the Great Pyrenees —a superb subject for Obedience work! As Obedience devotees will tell you, the well-rounded Pyrenees boasts letters after his name, as well as before.

The first Great Pyrenees to win a Companion Dog degree was Ch. Koranne of Basquaerie, in 1938. Up to the early seventies, a total of 94 Great Pyrenees added a C.D. to their names, and 12 a Companion Dog Excellent (C.D.X.). More than half of these degrees were won after 1967. During the past five years, 81 other Great Pyrenees have earned a C.D. degree, and nine can be counted as holders of the coveted C.D.X.

Considering the number of dogs involved, Canadian fanciers must be congratulated for finishing a total of 23 C.D. degree winners during the past ten years, with three winning a C.D.X., and one a Utility Degree. Champion Mynydd Cymru, owned by Vince Murphy of Ontario, is the distinguished holder of the U.D. degree.

265

Mention must be made of Roy and Margie Stehle's famous Britannic's Midsummer Knight—the first Great Pyrenees to earn the tracking degree, in 1970. "Sean" added the U.D.T. to his other long string of diplomas, which included a Canadian as well as an American C.D., a C.D.X., and a U.D. degree. He was the first male, and only the third Pyr in the U.S. to earn the U.D.. In 1975, Beau-Kay Wise Zest, C.D., owned by Suzanne Wallace, became the second Great Pyrenees to achieve the Utility Dog Tracking title.

Working the Shady Side of the Road

There is also another Pyrenean tradition which has, understandably, been given little public exposure. It, too, deserves a place in a chapter on the Working Pyrenees. What follows comes from the pen of Paul Strang:

> On the afternoon of the 26th of May, 1775, Louis Mandrin, the king of smugglers, was led to a scaffold erected in the front of the cathedral in the public square in Valence, France. Five thousand people jammed the area and crowded the surrounding rooftops. After a short speech, in which he warned the school children that crime does not pay, Mandrin was brutally executed.
>
> Mandrin's "crime does not pay" speech proved prophetic. He had been captured, illegally, by a commando-type French raiding party over the border in Savoy, which was then under the jurisdiction of Sardinia. Charles-Emmanual III, King of Sardinia, protested vehemently against the action and withdrew his ambassador to France. Louis XV, in turn, dispatched his most prestigious diplomat, the Count de Noailles, to smooth over the affair. Hostilities were averted but, in France, the public outcry refused to die down. Books and pamphlets rolled from the presses. Epic and heroic songs glorifying Mandrin became the rage. Thousands of portraits and engravings of the popular hero were sold.

Of particular interest is the fact the Mandrin legend mentions his huge and faithful companion, supposedly a mountain dog, purchased in Nice in 1748. And from some of the illustrations I have seen, it is apparent to me that this dog was a Great Pyrenees. We shall probably never know positively but in any case the association would be symbolic in the extreme for, from the earliest records of our breed we know him, not only as a protector of the flock, but as a smuggler's companion and helper.

Of all the animals that have been used to carry contraband goods, the dog is, of course, the most intelligent. Robert Leighton wrote in 1911:

> Travelers on the Continent may often notice the dogs kept at the various *octroi* cabins on the frontiers. They are used to assist in the detection and pursuit of smugglers, at which work they are remarkably clever; but there is even a more active and cunning class of dog employed by the contrabandists themselves who train them to evade the vigilant *dounier* and his canine assistants, and to carry consignments of illicit goods across the frontiers at night and in

stormy weather, the loads of silk, lace, tobacco, spirits, or other taxable commodities being packed in small compass about their bodies and covered with a false coat. The method of training these smuggling dogs is that of implanting in their minds a rooted fear of all men in uniform, and they are taught to make their journey by unfrequented paths; consequently they steer clear of the uniformed guards at the frontier stations, and make their way to their destination by secret routes which are frequently changed. The police dogs are seldom a match for these cunning four-footed contrabandists.

The situation in the Pyrenees is, in several respects, unique. In the East, towards the Mediterranean, live the Catelans, speaking an ancient Roman tongue not easily understood by outsiders. And in the West are the Basques who also have their own language. Quasi-control of the mountain passes between France and Spain has rested, for centuries, in the hands of these two population groups who are a closed society. Smuggling, for many, simply became a way of life. Imagine the difficulties of a detective sent from either Paris or Madrid in trying to obtain any information whatsoever in the mountains. One spoken word and he is immediately recognized as a potential danger!

Certainly any farm house, on either side of the border, had a perfectly legitimate reason for owning a big, strong Patou. He was there to "guard the sheep." The fact that he might be perfectly suited for a quick jaunt, over the border, in the dead of night, with a twenty-pound illicit pack on his back was incidental.

Actually, while the gradual disappearance of bears and wolves is usually given as the reason why our breed became scarce in his homeland there is another, and quite distressing reason, I have been told. This is the fact that trigger-happy border guards destroyed so many of the dogs in the early years of this century.

Most of the people I questioned on the use of Pyrs in the border traffic on my recent trip to the Pyrenees took great pains to assure me, "Yes, but that's all in the past." Planes, cars, boats and bribed officials have made smuggling a big business so there really was no place, in this day and age, for anything as unsophisticated as a dog.

Perhaps so. I must have been dreaming that morning, when, standing on the little balcony of my hotel room at dawn, in the tiny mountain village, I thought I heard a guarded whistle. And thought I saw something that looked like a Pyr carrying saddlebags disappear with his master behind quickly closed doors.

Using curved cards, Connie, sitting to the right, is preparing the rolags. Zatha, at the New Zealand Ashford wheel, is drawing the rolags out and winding them onto the bobbin.

Connie is spinning. A basket of rolags is on the right.

Spinning counter-clockwise, Zatha plys from a lazy kate.

268

20

Spinning Pyrenean Hair

by Zatha Hockridge and Constance Kousman

Mrs. Zatha M. Hockridge and Mrs. Constance B. Kousman, who live in Cornish, New Hampshire, are among the very few spinners who devote themselves full-time to working with dog hair. Mrs. Hockridge became intrigued with the craft in Nova Scotia 30 years ago. But at that time her Black Ledge Newfoundland Kennel was a big and successful operation with many top winners, so there was little time for spinning. Later, after providing foundation stock for the late Margaret Booth Chern's Little Bear Newfoundland Kennels, Mrs. Hockridge gave up her own program and moved to Vermont as Mrs. Chern's kennel manager. Mrs. Kousman's Mic-Mac Kennel in Maine was also affiliated with Little Bear for many years. These two ladies have spun the hair of Afghans, Lhasa Apsos, Old English Sheepdogs, Newfoundlands, Huskies, Shelties, Irish Wolfhounds and many others. But they say, "We haven't found anything that can match the lovely white of the Great Pyrenees."

THE LUXURIOUS COAT of the Great Pyrenees, shepherd, guardian and noble companion, has been for centuries a practical and economical source of extraordinarily warm, exceptionally beautiful clothing.

Proof against the severe climatic conditions of his mountainous homeland, the Great Pyrenees' long heavy coat provides an abundant supply of raw materials for the handspinner who recognizes its potential quality and elegance.

As Pyr combings include comparatively little of the long, straight, relatively coarse outercoat, it is the dense woolly undercoat, shed at regular intervals, upon which the spinner must primarily depend. Shorter and finer in texture, snow white or delicately shaded with lemon, gray or tan, these combings are softer and lovelier than many of the finest wools. The resulting products are lightweight with exceptional insulating properties. And, in our opinion, unsurpassed for warmth.

From Pyr Hair to Knitwear

When collecting Pyr hair for spinning, a few points kept in mind will prevent lost time and effort. Hair containing mats, burrs, or skin flakes should be discarded. Also reject clippings and unusually short hair. A small quantity of tail hair mixed in while carding ordinarily is not objectionable. However, because of its coarseness, some people prefer to omit it if the yarn is to be used for a delicate garment.

Spinning involves three basic steps: (1) carding or arranging the fibers; (2) drawing out the fibers; (3) twisting the fibers. Sheep's wool, having rough, crimped fibers that tend to cling together, is most easily spun. Therefore, until proper techniques are learned, this should be the starting point for beginners. When the craft is mastered, the smoother fibers of Pyr hair become less difficult to control—and a joy to spin!

Combings from a relatively clean dog need not be washed before spinning—a saving in time and handleability. When excessive dirt makes prewashing necessary, it must be done by hand in very small quantities to prevent felting. It may also need teasing, or pulling apart, to separate the fibers before carding.

Thorough carding, which disentangles and arranges the fibers, is most important as it increases the ability to maintain a smooth continuous draw. When the hair is well brushed, it is rolled off the card in the shape of a hollow tube or curl called a "rolag." The efficient spinner will make at least enough rolags to fill a bobbin to minimize interruptions.

Combings from short-haired breeds may be spun by mixing with the longer staple of wool. Pyr hair, however, is of sufficient length to be spun unadulterated into a strong yarn suitable for most projects.

Although yarn can be spun on the simple, primitive drop spindle, most handspinners today recognize the spinning wheel as the faster, more efficient method.

Whether spinning wool or Pyr hair, the fundamentals are essentially the same. As the rolag is fed into the orifice, the fibers are drawn out, twisted, and wound onto the bobbin simultaneously. Speed, rhythm, coordination, tension and other variables determine the quality and nature of the yarn. Thickness or size is a matter of individual preference—depending upon how the yarn will be used.

Plying, or twisting together two or more single strands of yarns, is also done on the wheel, using a counterclockwise spin and a bobbin rack called a "lazy kate". When spinning dog combings, a 2-ply yarn is most commonly used.

Miss Peggy Grant-Dalton spinning her Pyrenean hair. Moncal Suzette is in front and Moncal Laudley Yaronola is behind. — *Courtesy Mrs. C.R. Prince*

Mrs. Foy in her Pyrenean Mountain Dog fur coat. — *Courtesy Mrs. C.R. Prince*

Skeining can be done on a simple "niddy noddy" or the more efficient "wrap wheel". In lieu of either, a board wrapped with paper to protect the yarn from any possible roughness may be used. After tying loosely in at least two places, the skein is ready to be washed in warm, gentle suds. We recommend Ivory or Lux; carefully handling one skein at a time to avoid tangles.

We always give each skein at least two sudsings and rinse until the water is clear. We then add a few drops of baby oil to the last rinse water to replace any natural oils lost.

After gently squeezing, the skein is blotted by rolling in bath towels. Then, supported by strips of soft cloth, it is hung on a clothesline or rack to dry. When thoroughly air-dried, the skein is wound into a ball. This should be done loosely to prevent stretching.

It should be mentioned that Pyr hair yarn can be dyed in the skein. However, we doubt that any color can surpass the beautiful natural shadings provided by the Great Pyrenees himself.

Now! This is the moment the spinner has been working patiently and diligently toward — the final adventure in the transformation from Pyr hair to sweaters, skirts, scarves, mittens, afghans, blankets or an infinite variety of projects which are limited only by the imagination and skill of the craftsman. Pyr hair yarn is strong, knits easily, and can be raveled, becoming more fluffy as it is handled. Therefore, we recommend rather large knitting neddles in order to best display its soft, natural beauty. As individual knitting and spinning techniques vary, it is better to plan on a little more yarn than the pattern calls for; and advisable that all yarn for a specific project be spun by the same person.

Garments made from Pyr hair are easily handwashed. Just follow the instructions given for yarn in the skein. Add four or five drops of oil to the last rinse water, blot, block and dry flat. When thoroughly dry, additional fluff can be gained by tossing it in the dryer for two or three minutes. With reasonable care, the garment should last for years—becoming softer and fluffier with each wash.

Spinning is an ancient art which has been revitalized by the current focus on crafts. For obvious reasons, wool has been emphasized, and this subject has been thoroughly covered in a number of good books.

Although yarn spun from dog combings can be used for knitting, crocheting, hooking, weaving and crewel work, it has received little attention. Yet viewed in proper perspective, its value should not be overlooked. From sentimental, economical and practical viewpoints, the rewards are many. And they are available to each and every Pyr owner.

272

21

Special Health Problems in the Great Pyrenees

by Robert Brown, D.V.M.

AN IDIOSYNCRACY in the Great Pyrenees breed is a rolling cephalic vein on the front legs. This fact is important since these veins are the usual site for intra-vascular injections. Intravenous anesthesia, one type of anti-parasitical, and arsenic for treatment of heart worm infection, are among the preparations given through this vein. Many preparations will cause a severe tissue reaction if inadvertently injected outside the vein. The cephalic vein must be trapped and held until a needle can be inserted well into its lumen.

The Great Pyrenees has a lower metabolic rate than many other breeds. Adult nutritional requirements are considerably less than one would estimate on weight of dog alone. The body temperature may be 100 degrees instead of the usual 101.5. The lower metabolic rate is reflected in his typically easy going manner.

Generally, the Great Pyrenees will require a surprisingly small amount of sedative and anesthetic. This phenomenon may be due, in part, to the fact that Pyr weight is often "guestimated." A second factor is their lower metabolic rate which requires less drug to achieve the same end. As a rule of thumb, I figure half of the usual dosage as determined for the weight of a dog, and then if the desired plane of anesthesia has not been achieved, more anesthesia can be given to effect.

Many veterinarians do not have a scale that can accurately weigh a dog over 100 pounds and will ask you what your dog weighs. I find that Great Pyrenees owners usually overestimate the weight of their dogs by about 35 pounds. Make it a practice to take your Pyr to a freight scale or a farm elevator that has a high capacity scale and weigh him accurately. It may save his life.

Heartworms are becoming an increasing source of morbidity among dogs in the United States. The Pyrenees is no exception, being as susceptible as other breeds. In some communities, 30% of the dog population is infected. Heartworms are found in all states in the southern zone; as far north as Minnesota and Maine. In areas where the disease may be endemic, routine blood studies should be made twice yearly to identify Pyrs harboring the disease.

Heartworm preventives (*Caracide, Sterid-Caracide*) are 100% effective when used as directed. They should be started before the mosquito season and continued beyond the first frost. In southern climates, the preventive should be given year-round. The dosage is given according to the weight of the dog. These compounds may safely be given to older puppies.

Great Pyrenees are very susceptible to *heat stroke.* This almost always occurs because someone has forgotten the animal and left him enclosed in a car parked directly in the sun. In summer, a Pyrenees should always be transported in *open wire crates* so that the windows of the car can be rolled down completely. Always park in the shade and return often to check on the dog and be sure the car remains in the shade.

A Pyrenees' food intake should be reduced in hot weather and he should be given plenty of fresh water at all times. This breed requires more water than do most others. A Pyrenees should never be forced to take vigorous exercise during the heat of the day.

The Lame Dog

A Pyrenees who suddenly begins to favor one of his legs may be suffering from a minor sprain, a pulled muscle, or a tendonitis. Such minor injuries are not uncommon in the active dog. Usually, with moderate rest and restriction, the dog will recover.

On the other hand, a serious limp in a Great Pyrenees, especially one which appears during the first year of his life and doesn't clear spontaneously, may be due to one of several conditions of a more serious nature. In the differential diagnosis, one would need to consider whether the limp involves one or more extremities, and whether it involves the front or the rear.

Front limps may be due to *osteochondritis dessicans, elbow dysplasia,* or *panosteitis.* Rear-end limps are commonly due to *canine hip dysplasia, the hyperextension syndrome* (popping Hocks), *osteochondritis dessicans* and *panosteitis.* If, after a careful veterinary examination, one of these conditions is found to be the cause, the animal should be considered unacceptable for stud work or breeding. With the possible exception of popping hocks, all of these conditions have a hereditary basis and affected animals can pass them along to their offspring.

Canine Hip Dysplasia is the most important of these conditions because there is no satisfactory treatment for the badly crippled animal. In addition, the disease is not uncommon in the breed, with certain bloodlines showing a higher incidence of clinical and radiological involvement. Currently, 15% of Pyrenees' X-rays sent to the Orthopedic Foundation of America are read as showing various grades of dysplasia. This does not reflect the true incidence, since the X-rays are screened by local veterinarians before they are submitted.

Hip dysplasia is moderately heritable. It depends upon a combination of genes. Although afflicted dogs do not always throw dysplastic puppies, the disease, once established in the bloodline, reappears often enough to warrant strong measures to see that it is eliminated completely.

The problem resides in the structure of the hip joint. The head of the femur should sit solidly in the cup (*acetabulum*) of the pelvis. Loose ligaments allow the head to work loose, or begin to "subluxate." A shallow acetabulum also predisposes to joint laxity. Finally, the mass or tone of the musculature around the joint socket is an important determinant.

Tight ligaments, a broad pelvis with a well cupped acetabulum, and a good ratio of muscle mass to size of bone, are all factors which predispose to good hips. The reverse is true of animals who are likely to develop the disease. Environmental factors, including the weight of the puppy, and joint stress, all figure into the final outcome.

The first signs usually appear during a period of rapid growth (four to nine months), during which time the Pyrenees puppy may show pain in the hip, walk with a limp or swaying gait, bunnyhop when he runs, and show difficulty getting up on his hind legs. Once established, the disease usually progresses. Radiographically, hip joints grow worse with time.

Properly taken X-rays are essential to the diagnosis. Usually this is done under sedation or general anesthesia. The OFA currently certifies dogs who are 24 months of age, or older.

Some veterinarians claim to be able to tell whether a puppy is going to be dysplastic by palpation, which is an attempt to subluxate the hip joints of the anesthetized animal. This would appear to correlate mainly with joint laxity; and it must be remembered that by no means do all Pyrenees with joint laxity become dysplastic.

The incidence of canine hip dysplasia can be controlled by carefully selecting and using only breeding stock known to be free of the problem. It is to the advantage of the buyer to investigate the records of the bloodlines in question and to come to an understanding with the breeder about any warrantees covering dysplasia. This should be done before the puppy is purchased.

Elbow Dysplasia, or ununited anconeal process, is uncommon. This process normally fuses with the ulna bone by four months of age. If it doesn't, the result is lameness in the front leg, a characteristic deviation, and instability of the joint by palpation. Surgical removal of the ununited process alleviates the lameness.

Osteochondritis Dessicans (O.D.) is more common in the shoulder joint but may be found in the stifle joint also. Ordinarily, young males are the ones affected. The condition is due to an injury to the cartilage overlying the head of one of the long bones. A puppy who jumps off a high perch might sustain such an injury. The tendency for cartilage to be easily damaged is based on hereditary factors. The condition can be treated by total cage rest, or if not successful, by surgical removal of the damaged cartilage.

Eosinophilic Panosteitis ("growing pains", "wandering lameness") is a rare condition which has recently been found to affect Great Pyrenees. Various degrees of lameness appear in one leg and can, from time to time, shift from one leg to another. Males over six months of age are the ones usually affected. The disease is accompanied by fever, joint inflammation, muscle wasting, and unthriftiness. Anti-inflammatory drugs are usually prescribed. The etiology is unknown but there is a tendency for the disease to run in bloodlines.

Popping Hocks ("slipping hocks", the hyperextension syndrome) is a condition which is accompanied by laxity of the supporting structures around the hock joints. The result is that the hock "slips out of place," either forward or to the side, when the joint is extended. Pyr pups who are repeatedly allowed to jump up on their hind legs, with their front feet on people or a fence, could potentially stretch the ligaments and tendons which stabilize the hock joint. An underlying weakness of these structures may be a contributing cause also. It is usually observed in pups from four weeks to six months of age, and is more common among animals with very straight rear-end angulation. Proper early immobilization may possibly reverse the condition in young pups.

Bone Cancer

Osteogenic sarcoma is the most common form of cancer in Great Pyrenees. It ordinarily affects the long bones. While it can strike at any age, it is usually a disease of the middle years. Unfortunately, by the time the Pyr exhibits lameness or swelling in the area of the cancer, it is too late to treat. This form of cancer spreads early and to the lungs.

Skin Disorders

Beneath his heavy coat, the Great Pyrenees actually has a sensitive skin. A few guidelines will help to keep it as healthy as possible.

Do not clip or shave a Pyrenees in the summer as he will easily sunburn.

Since our breed possesses a double coat, when the soft woolly undercoat dies and starts to loosen, it should be removed. A dead undercoat is irritating to the skin and can start a bad case of acute moist dermatitis ("hot spots"). Hot spots are always indicative of some underlying problem. Other causes are fleas, and ear and anal gland infections.

White-coated breeds are somewhat more disposed to develop skin allergies. Various soaps and chemicals applied to the coat, as well as food allergens, may cause an atopic dermatitis. The use of allergy testing may be necessary to determine the cause. Pyrenees should be bathed only with appropriate dog shampoos—*never* shampoos used on people.

A Pyrenees who scratches himself for any reason may abrade his skin and convert a hot spot or skin allergy into a secondarily infected bacterial dermatitis. This can be a serious problem. Medical consultation should be sought rather than treating such a disorder with patent preparations.

Being a long-coated breed does not necessarily protect the Great Pyrenees from demodectic mange. This can be diagnosed by skin scrapings and treated accordingly.

Eye Problems

Some strains of Great Pyrenees exhibit a condition in which the eyelashes of one or both lids turn inward and scratch the cornea (*entropion*). If the irritation is severe, the dog will tear excessively, as indicated by a reddish-brown discoloration at the inner corner of his eye. Tearing, of course, can also be due to mild forms of allergic conjunctivitis and contagious infections.

A Pyrenees with excessively loose lids will exhibit the opposite condition (*ectropion*). This is characteristic of Pyrs with coarse heads and heavy flews which pull the lower lids away from the globes.

If either condition is found to run in bloodlines (it is hereditary) the animal should not be used for breeding. Cosmetic surgery will correct both disorders. Of course, this eliminates the dog from dog show competition.

The Bite

A number of undesirable dental problems can appear in the Pyrenean. The *overshot mouth* (parrot jaw) appears in very young puppies. An animal with an overshot bite has a great deal of difficulty in grasping food with his incisors since they don't line up in correct apposition. An overshot bite may improve as the animal grows; but if it hasn't done so by eight months of age, it's unlikely it ever will.

The *undershot mouth* is a more severe malocclusion problem since the teeth wear abnormally, especially the canines. A pup may have a normal bite until he is three months old, and then he could begin to "go under." If proper preventative measures are started at the earliest sign of deviation (at 12 weeks), the condition can be corrected. While the overshot mouth in an adult is definitely hereditary, the undershot mouth *may* be hereditary, or it may be due to the breeding of two strains of Pyrenees with different muzzle lengths.

The *wry mouth* is the worst of the malocclusion problems. In this situation the teeth on one side of the mouth are in a different plane from the same teeth on the other side. In simple terms, the jaw is crooked. A bitch with this condition has a hard time severing umbilical cords properly, and subsequently licking newborns in the usual aftercare. Great Pyrenees with this condition will be severely penalized in the show ring.

All Pyrenees with dental malocclusion problems should be eliminated from breeding programs.

Pyrenees cut their baby teeth more rapidly than smaller breeds. In the majority of cases, the replacement of teeth occurs quite naturally and never comes to the owner's notice. Occasionally, a milk tooth does not fall out. This can deflect a permanent tooth or even cause a double row of teeth. It should be watched closely. If it exists at four months of age, an extraction may become necessary.

The Anal Glands

These are two secretory sacs, analogous to the scent glands of the skunk, which are located on each side of the anus. They are normally emptied by activity, or during a bowel movement. However, on occasion these glands may become impacted. Usually a Pyrenees who rubs his bottom on the ground, or who scoots, is having an anal gland problem. Chewing at the base of his tail may be a sign of infection. If impaction of secretion is suspected, the anal sacs should be examined. It is a good idea to check these each time the dog is groomed or bathed.

22

The Great Pyrenees Club of America

THE GREAT PYRENEES CLUB OF AMERICA was founded on December 2, 1934, as the result of the efforts of Mr. and Mrs. Francis Crane. The first President was Professor Will Monroe.

It was through Professor Monroe's untiring researches in the libraries of London and Paris that much of the historical background of our breed was originally uncovered. His is also the honor of having owned the first-born pup of the first litter raised in the United States: Basque of Basquaerie (Ch. Urdos de Soum—Blanchette).

From among the early members of the GPCA, only Mrs. Crane and Paul Strang remain active in the affairs of the Club. Mrs. Crane was its first Secretary and held this post for nearly twenty years. She remains active on the Board of Directors, serving in 1975 as the Club's President. Both Mrs. Crane and Mr. Strang were twice appointed to a recent committee to study the Standard and recommend changes.

The first Club Handbook was published in 1936 (200 copies). It was expanded and revised in 1941, and again in 1949. For many years, a copy of the last edition was made available to new Club members. Today, the possession of any one of these books is a valuable addition to the library of any student of the Great Pyrenees.

The GPCA held its first Specialty Show in 1935 at the Morris and Essex Kennel Club show. The Annual Meeting was held for many years in conjunction with the Westminister Kennel Club Show in New York. Later, it was held in conjunction with the annual National Great Pyrenees Club of America Specialty, which in the sixties was held at the Trenton Kennel Club show.

During the seventies, with the emerging importance of the breed across the country, the GPCA began a policy of moving the National Specialty and the

Annual Meeting during successive years from the East Coast to the Midwest, from the Midwest to California, and then back to the East Coast. Pyrenees who have won at a number of the National Specialties are pictured on the accompanying pages.

The current activities of the GPCA include the publication of a bi-monthly *Bulletin,* containing a Breeder's Directory and articles of interest submitted by club members. An important and on-going project is *The Great Pyrenees Titleholders.* This is a pictorial and pedigree record of all Pyrenees to gain a championship or Obedience degree in the year of publication. The *Titleholders* is being back-dated to 1949, to coincide with the complete records of Mrs. Crane, and together this will provide an historical record of every Pyrenees to win a championship degree in America.

The International Film Exchange is an independently run project which is supported, in part, by a contribution from the club fund. The Film Exchange maintains an international library of movies under the supervision of Mrs. Joyce Stannard in England and Mrs. Joan Gross in America. Included are movies taken by Mr. and Mrs. Crane during trips to the Pyrenees Mountains in the late thirties. Club members may borrow movies from the library.

The GPCA sponsors an annual National Specialty and authorizes several Regional Specialty shows each year, under the direction of regional Clubs in New England, the National Capital area, the Michigan area, the Greater Chicago area, the Rocky Mountain area and California.

Membership in the GPCA is open to any interested fancier in good standing with the American Kennel Club.

The regional Clubs active at the present time are:

The Great Pyrenees Club of Alaska
Great Pyrenees Club of Greater Austin
Great Pyrenees Club of California
Great Pyrenees Club of Greater Chicago
Mile-Hi Great Pyrenees Club (Colorado)
Great Pyrenees Club of Michigan
National Capital Area Great Pyrenees Club
Pyrenean Fanciers of the Northwest
Heart of Ohio Great Pyrenees Club
Great Pyrenees Club of the Pacific Northwest

Should the reader be interested in obtaining further information, the name and address of the secretary of the parent or any of the regional clubs can be obtained from the American Kennel Club, 51 Madison Avenue, New York, N.Y. 10010.

280

Professor Will S. Monroe with his Basque of Basquaerie, the first AKC registered Great Pyrenees to be born in America. — *Courtesy Mrs. Francis V. Crane*

The Bergerie Knur Trophy, donated by Mr. and Mrs. F. S. Prince to the Great Pyrenees Club of America. Awarded to the Best of Breed winner at the annual National Great Pyrenees Club of America Specialty. A limited edition bronze sculptured by Mr. Geoffrey Davien. — *Courtesy Mrs. C. R. Prince*

The Great Pyrenees National Specialty, June 8, 1952. From left to right: Mrs. Frank Butcher with her Ch. Cote de Neige Paon, Best Opposite Sex; Judge, Louis J. Murr; Mrs. Francis Crane with her Ch. Basquaerie Ballerina, Best of Breed. — *Shafer*

Ch. Quibbletown Easter Token, pictured with his owner C. Seaver Smith, Jr., going Best of Breed at the National Specialty '54. Token was also BOB at the National Specialty in '55 and '56.

— *Shafer*

Mr. C. Seaver Smith, Jr., with his Ch. Quibbletown Meringue, Best of Breed, National Specialty '55. — *Shafer*

Ch. Quibbletown Duch de Nemours went Best Opposite Sex at four National Specialties. Owned by Mr. and Mrs. C. Seaver Smith, Jr. — *Gilbert*

Ch. Quibbletown Bon Chance, Best of Breed at the National Specialty in 1961 under the late R. Kerns. Bon Chance also won three other Nationals and several Groups. Owned by Mr. and Mrs. Lineweber.—*Shafer*

Ch. Quibbletown Jim Dandy, Best of Breed at the National Specialty in 1966. Here pictured with his owner C. Seaver Smith, Jr. The judge is the late Mr. Alva Rosenberg.

The Trenton National Specialty '67. Pictured left to right: Going Best Opposite Sex is Ch. Tip'N Chip's Quibbletown Impy; judge Mary W. Crane; and Ch. Tip 'N Chip's Luchon, handled by Judith G. Bankus, going Best of Breed. — *Gilbert*

Ch. Quibbletown Falstaff, Best of Breed at the National Specialty in 1971. The judge is Mr. F. S. Prince of England. Owned by Frankie Glover. — *Gilbert*

Ch. Soleil Pierre de Blu Crest, Best of Breed at the National Specialty
'74—from the Veterans' class to a Group Third at ten years of age.
Pictured left to right are the judge, Mrs. Joan Passini-Birkett of England, Pierre's owner, Victor Capone and Pierre's breeder, Jack Magoffin. — *Sonya Larsen*

Ch. Tip 'N Chip Sonny's Side Up pictured winning Best of Breed at
the first Independent National GPCA Specialty under judge Mrs.
Francis Crane, 1976. Handled by Stuart Rogell. Owned by Mr. and
Mrs. Waldemar Hauff. — *Schley*

Karolaska Puffin, pictured going Best Opposite Sex under judge James Bennett at the Golden Gate Specialty in California, January 31, 1976. Puffin was also Best Opposite Sex at the first Independent National Specialty in 1976. Shown here with her owner and handler, Mrs. Carol Kentopp. — *Roberts*

Ch. Karolaska's Captivator winning the Group at New Brunswick KC, September 1976 under judge Langdon Skarda. Two days earlier, Captivator had come from the classes to go Best of Breed at the first Great Pyrenees Club of America Eastern Specialty under Mr. Skarda. Owned by Joseph and Maryann Gentzel, and handled by Robert Forsyth.

BIBLIOGRAPHY

ALL OWNERS of pure-bred dogs will benefit themselves and their dogs by enriching th
knowledge of breeds and of canine care, training, breeding, psychology and other important aspe
of dog management. The following list of books covers further reading recommended by judg
veterinarians, breeders, trainers and other authorities. Books may be obtained at the finer bo
stores and pet shops, or through Howell Book House Inc., publishers, New York, N.Y.

Breed Books

AFGHAN HOUND, Complete	Miller & Gilbert
AIREDALE, Complete	Edwards
ALASKAN MALAMUTE, Complete	Riddle & Seeley
BASSET HOUND, Complete	Braun
BEAGLE, Complete	Noted Authorities
BLOODHOUND, Complete	Brey & Reed
BOXER, Complete	Denlinger
BRITTANY SPANIEL, Complete	Riddle
BULLDOG, New Complete	Hanes
BULL TERRIER, New Complete	Eberhard
CAIRN TERRIER, Complete	Marvin
CHIHUAHUA, Complete	Noted Authorities
COLLIE, Complete	Official Publication of the
Collie Club of America	
DACHSHUND, The New	Meistrell
DOBERMAN PINSCHER, New	Walker
ENGLISH SETTER, New Complete	Tuck & Howell
ENGLISH SPRINGER SPANIEL, New	
Goodall & Gasow	
FOX TERRIER, New Complete	Silvernail
GERMAN SHEPHERD DOG, Complete	Bennett
GERMAN SHORTHAIRED POINTER, New	Maxwell
GOLDEN RETRIEVER, Complete	Fischer
GREAT DANE, New Complete	Noted Authorities
GREAT PYRENEES, Complete	Strang & Giffin
IRISH SETTER, New	Thompson
IRISH WOLFHOUND, Complete	Starbuck
KEESHOND, Complete	Peterson
LABRADOR RETRIEVER, Complete	Warwick
MINIATURE SCHNAUZER, Complete	Eskrigge
NEWFOUNDLAND, New Complete	Chern
NORWEGIAN ELKHOUND, New Complete	Wallo
OLD ENGLISH SHEEPDOG, Complete	Mandeville
PEKINGESE, Quigley Book of	Quigley
POMERANIAN, New Complete	Ricketts
POODLE, New Complete	Hopkins & Irick
POODLE CLIPPING AND GROOMING BOOK,	
Complete	Kalstone
PUG, Complete	Trullinger
PULI, Complete	Owen
ST. BERNARD, New Complete	
Noted Authorities, rev. Raulston	
SAMOYED, Complete	Ward
SCHIPPERKE, Official Book of	Root, Martin, Kent
SCOTTISH TERRIER, Complete	Marvin
SHETLAND SHEEPDOG, New	Riddle
SHIH TZU, The (English)	Dadds
SIBERIAN HUSKY, Complete	Demidoff
TERRIERS, The Book of All	Marvin
TOY DOGS, Kalstone Guide to Grooming All	
Kalstone	
TOY DOGS, All About	Ricketts
WEST HIGHLAND WHITE TERRIER,	
Complete	Marvin
WHIPPET, Complete	Pegram
YORKSHIRE TERRIER, Complete	
Gordon & Bennett	

Care and Training

DOG OBEDIENCE, Complete Book of	Saunde
NOVICE, OPEN AND UTILITY COURSES	Saunde
DOG CARE AND TRAINING, Howell	
Book of	Howell, Denlinger, Merri
DOG CARE AND TRAINING FOR BOYS	
AND GIRLS	Saunde
DOG TRAINING FOR KIDS	Benjan
DOG TRAINING, Koehler Method of	Koeh
GO FIND! Training Your Dog to Track	Da
GUARD DOG TRAINING, Koehler Method of	
Koehler	
OPEN OBEDIENCE FOR RING, HOME	
AND FIELD, Koehler Method of	Koeh
SPANIELS FOR SPORT (English)	Radcl
SUCCESSFUL DOG TRAINING, The	
Pearsall Guide to	Pears
TRAIN YOUR OWN GUN DOG,	
How to	Goo
TRAINING THE RETRIEVER	Kers
TRAINING YOUR DOG TO WIN	
OBEDIENCE TITLES	Mors
UTILITY DOG TRAINING, Koehler Method of	
Koehler	

Breeding

ART OF BREEDING BETTER DOGS, New	Onst
HOW TO BREED DOGS	Whitn
HOW PUPPIES ARE BORN	Pr
INHERITANCE OF COAT COLOR	
IN DOGS	Li

General

COMPLETE DOG BOOK, The	
Official Pub. of American Kennel Cl	
DOG IN ACTION, The	Ly
DOG BEHAVIOR, New Knowledge of	
Pfaffenberger	
DOG JUDGING, Nicholas Guide to	Nichol
DOG NUTRITION, Collins Guide to	Coll
DOG PSYCHOLOGY	Whitn
DOG STANDARDS ILLUSTRATED	
DOGSTEPS, Illustrated Gait at a Glance	Elli
ENCYCLOPEDIA OF DOGS, International	
Dangerfield, Howell & Riddle	
JUNIOR SHOWMANSHIP HANDBOOK	
Brown & Mason	
SUCCESSFUL DOG SHOWING, Forsyth Guide to	
Fors	
TRIM, GROOM AND SHOW YOUR DOG,	
How to	Saunde
WHY DOES YOUR DOG DO THAT?	Bergm
WORLD OF SLED DOGS, From Siberia to	
Sport Racing	Coppin
OUR PUPPY'S BABY BOOK (blue or pink)	